IMAGES
of Modern America

ALTOONA

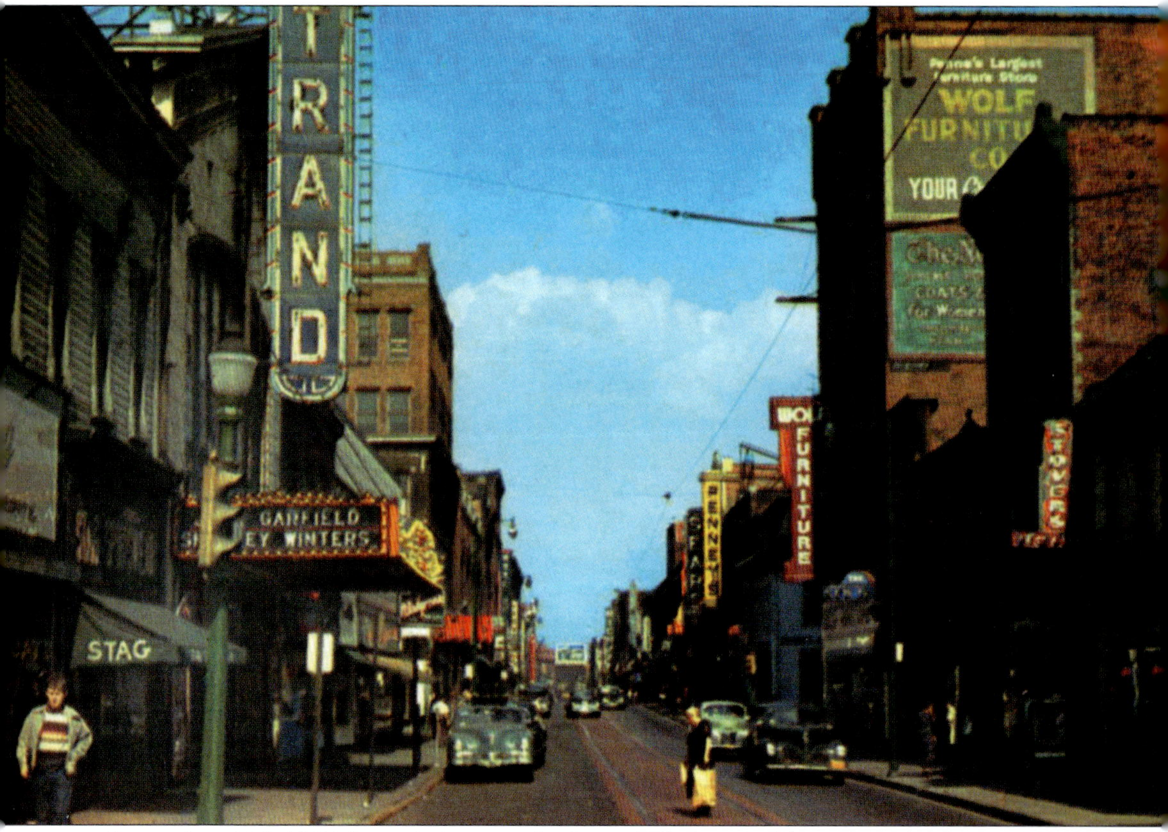

Situated at 1510–1512 Eleventh Avenue, the Strand Theatre could accommodate 1,600 patrons. Pictured here in 1951, the marquee is advertising the John Garfield and Shelley Winters crime film *He Ran All the Way*. The theater was demolished in 1962 after closing in 1954. Notice Wolf Furniture, J.C. Penney, and Sears on the right in addition to the streetcar line in the center. (Courtesy of David Seidel.)

On the Front Cover: Clockwise from the top left, female cyclists embark on a stage of the July 2011 International Tour de 'Toona (photograph by Bob Airhart); a passenger train rolls around the Horseshoe Curve (courtesy of *Altoona Mirror*); an evening vista of Peoples Natural Gas Field (courtesy of Explore Altoona); circus master Eric Paul Scites performs a show at Fort Roberdeau in October 2013 (author's collection); and Vice Pres. Richard Nixon and his wife, Pat, are greeted by Rep. James Van Zandt and his wife, Esther, during an October 1956 visit (courtesy of *Altoona Mirror*).

On the Back Cover: From left to right, the iconic Cathedral of the Blessed Sacrament (author's collection); a Pennsylvania Railroad caboose is among vibrant landscaping at Benzel's Bretzels Factory (courtesy of Benzel's Bretzels); and reenactor Mark Frederick interacts with visitors Andrea and Jack Slusser for Baker Mansion's 2014 World War II Weekend (author's collection).

IMAGES
of Modern America

ALTOONA

Jared Frederick

ARCADIA
PUBLISHING

ISBN 978-1-4671-2286-3

Published by Arcadia Publishing
Charleston, South Carolina

Printed in the United States of America

Library of Congress Control Number: 2014945840

For all general information, please contact Arcadia Publishing:
Telephone 843-853-2070
Fax 843-853-0044
E-mail sales@arcadiapublishing.com
For customer service and orders:
Toll-Free 1-888-313-2665

Visit us on the Internet at www.arcadiapublishing.com

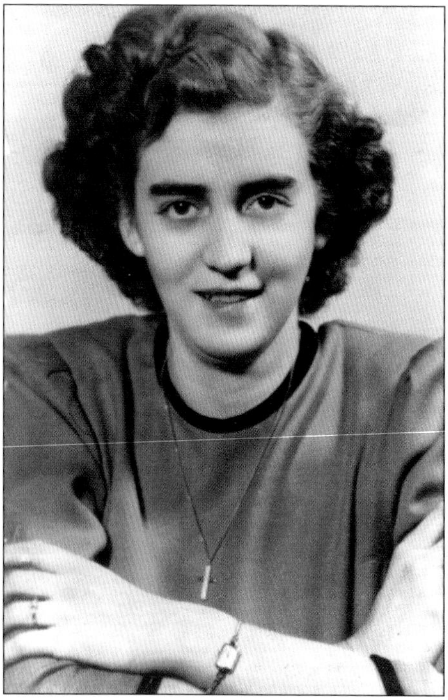

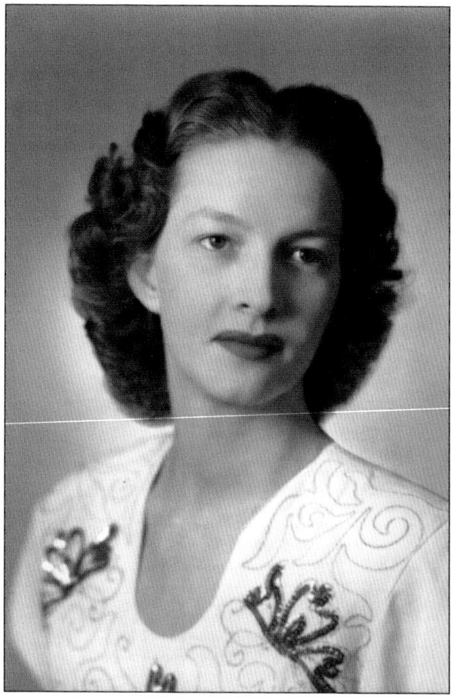

This book is dedicated to my grandmothers, Marguerite Frederick and Gertrude Nycum, my two favorite Altoona gals!

Contents

Acknowledgments

History is a matter of perception. I discovered at the outset of this project that interpreting every noteworthy event or place in my hometown would not be possible. That said, this book is not meant to be a comprehensive history of Altoona. While this series is Images of Modern America, I used the year 1945 as a point of departure for exploration. Like countless communities, World War II and its long-term ramifications had profound consequences on Altoona.

While I was a park ranger at Gettysburg National Military Park, I learned history is best served to the masses from personal perspectives. Taking the same approach with this chronicle, I strived to give the people of Altoona a voice with the primary sources. Unless otherwise noted, all direct quotes are from original newspaper issues of the *Altoona Mirror.*

Scores of friends and colleagues also assisted me in this endeavor. In addition to all those mentioned in photograph credits, I would like to thank the following people who offered me photographs, assistance, and inspiration: Gary Baranec, Ann Benzel, Dr. Brian Black, Marissa Carney, J.D. Cavrich, Gail Clapper, Barbara Cowan, Todd Davis, Dustin Faust, Paula Foreman, Sgt. Brian Freiwald, Harriett Gaston, Trisha Gates, LuAnn Hallinan, Pastor Edward Harshbarger, Mark Ickes, John Meise, Patty Morgan, Neil Rudel, Linda Stotler, Tim Van Scoyoc, Bill Wallen, and Dr. Ken Womack.

I would like to express special appreciation of photographers Bob Airhart, William Burket, and David Seidel for allowing me to use many of their images throughout this book. Above all else, I thank my parents, John and Kathy, and my brother Mark for their continued patience and encouragement.

Courtesy lines are indicated by the following where applicable: Altoona Area High School (AAHS), *Altoona Mirror* (AM), Altoona Police Department (APD), Altoona Railroaders Memorial Museum (ARMM), Blair County Arts Foundation (BCAF), Blair County Chamber of Commerce (BCCC), and Penn State Altoona (PSA).

Introduction

Altoona, Pennsylvania, sits at an intersection of history. Shaped by geography, created by a railroad, fueled by industry, forged by war, and remade through innovation, the city's tale is a microcosm of the American story. Purportedly named after the Cherokee word *allatoona*, meaning "high lands of great worth," the city could just as well have been named after Allatoona, Georgia, the site of a major railroad junction. Established in 1849 by the enterprising Pennsylvania Railroad (PRR), Altoona was a town of constant bustle. An aspiring Andrew Carnegie began his career there. In 1862, Northern governors held a covert meeting in the city to discuss momentous issues of the Union cause. The first generation of Bell telephones were connected to Altoona's railroad shops in 1877. Babe Ruth hit a home run at nearby Cricket Field in 1924. Nazi saboteurs were thwarted in a daring plot to demolish the city's industry 18 years later. As all these forces were at work, Altoona thrived as the largest railroading center in the world.

During World War II, trains whizzed through the picturesque Horseshoe Curve every 15 minutes. Despite wartime woes and rationing, the city remained a flourishing hub of activity. Unfortunately for Altoona, the end of the costliest war in history also marked the gradual decline of the town and the business empire that conceived it. While many of the PRR's competitors converted to diesel engines, the Pennsylvania Railroad did not do so until after the war. Even then, fewer workers were needed to repair more efficient trains. Railroad misfortunes multiplied with the advent of commercial airliners, the death of the Altoona & Logan Valley Electric Railway in 1954, and the rise of the affordable family car.

During the 1950s, Altoona facilities and laborers continued to diminish in the face of corporate woes and rapidly changing times. In June 1952, the PRR began to dismiss employees not involved in the diesel or car-repair programs. The decision marked the end of an era. The demise of steam engines came the following year, and Altoona would never be the same. The PRR was gone forever 15 years later, and the community found itself consumed by uncertainty. Consecutive railroading tenures by the Penn Central, Conrail, and Norfolk Southern placed Altoonans within a seemingly constant ebb of transition.

The lasting consequences of the region's labor exodus ushered nearly unfathomable change—as is best represented by Altoona's dramatic decline in population. Reaching its numerical peak in 1930 with over 82,000 residents, the city is home to approximately 45,000 citizens as of 2014. This demographic shift, in turn, led to a rapid increase in urban blight and gradual deterioration of a formerly enterprising business district. Subsequently, franchises located downtown began to relocate within the new cultural landscapes of suburbanization and urban sprawl. Constructed in 1959, the Pleasant Valley Shopping Center was among the first of these new strip malls that created an entirely new commercial vista. The areas of Plank Road and Interstate 99 are now dotted with major retailers marketing to Altoonans and passing motorists.

As Altoona residents looked beyond the traditional city limits for growth, local leaders attempted to stem the infectious tide of blight from within. Throughout the late 1960s and early 1970s, hundreds of structures were razed between Fifth and Twelfth Avenues to make way for potential redevelopment, plazas, and modernized facilities for Altoona High School. While many historical structures were lost in this seesaw process, activists saved others, including the majestic Mishler Theater. Reinventing what was once the heart of the community remains an ongoing evolution into the 21st century.

While certain episodes of the city's past are bleak, much is also to be commended. Iconic treasures such as Baker Mansion and the Horseshoe Curve stand resilient against the tests of time. Corporations such as Norfolk Southern, Sheetz, Ward Trucking, and Wolf Furniture operate as regional economic pillars. This characteristic is equally true of community institutions such as the Altoona Area School District, Blair Medical Associates, Penn State Altoona, and the University of Pittsburgh Medical Center's Altoona campus. At the same time, the successful Altoona Curve baseball club has infused an immense level of civic pride among area residents.

Ultimately, this book seeks to holistically examine both the accomplishments and pitfalls that have inexorably shaped Altoona and its people. To illustrate the numerous tragedies and triumphs Altoona has experienced over the course of seven decades, this book is divided into four chapters. Chapter one delves into the lives, products, and practices of Altoona businesses, ranging from humble diners to a multibillion-dollar corporation. While the city is synonymous with railroading, other enterprises and infrastructure were necessary to sustain the colossal industrial undertaking. This section is counterbalanced by an additional chapter interpreting the significances of railroad culture within the community. In doing so, the author attempts to convey a human drama as much as a mechanical one.

Chapter three analyzes the role of civic organizations and foundations within the community, including schools, churches, the arts, and landmarks. Recognition of such hallowed institutions is a vital component of understanding a community's character. Accordingly, a final section reveals the significance of sports and leisure in relation to Altoona's identity. In doing so, this book considers the value of community spirit that local teams have evoked. Equally noteworthy are the parks, stores, and places of recreation that bound together families and neighbors. All told, these varied episodes, people, and places stitch together a rich mosaic of a classic Pennsylvania city.

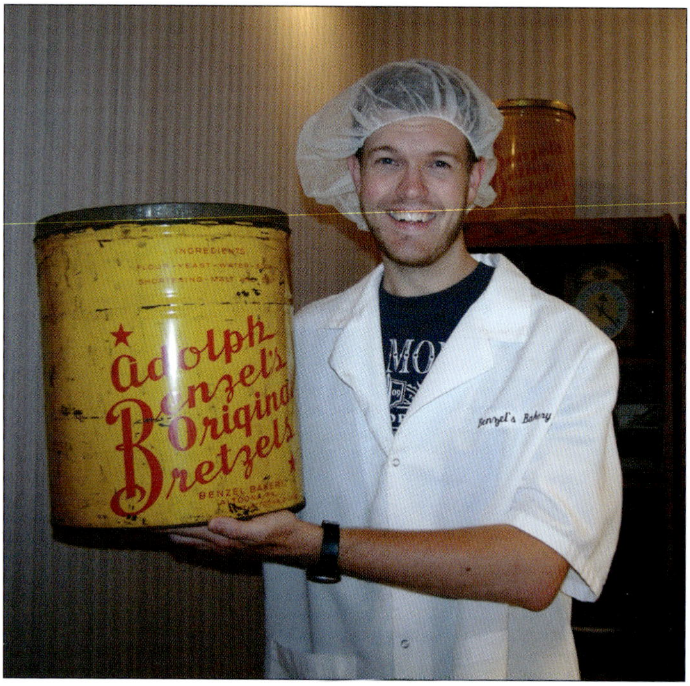

As one of several benefits of composing this book, author Jared Frederick gained access to many of Altoona's most iconic landmarks—including Benzel's Bretzel Bakery on Sixth Avenue. (Photograph by Ann Benzel.)

One

A Town at Work

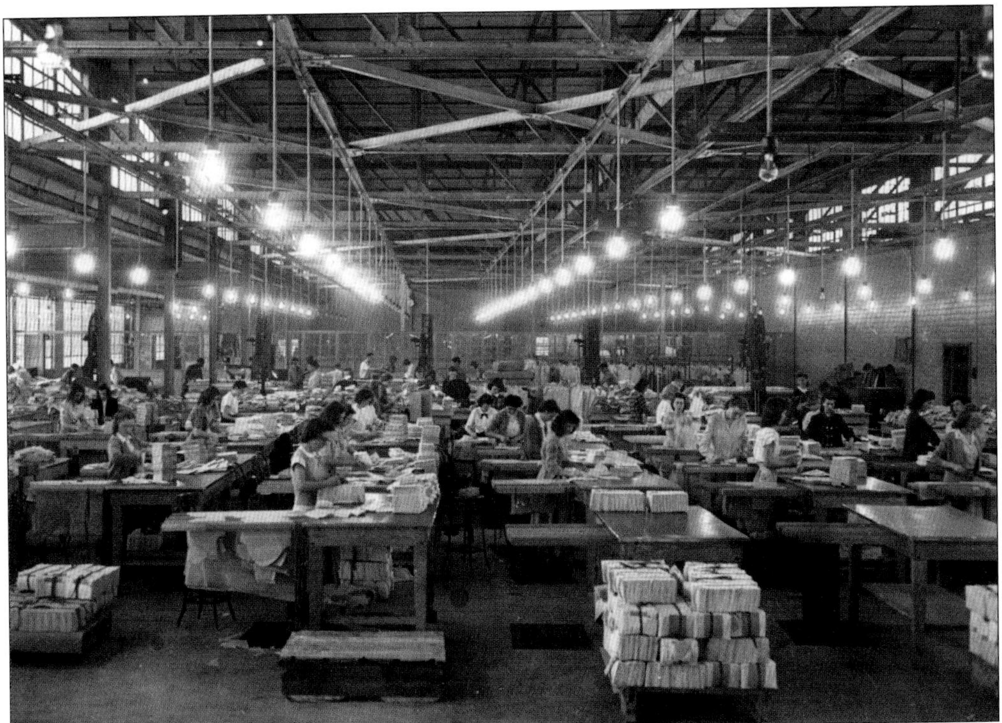

The 1947 construction of the Butterick Pattern Company plant on Beale Avenue was emblematic of America's postwar ascendance as a consumer nation. According to supervisor Eugenia Miswick, each of the 60 female workers seen here could package at least 1,100 clothing patterns per hour. (Courtesy of AM.)

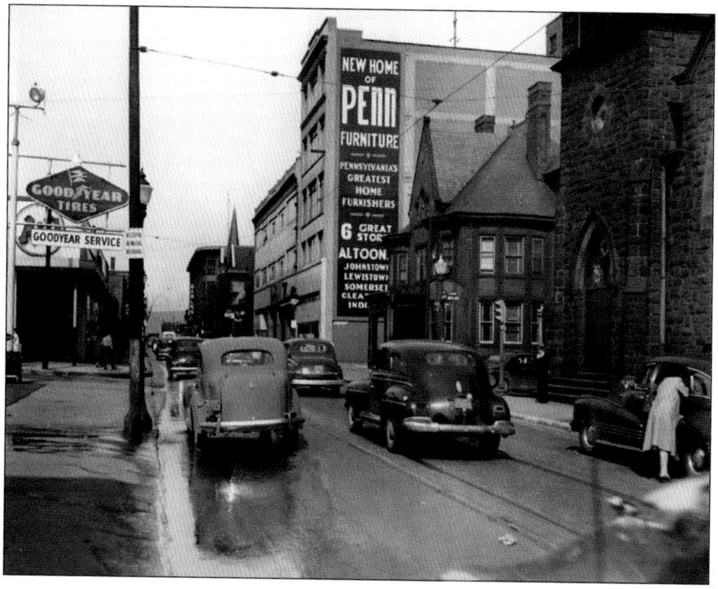

By 1950, Penn Furniture on Twelfth Avenue was a premier furnishings outlet in Pennsylvania. Encouraging housewives to be responsible yet fashionable, Penn Furniture hosted interior design lectures on refurbishing an entire living room for $200 or less. The store closed in 1985 and is now the Heritage Discovery Center. (Courtesy of BCCC.)

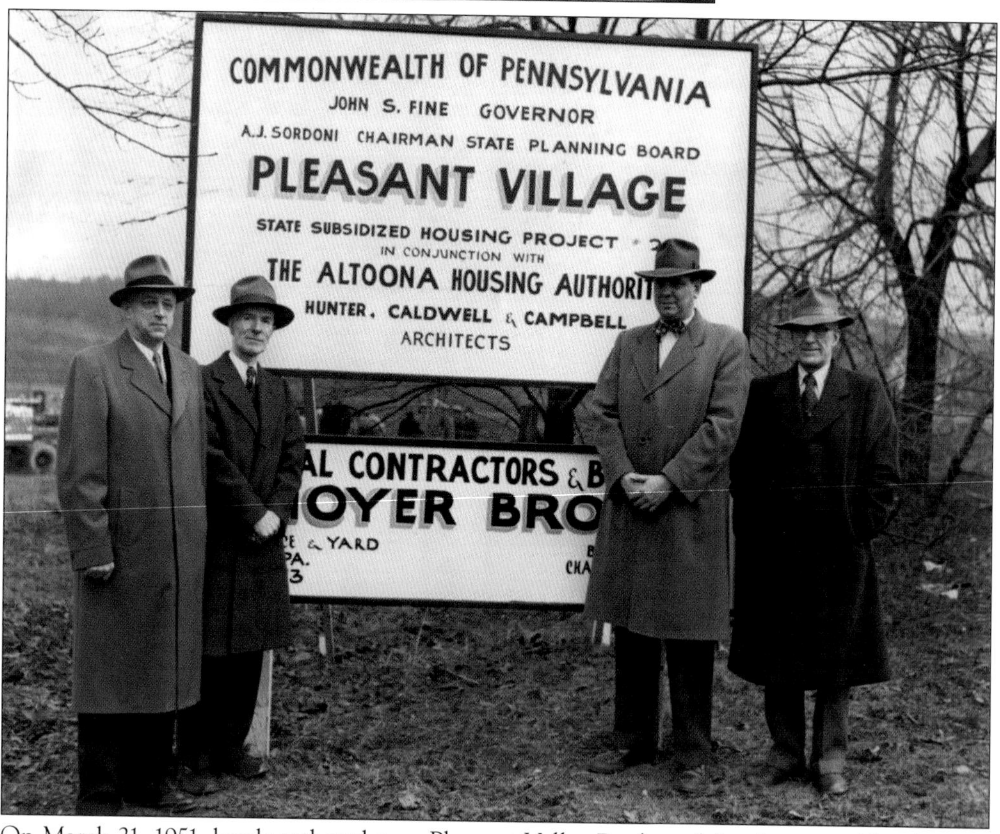

On March 21, 1951, locals gathered near Pleasant Valley Boulevard for the ground-breaking of Pleasant Village, a 120-unit complex constructed to accommodate returning veterans. Chamber of commerce president J.E. Holtzinger noted, "We all will benefit from having better living conditions for our citizens." From left to right are local leaders Paul Hayward, W.A. Morgan, Frank Marsh, and Lawrence Schzenk. (Courtesy of AM.)

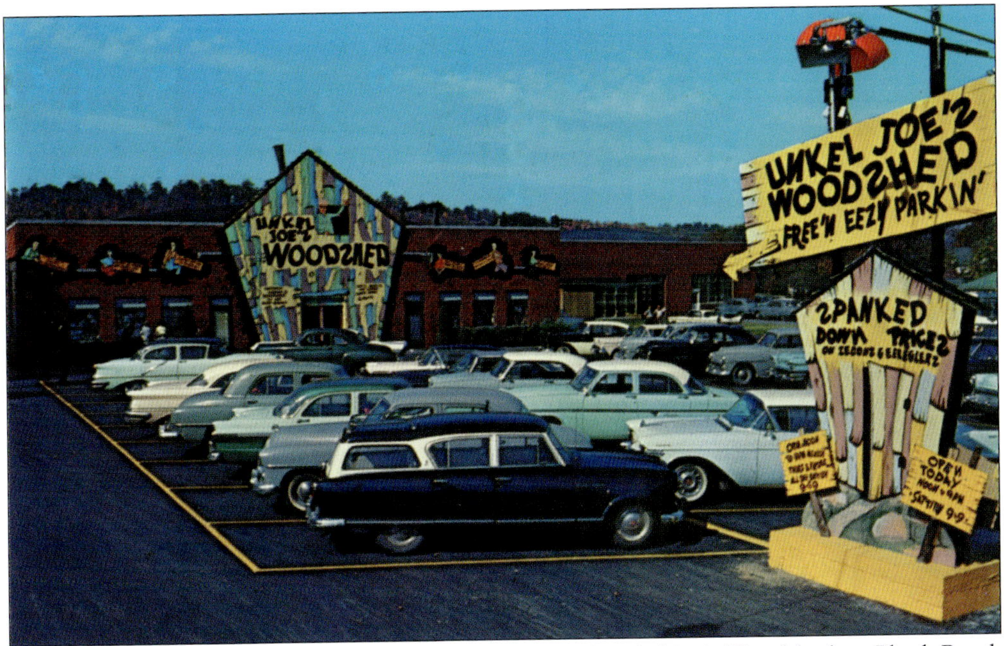

In 1958, World War II veteran Robert Baker established Unkel Joe's Woodshed on Plank Road. Embracing the representation of hillbillies in pop culture, a 1959 store advertisement exclaims, "Ain't Never Opin Sundys—Mundys—Toosdys!" The family-owned household store is now located in the Pleasant Valley Shopping Center. (Courtesy of William Burket.)

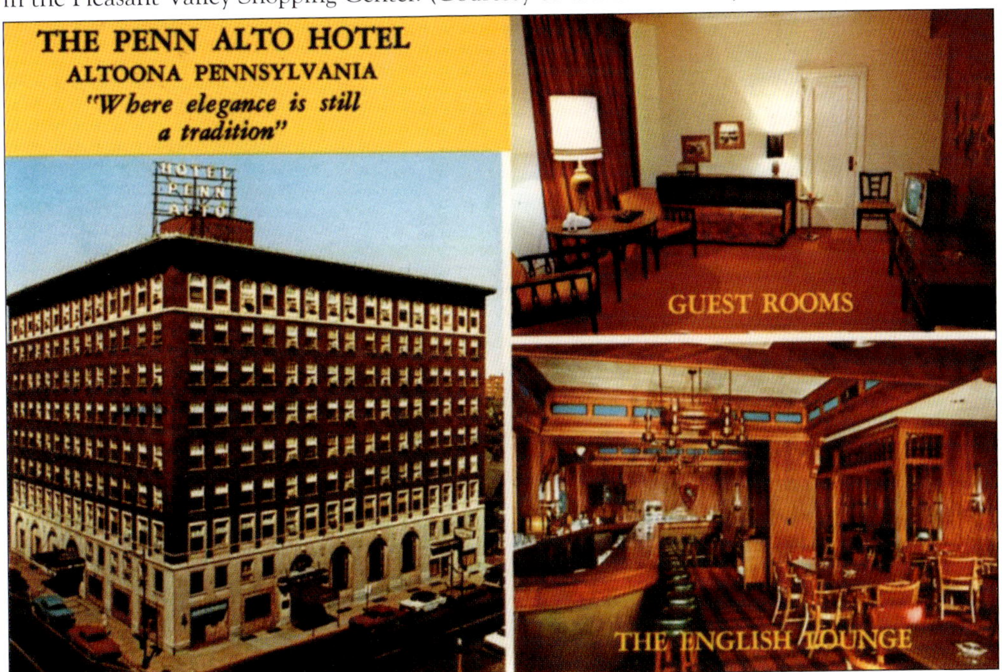

Constructed in 1921, the Penn Alto Hotel on Twelfth Street and Thirteenth Avenue was the Ritz of Altoona for over half a century. On April 1, 1963, the hotel's celebrated English Lounge opened, guaranteeing customers a sentimental flashback "to the romantic and elegant era" of 1800s Britain. The once-opulent hotel is now subsidized housing. (Courtesy of David Seidel.)

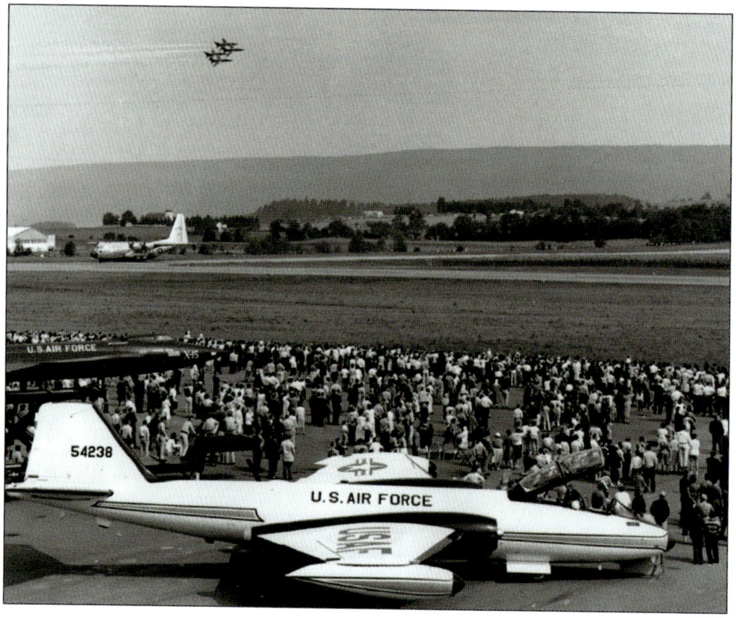

Many residents hoped the new Altoona-Blair County Airport in Martinsburg would help fill the void of the slowly diminishing railroad. Opening on September 17, 1960, the airport's dedication featuring the Blue Angels was rained out. On October 1, 1961, however, the Blue Angels arrived for a rescheduled appearance. (Courtesy of BCCC.)

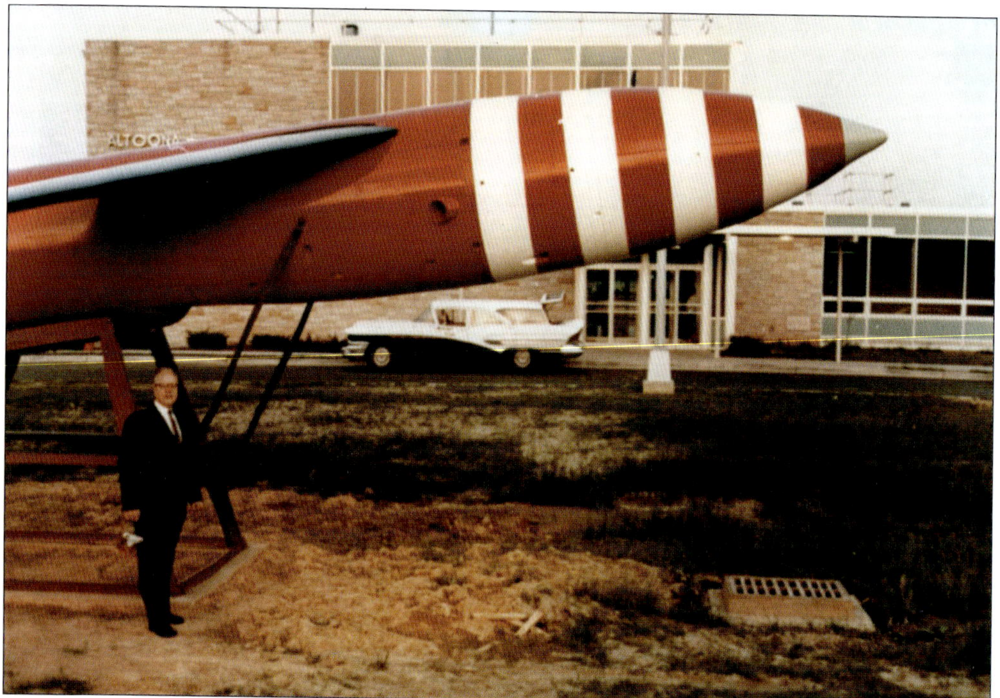

The Altoona-Blair County Airport obtained an unlikely lawn ornament for the Fourth of July in 1961 when it received a junked MGM-1 Matador cruise missile. Requisitioned by Gen. R.M. Montgomery, an Altoona native, the decommissioned atomic weapon was previously stationed in Europe. (Courtesy of BCCC.)

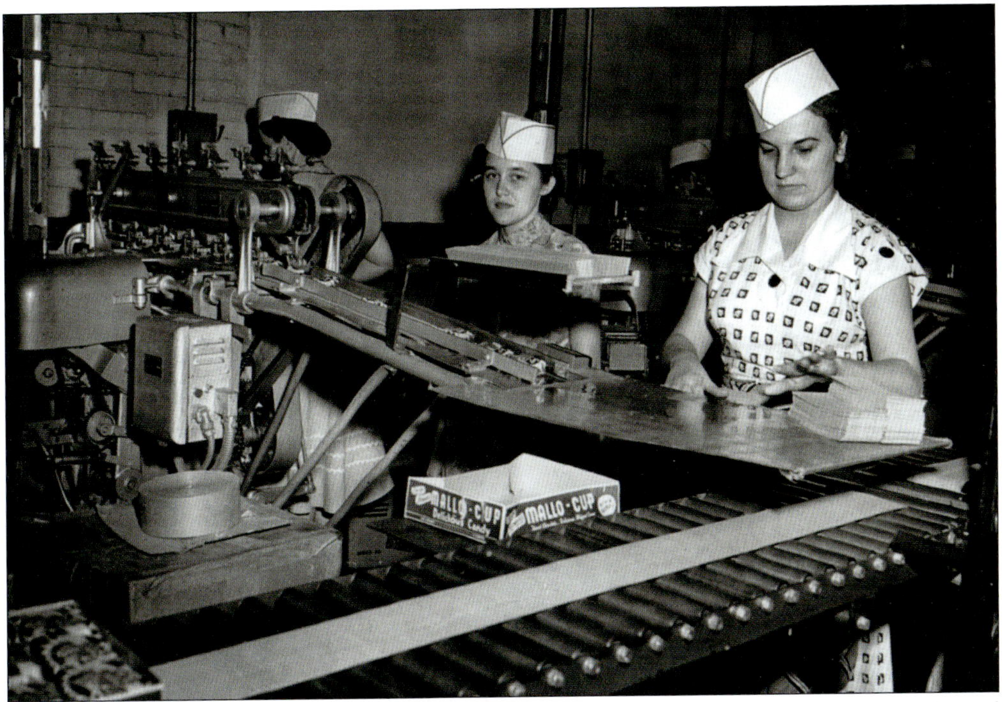

In what began as a small family venture in 1936, Boyer Candy has since become a celebrated institution. Based out of its original plant on Seventeenth Street, Boyer produces the Mallo Cup: a popular marshmallow treat laced in coconut and covered with chocolate. (Courtesy of BCCC.)

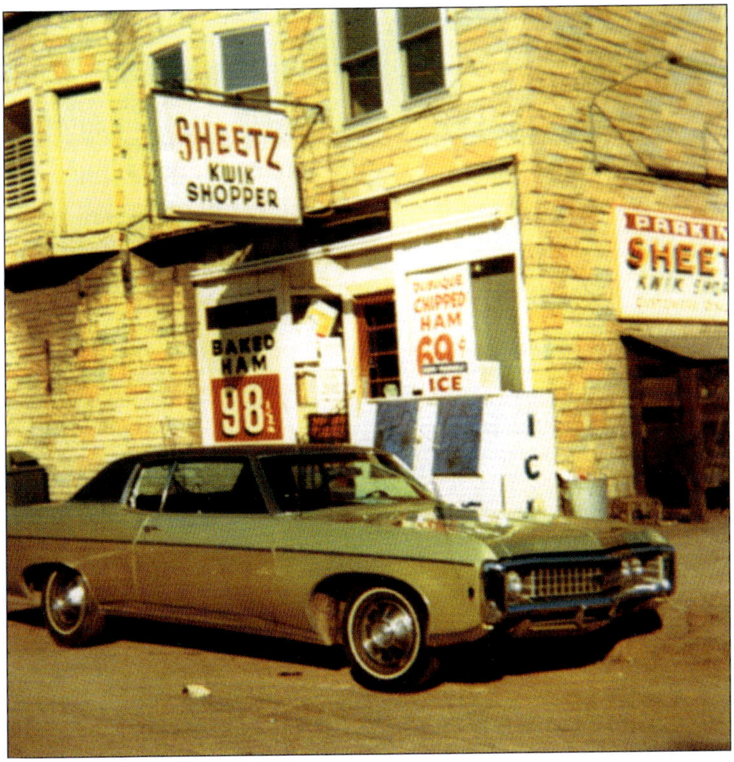

The massive Altoona-based Sheetz Inc. began as a small dairy and deli on Fifth and Union Avenues. Purchasing the property from his father in 1952, Bob Sheetz sold hundreds of pounds of chipped ham weekly. Still, Sheetz yearned for something bigger and had grand plans in store. This 1970s photograph shows the birthplace of a future corporation. (Courtesy of Sheetz.)

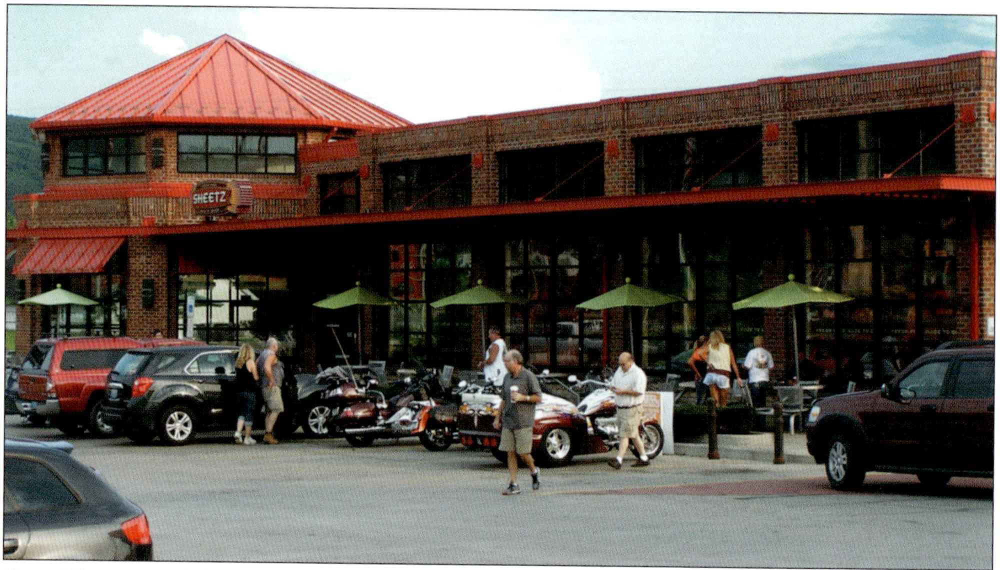

Over 50 years and 500 stores later, Sheetz stands as one of the largest gas and convenience store franchises in the country. With an annual revenue exceeding $5 billion, Sheetz has met great success in selling fuel as well as hoagie sandwiches known as MTOs (made to order). Modern locations such as Seventeenth Street's Super Sheetz demonstrate how far the corporation has come since the first Sheetz Kwik Shopper. (Author's collection.)

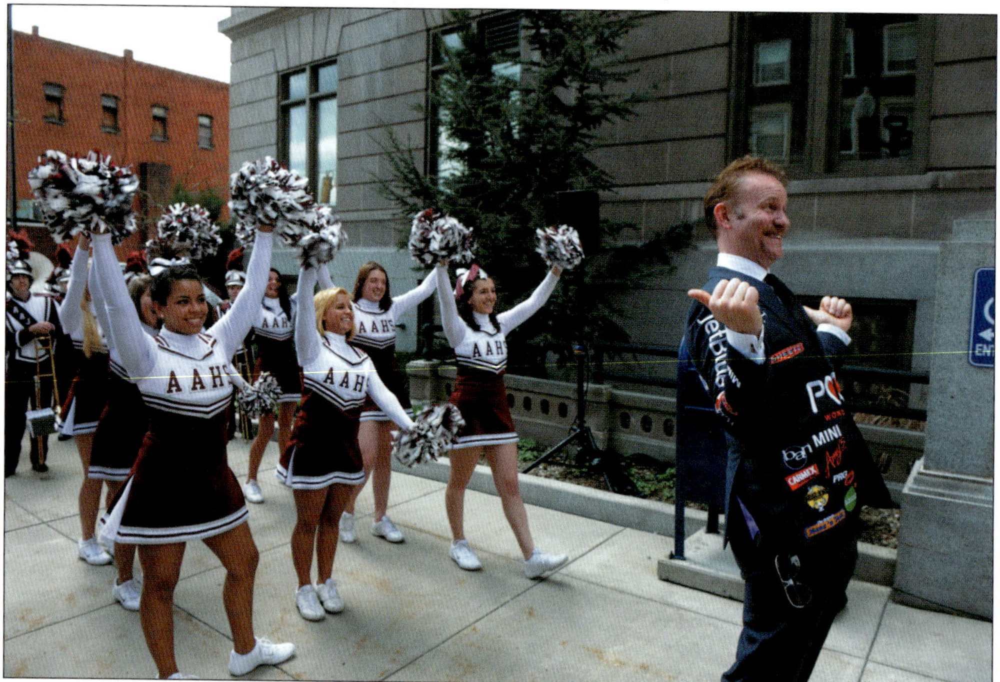

On April 27, 2011, documentarian Morgan Spurlock paraded in front of city hall to promote his film humorously examining corporate sponsorship. In conjunction with Sheetz, the director paid the city $25,000 to change its name to "POM Wonderful Presents: *The Greatest Movie Ever Sold*, Pennsylvania" for 60 days. Jubilantly sporting a suit adorned with corporate logos, Spurlock remarked, "This is possibly the greatest day ever." (Courtesy of AM.)

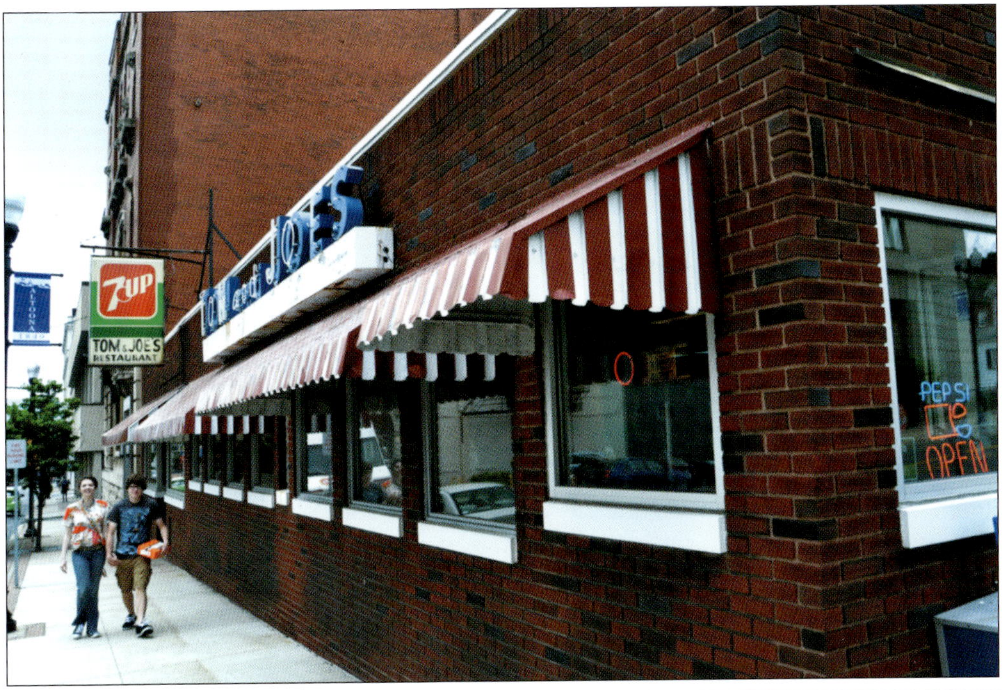

Founded in December 1933 by brothers Tom and Joe Batrus, Tom and Joe's Restaurant on Thirteenth Avenue remains one of the few eateries in the downtown district. Conveniently located across from city hall, the family-owned diner remains a favorite lunch spot. Pictured here are Veronica Compton and Matt Adams of Altoona headed in for a bite to eat. (Author's collection.)

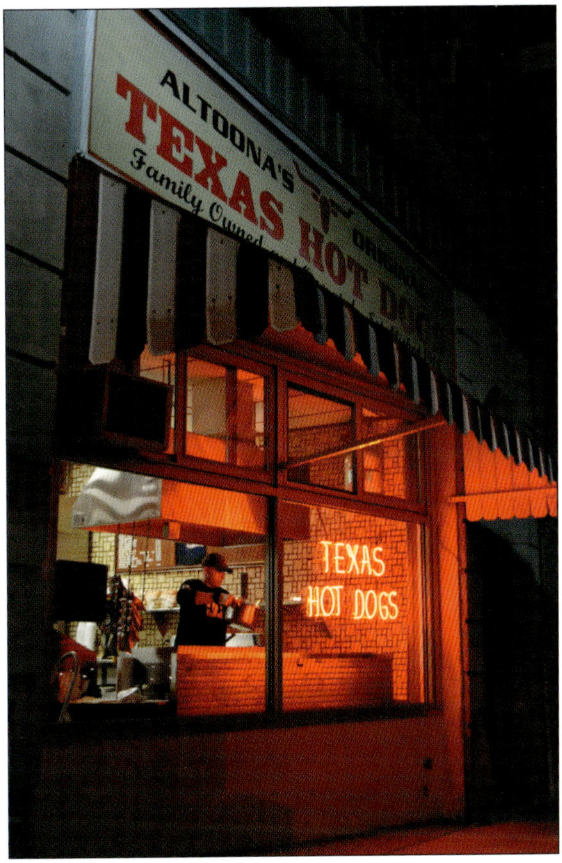

Said to be the birthplace of the original Texas Weiner, Texas Hot Dogs, founded by Greek immigrant Peter George, has been in continuous operation since World War I. A customer favorite at the Twelfth Avenue shop is the Everything, a hot dog smothered in specialty chili sauce, brown mustard, and diced onions—George's original recipe. (Courtesy of Mark Frederick.)

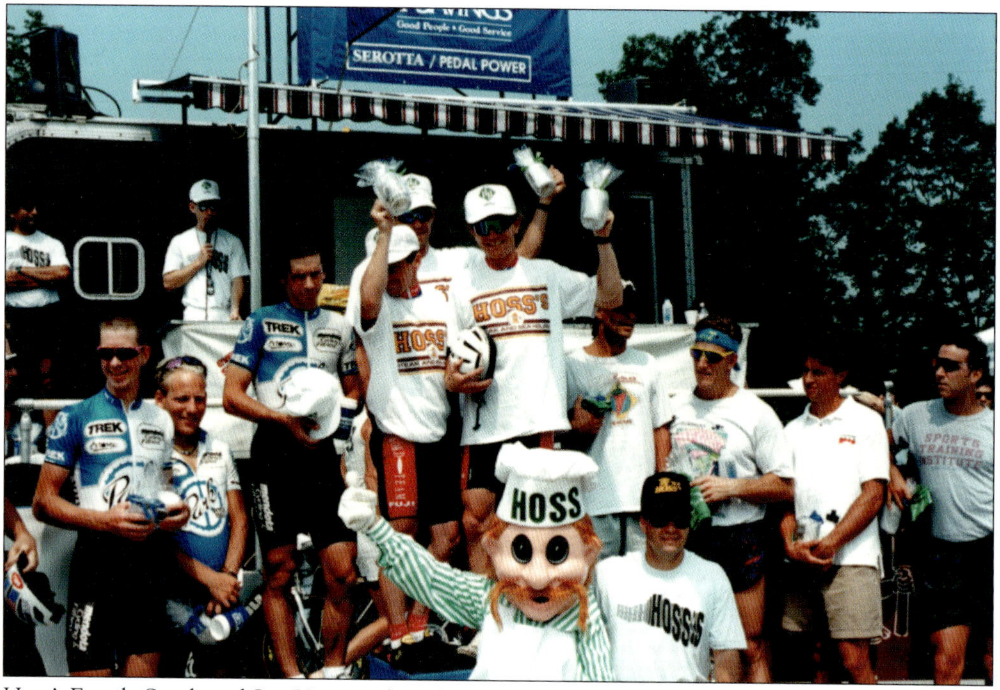

Hoss's Family Steak and Sea House is based out of Blair County and opened under the leadership of William Campbell in 1983. Boasting some three dozen restaurants, the chain has been rated among the best places to work in Pennsylvania for multiple years. In its corporate history, Hoss's has sponsored numerous charities and community events, including the 1993 International Tour de 'Toona bicycle race. (Courtesy of Hoss's.)

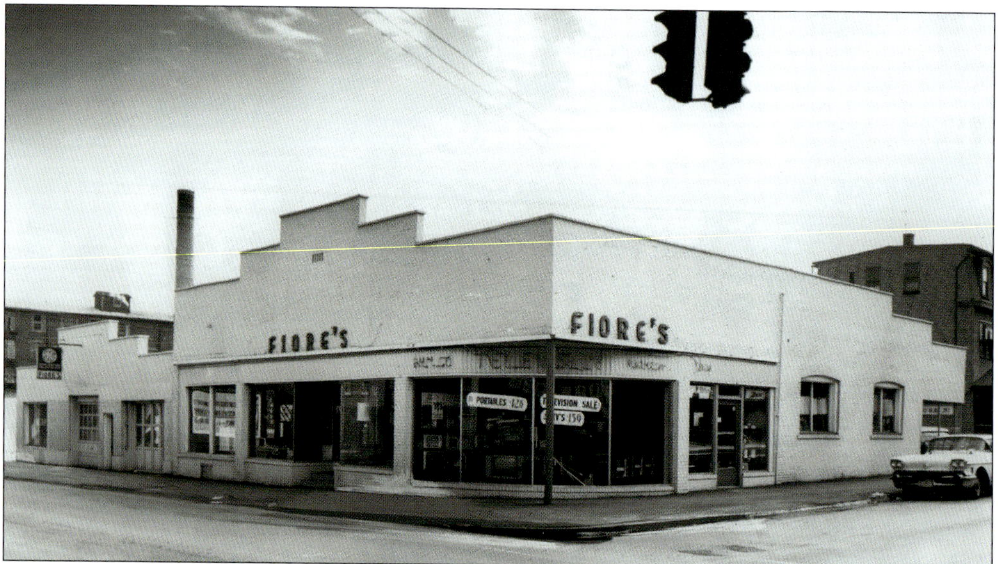

This view of Fiore Furniture at the corner of Twenty-fourth Street and Beale Avenue was taken in 1963 to mark the store's 24th anniversary. Managed by Anthony, Frank, and Joseph Fiore, the store held an anniversary sale and prize drawing. The grand winner received an Admiral stereo phonograph valued at $395. While this structure still stands, the current store's location operates on Cayuga Avenue. (Courtesy of AM.)

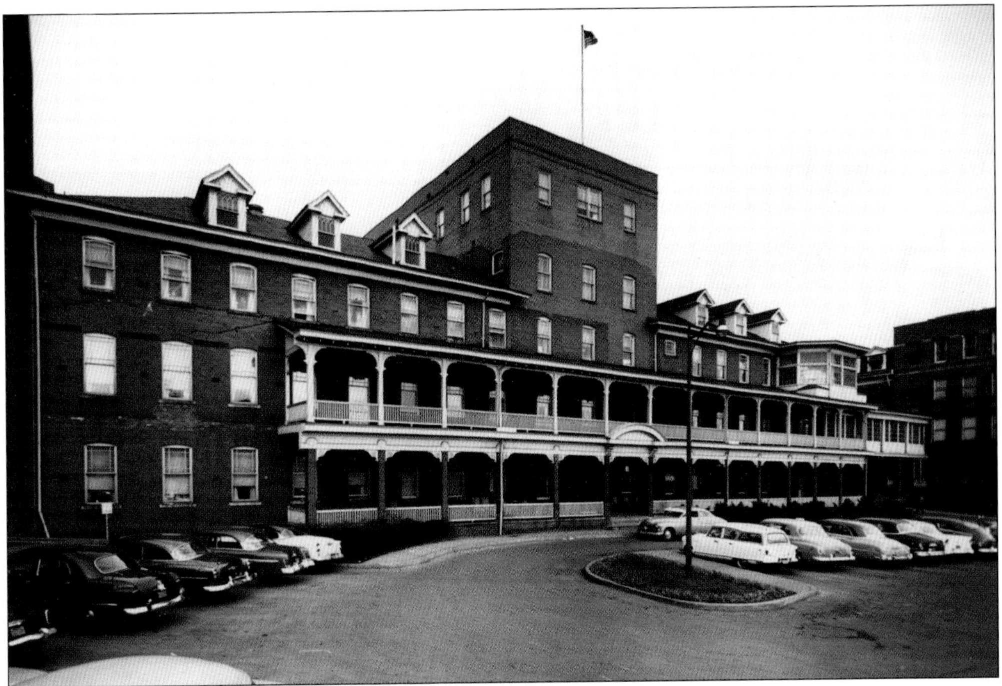

In 1886, the Pennsylvania Railroad founded the Altoona Hospital, which was morbidly but pragmatically built next to Fairview Cemetery. In 1950–1951, two wings were added for additional facilities. Of the $1.1 million spent on construction, $650,000 was donated. Fundraiser Clair Clugh exclaimed in a final campaign blitz, "We must succeed!" (Courtesy of AM.)

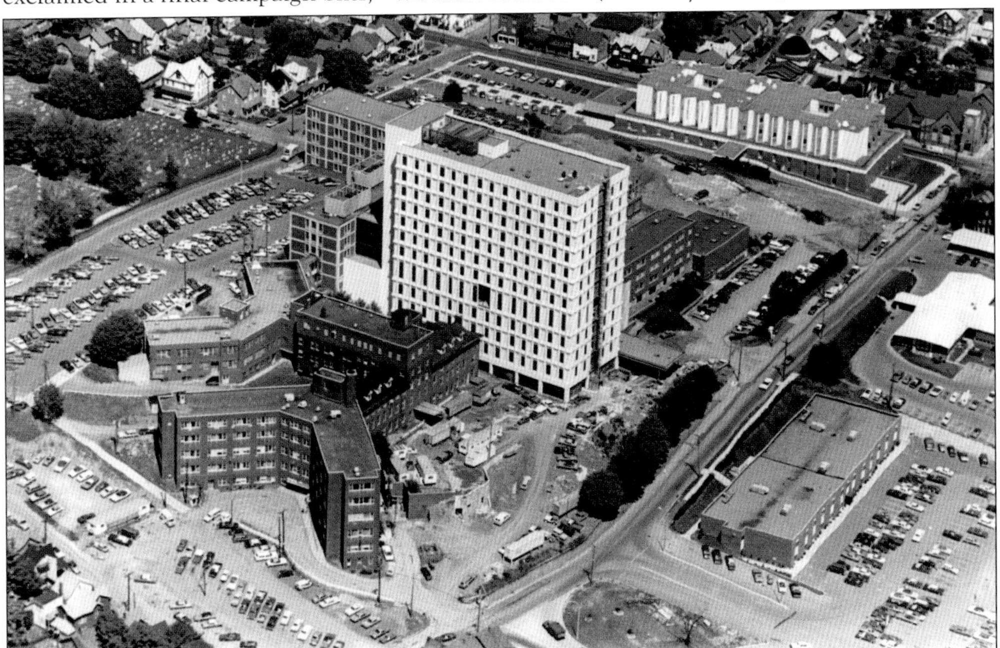

The hospital expanded again in 1978 as a 13-floor addition was added, offering needed space for 116 new beds and echocardiography equipment. Nine years later, the hospital's first open-heart surgery occurred. The earlier brick wings were demolished for expansion. (Courtesy of AM.)

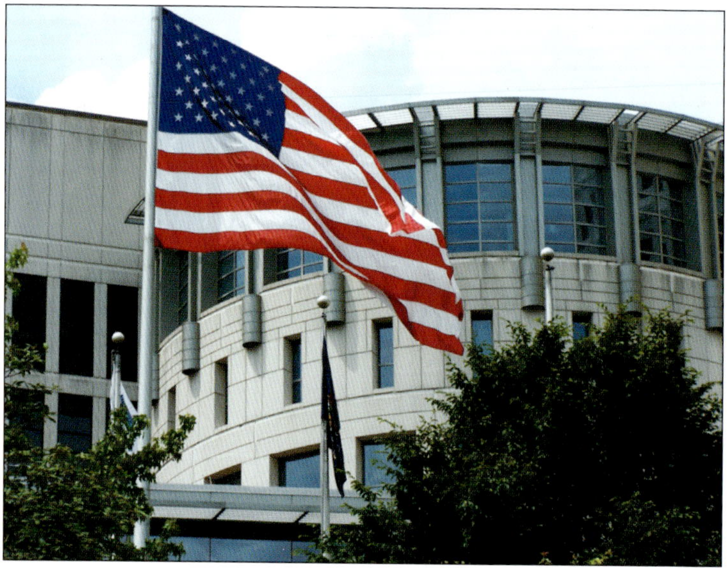

Merging with Bon Secours-Holy Family Hospital in 2004, the hospital (with its new outpatient center seen here) changed its title to the Altoona Regional Health System. In 2013, the institution was acquired by the University of Pittsburgh Medical Center. Today, UPMC Altoona serves as a stroke and trauma center for multiple counties. (Author's collection.)

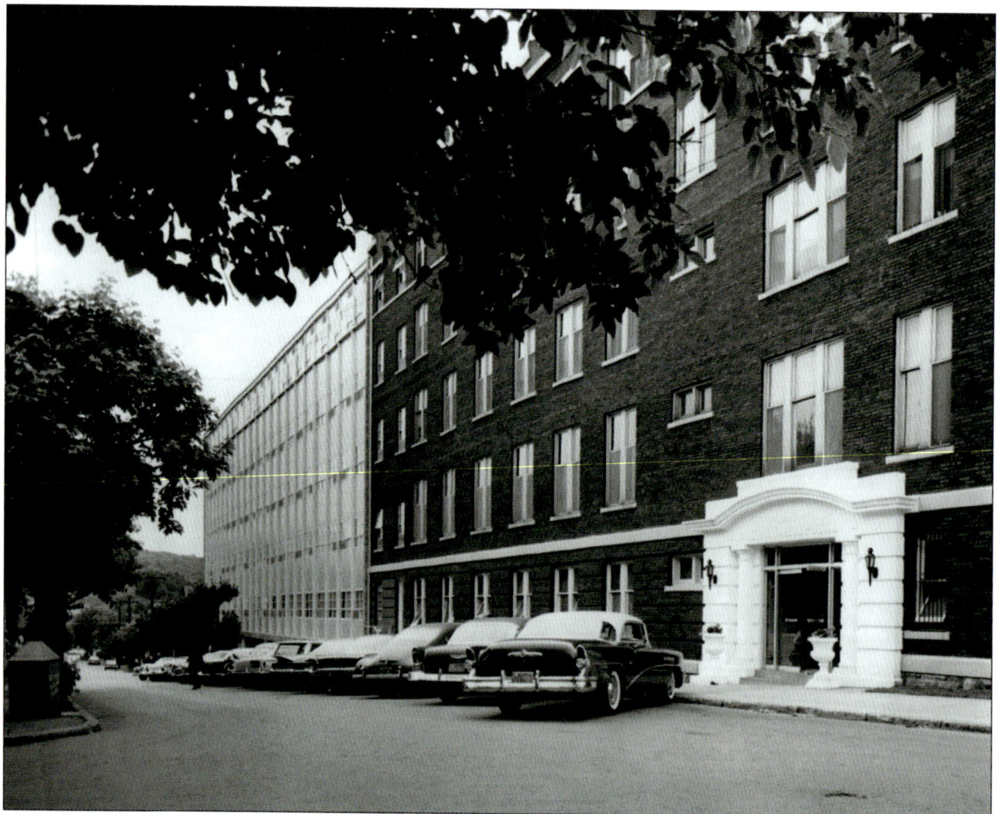

This June 1962 photograph exhibits a new addition onto Mercy Hospital on Seventh Avenue. Initially located in the home of Thomas McCaulley, the hospital was eventually staffed by the Sisters of the Holy Family of Nazareth. The institution merged with Altoona Hospital in 2004 but ultimately closed in 2012 amid consolidation. (Courtesy of AM.)

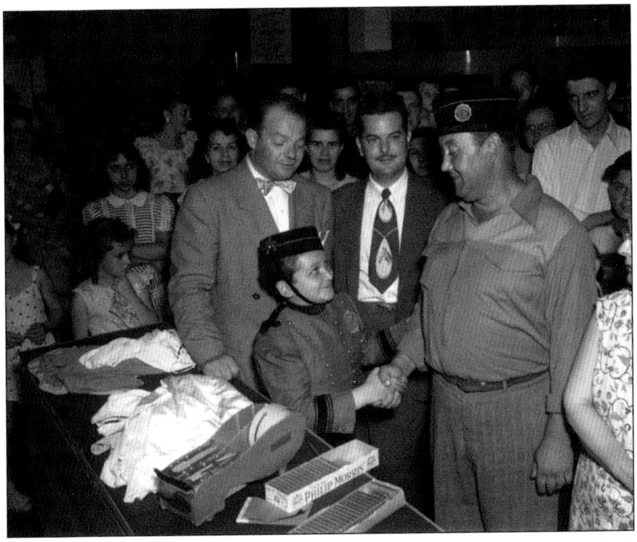

A wide array of ceremonies commemorated Altoona's 1949 centennial. Philip Morris district representative I.C. Duffey (wearing necktie) guided mascot "Johnny" Philip Morris to events. City council appointed Johnny honorary fire chief in recognition of Philip Morris placing "Please Be Careful" smoking cards in hotels. Here, Johnny distributes complementary cigarettes at the Lorraine Shop at 1333 Eleventh Avenue on August 10, 1949. (Photograph by Gelon Smith, courtesy of William Burket.)

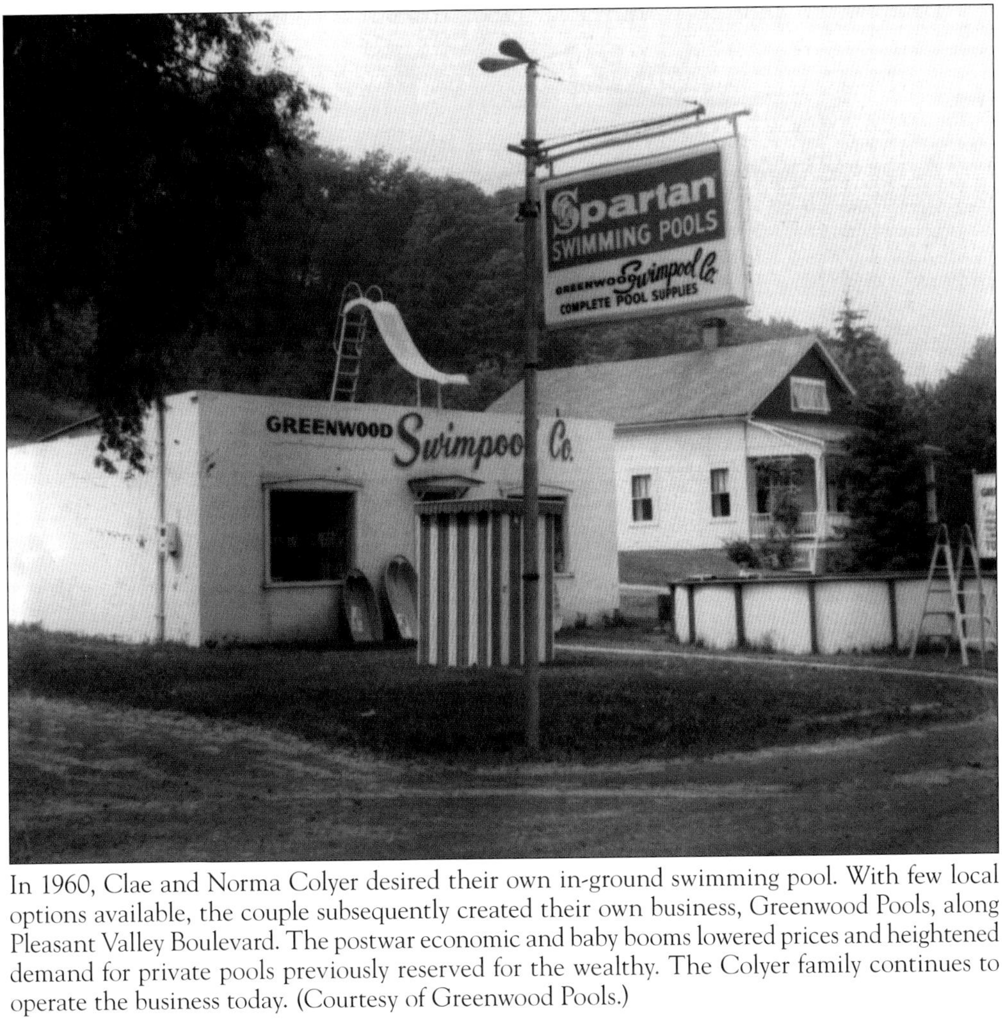

In 1960, Clae and Norma Colyer desired their own in-ground swimming pool. With few local options available, the couple subsequently created their own business, Greenwood Pools, along Pleasant Valley Boulevard. The postwar economic and baby booms lowered prices and heightened demand for private pools previously reserved for the wealthy. The Colyer family continues to operate the business today. (Courtesy of Greenwood Pools.)

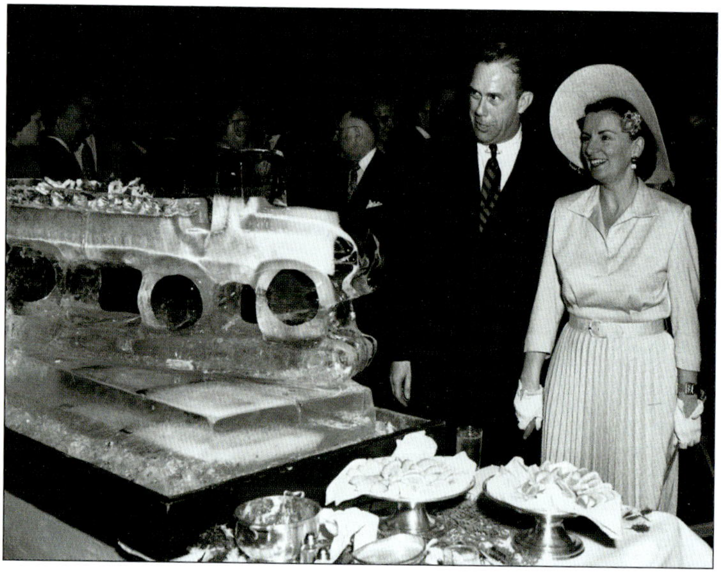

Ward Trucking president William Ward and his wife and vice president, Dorothy, greet guests next to an ice sculpture during an open house at their new Seventh Avenue freight terminal on November 10, 1951. Today, Ward Transport and Logistics is in its third generation of family ownership and offers shipment coverage throughout half the nation. (Courtesy of AM.)

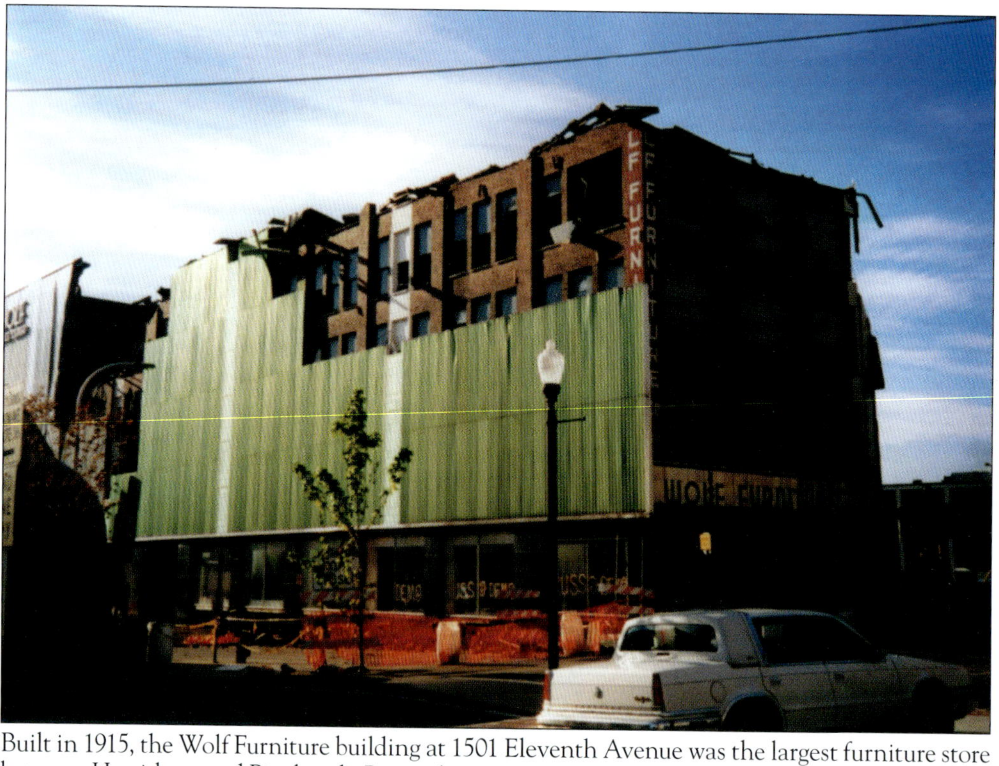

Built in 1915, the Wolf Furniture building at 1501 Eleventh Avenue was the largest furniture store between Harrisburg and Pittsburgh, Pennsylvania. Later updated with a modernistic green facade, the building was dismantled in November 1997. The site is currently Wolf Court apartments. Now with over one dozen stores, Wolf Furniture is one of the largest home furnishing retailers in the Mid-Atlantic region. (Courtesy of David Seidel.)

Upon its opening in August 1946, Kaufman's was hailed as "Altoona's newest fashion center." As seen in this April 9, 1962, photograph, the business offered stylish apparel. Kaufman's closed amid bankruptcy in 2005 and was demolished in November 2007. Passerby Frank Birkl lamented at that scene of destruction, "They never save anything for posterity." (Courtesy of AM.)

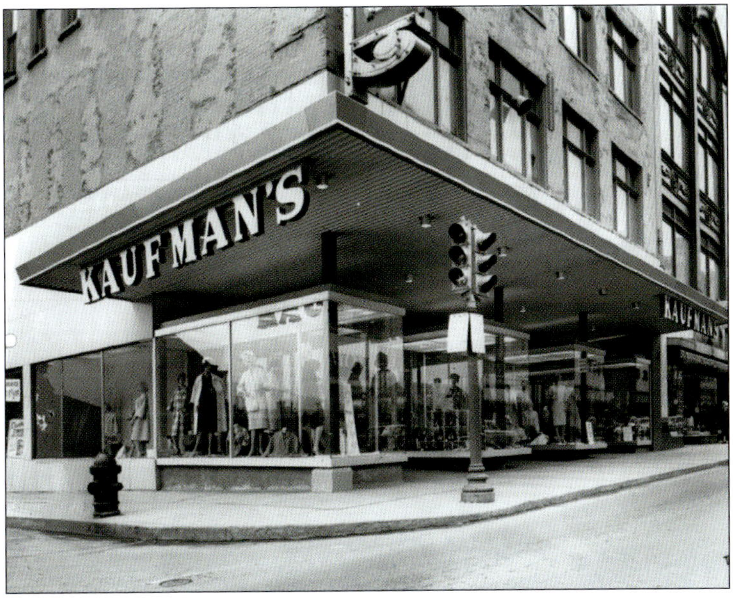

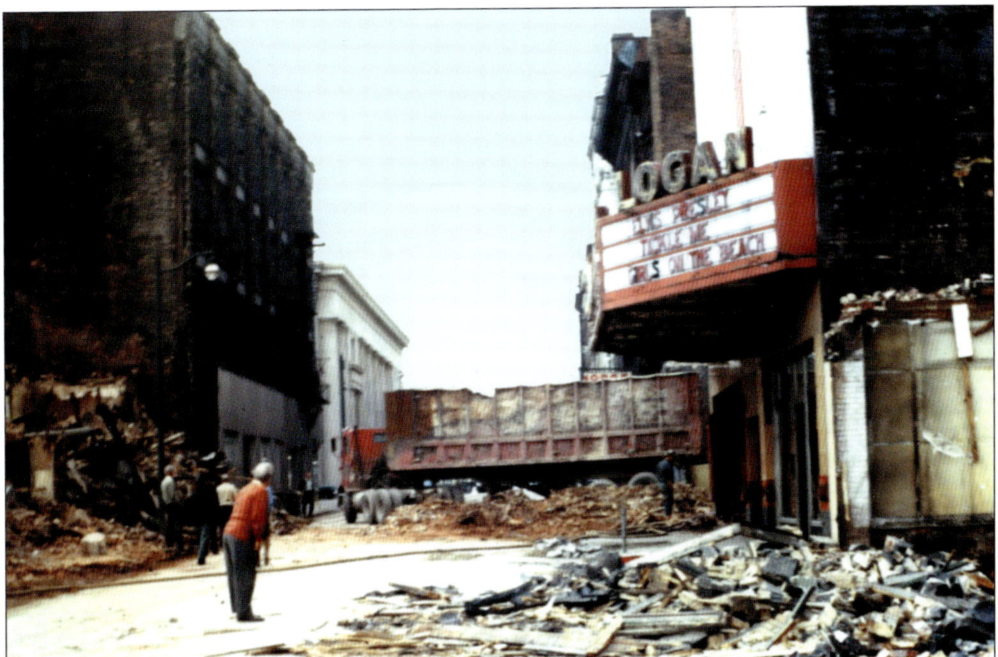

Opened by Jacob and Isaac Silverman in 1938, the Art Deco–style Logan Theatre at 1116 Eleventh Avenue played films until 1965. The cinema charged 25¢ per adult for evening tickets. Among the last movies to roll at the Logan was the Elvis Presley musical *Tickle Me*. The theater was torn down in September 1969. (Courtesy of David Seidel.)

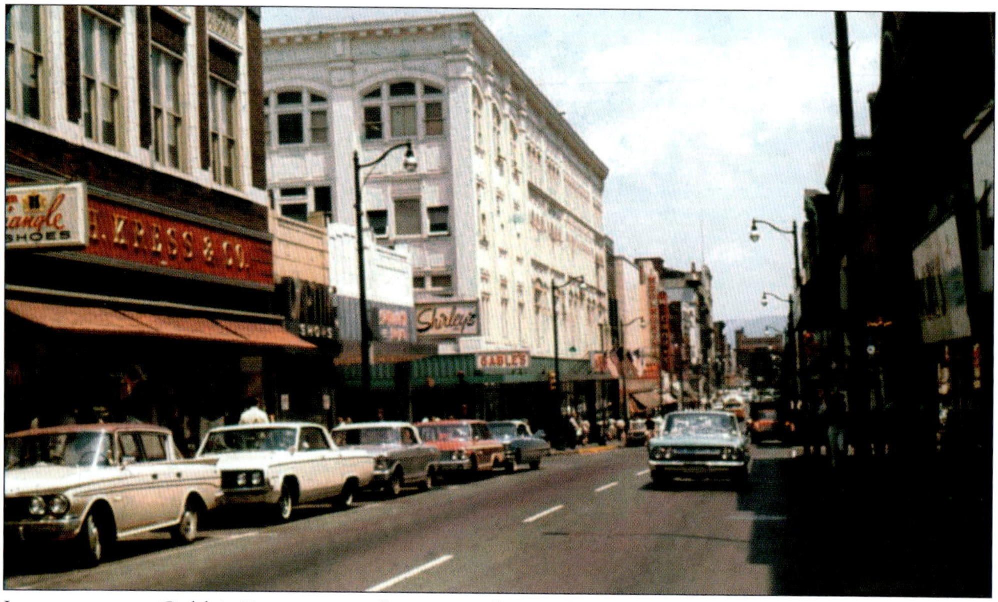

In many ways, Gable's Department Store was the nucleus of downtown life. Opening in 1884, William F. Gable's business relocated to Eleventh Avenue in 1892. The massive store eventually boasted some 40 departments. This mid-1960s photograph also shows Shirley's Shoes at the corner of Fourteenth Street and Eleventh Avenue. (Courtesy of David Seidel.)

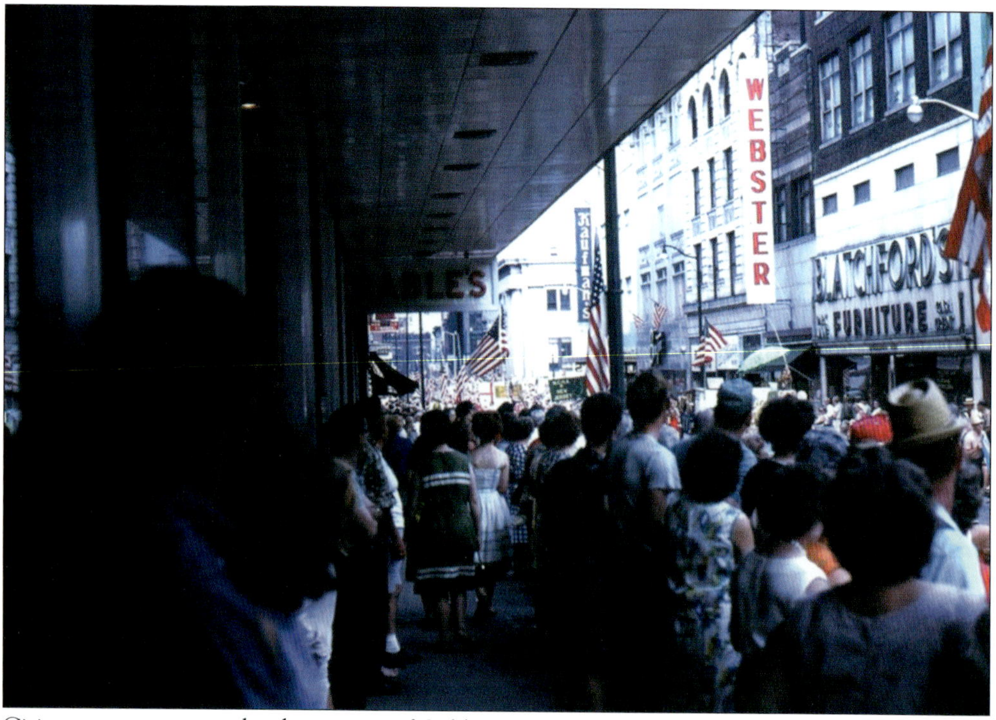

Citizens congregate under the portico of Gable's on July 13, 1967, to enjoy the National Campers and Hiker's Association Campvention that marked the opening of Prince Gallitzin State Park. Some 25,000 people participated in the festivities. The *Altoona Mirror* editorialized, "We are for more parades." (Courtesy of David Seidel.)

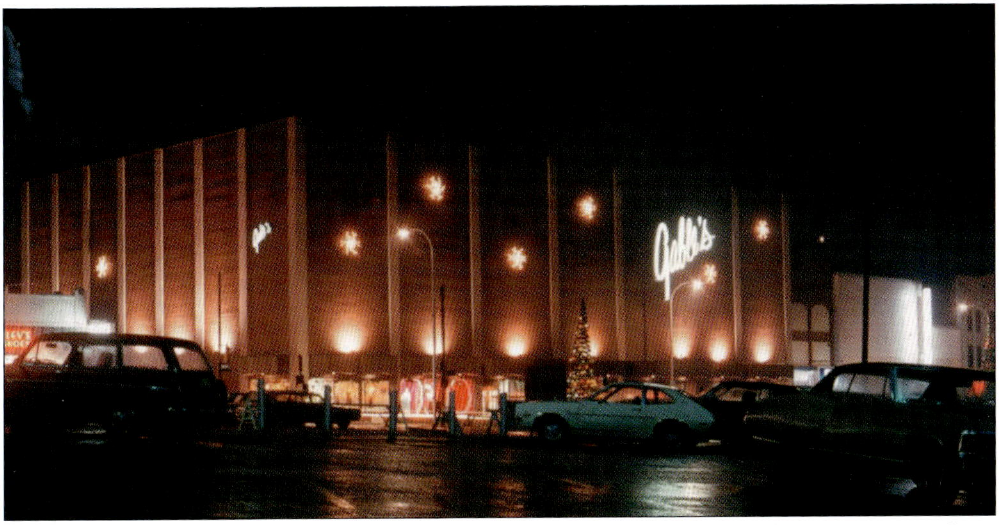

By Christmas 1975, Gable's underwent a massive face-lift that concealed its ornate storefront in the name of modernization. Two feet of space currently separates this brick veneer from the original walls encased within. Many residents hope the structure can be restored to its original appearance. Today, the old department store is home to various businesses and community organizations. (Courtesy of David Seidel.)

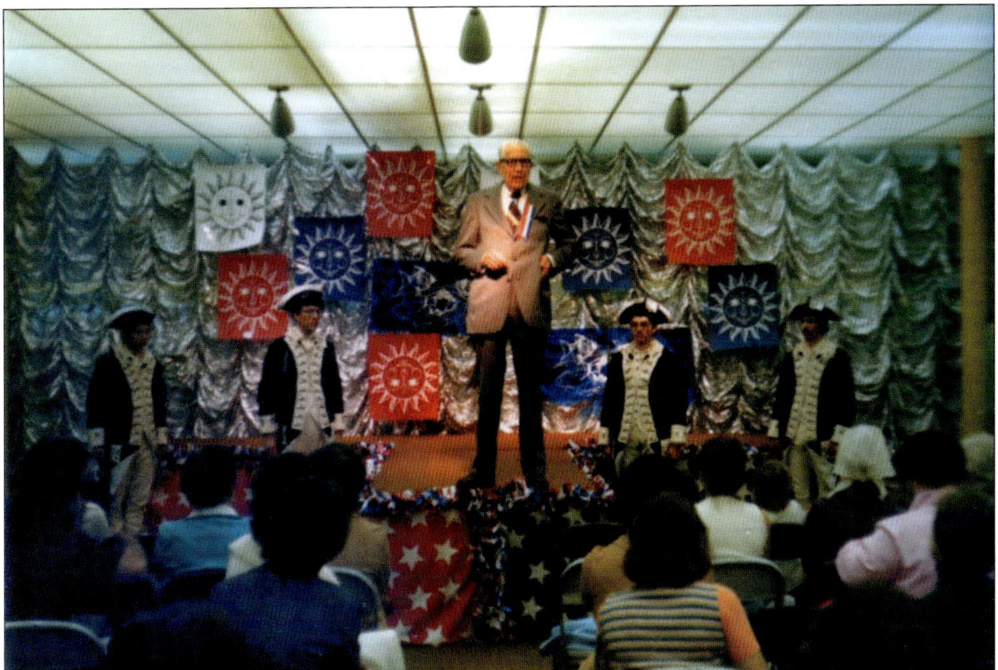

In recognition of the national bicentennial in 1976, Gable's employee David Little introduces Miss Pennsylvania Connie Harness, who was sponsored by the department store at the Miss America pageant the prior year. In the background, Penn State Altoona ROTC cadets stand at attention in Continental uniforms. (Courtesy of David Seidel.)

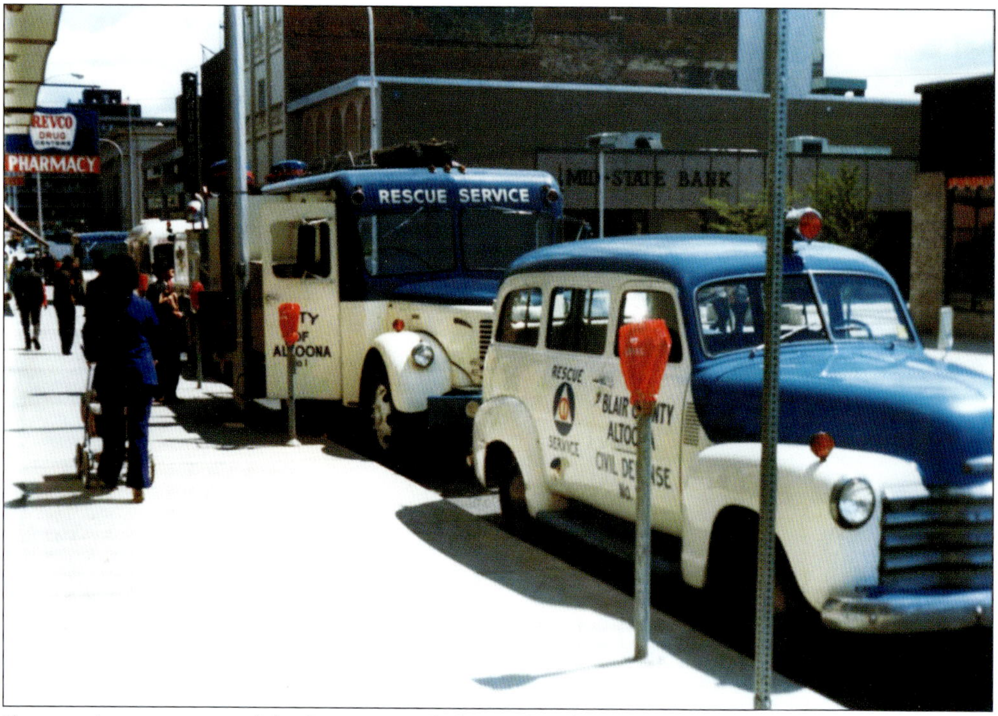

Despite the pageantry of the bicentennial, fears of nuclear conflict with the Soviet Union still troubled Altoonans. These civil defense vehicles displayed outside Gable's during bicentennial events served as subtle reminders of Cold War anxieties. Simultaneously, Gable's faced troubles of its own, ultimately closing four summers later. Altoona residents wrote to the store's employees, "We will miss all of you people very much." (Courtesy of David Seidel.)

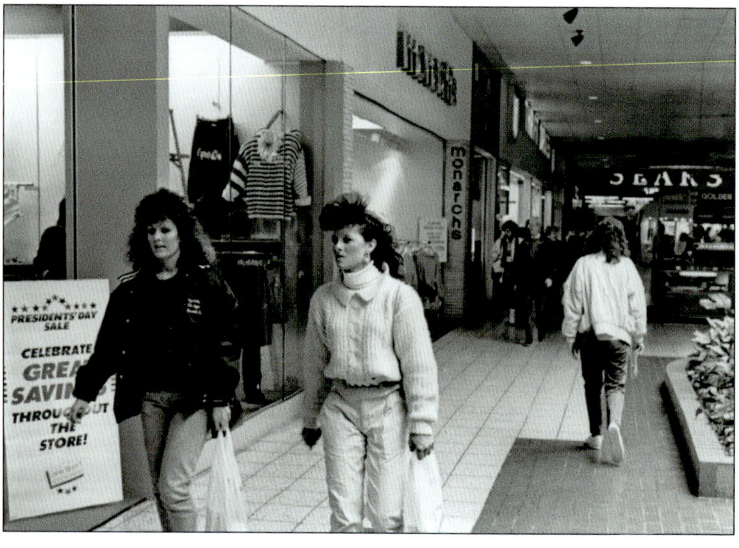

With downtown shopping largely extinct due to the rise of suburban sprawl, new retail centers such as the Logan Valley Mall, opened in 1965, filled Altoona's commercial void. In this 1980s photograph, shoppers take advantage of a Presidents' Day sale. (Courtesy of AM.)

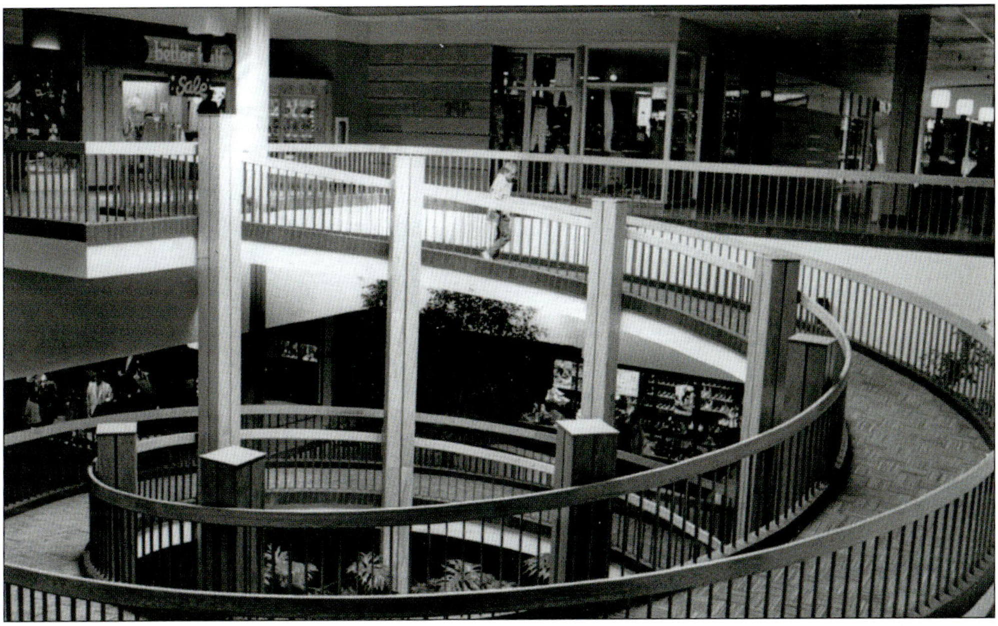

A central feature of the Logan Valley Mall was this unique spiral walkway located near an equally novel glass elevator. The walkway was removed after a 1994 fire ravaged the complex. As is seen in this 1988 photograph, the architectural feature was a favorite play spot for children. (Courtesy of AM.)

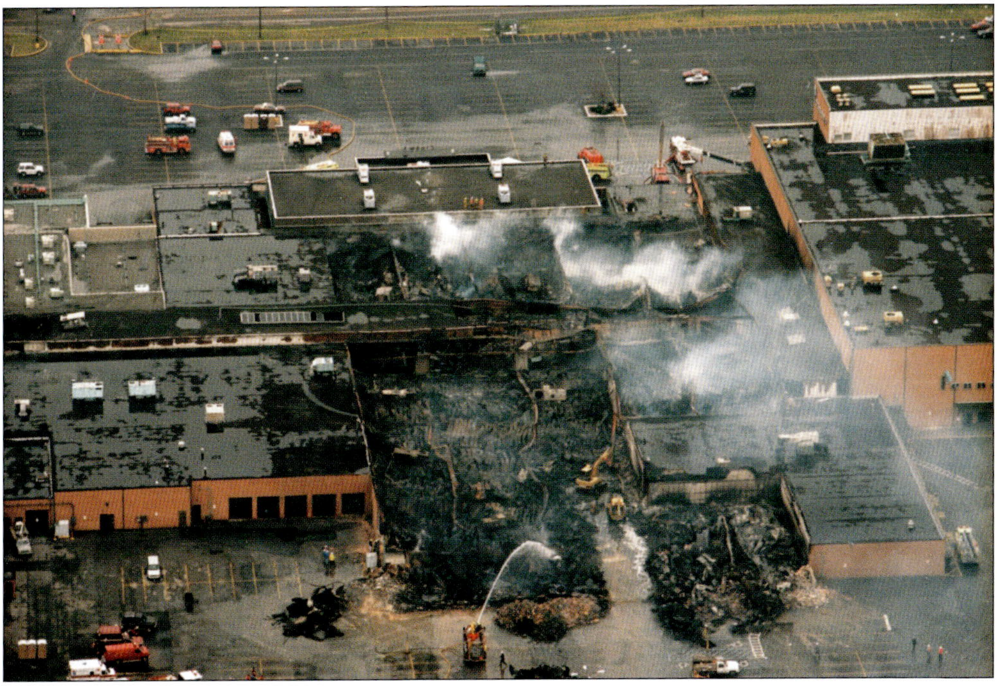

Shortly after 2:00 a.m. on December 16, 1994, an inferno erupted at the Logan Valley Mall's G.C. Murphy store. Over 400 emergency officials responded to the blaze, which damaged nearly 50 stores; however, J.C. Penney Company survived and reopened the following day. (Photograph by J.D. Cavrich, courtesy of AM.)

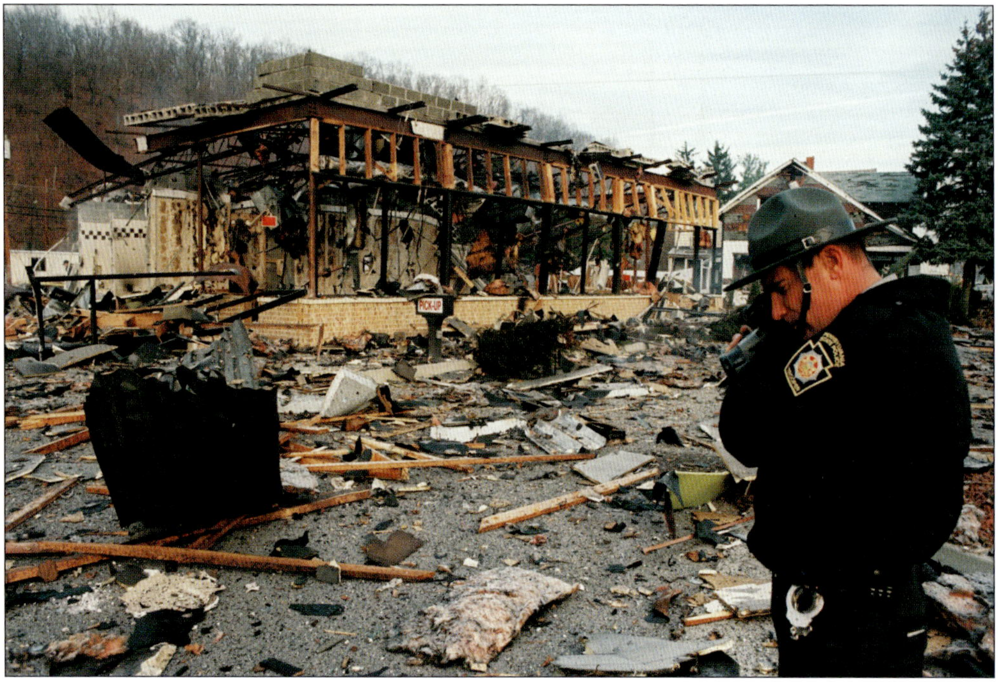

On December 10, 1994, the Boardwalk Pizzeria at 320 Logan Boulevard was consumed by a massive fireball resulting from a leak of 70,000 cubic feet of natural gas. The explosion blew out windows and rocked surrounding Lakemont. "We think about it every 10th of December," resident John Heininger remembered. (Courtesy of AM.)

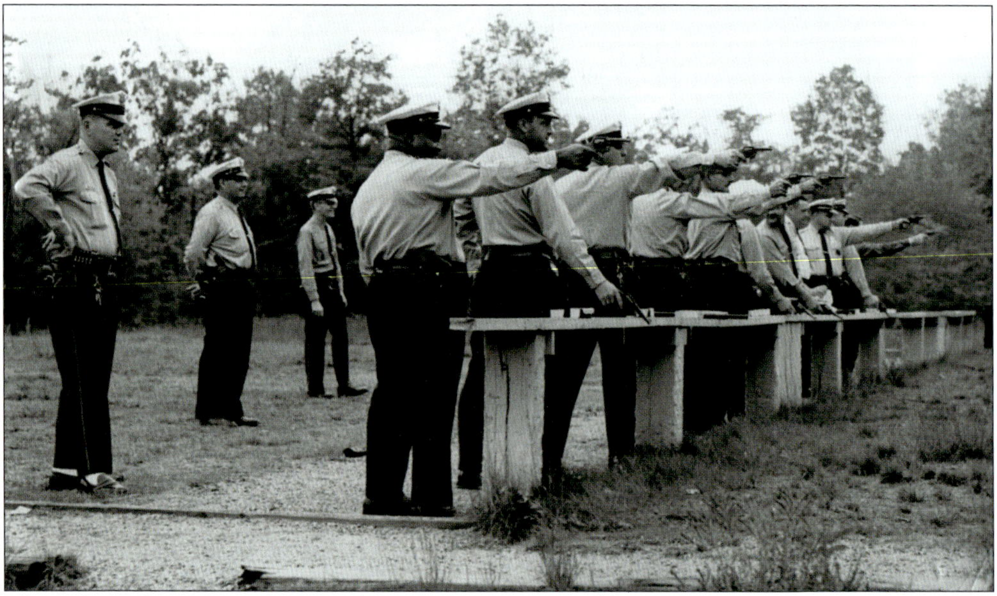

Throughout the 1960s, Altoona police participated in weekly training at the PRR shooting range in East Juniata. Chief William Stephens instituted drills so an officer could "defend not only the lives of others, but his own." In the back, Bob Roessing (left) and Vince Kimmel (center) observe the shooters' stances. Milford Pittman and Joe Franks are the first two marksmen in the foreground, and Orman Ostrander is the left-handed officer near the end of the line. (Courtesy of APD.)

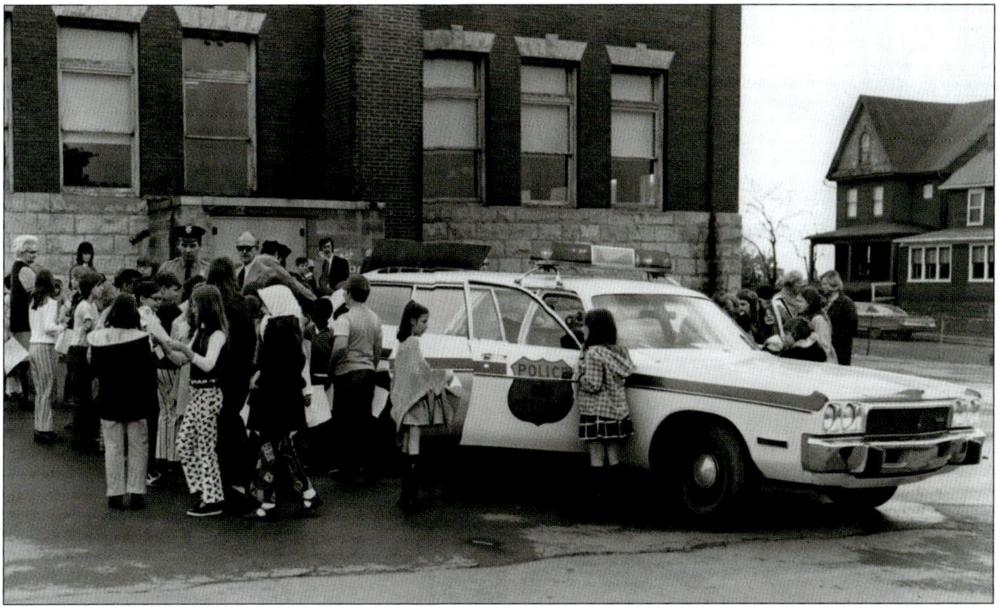

Garfield Elementary School on Twentieth Street and Fourteenth Avenue featured a popular playground operated by the recreational commission. In this 1973 photograph, police chief Jack Kuhn and officer Fred Lowery show students the interior of a squad car. One of several notable city veterans, Chief Kuhn scaled the cliffs of Pointe du Hoc on D-Day. (Courtesy of APD.)

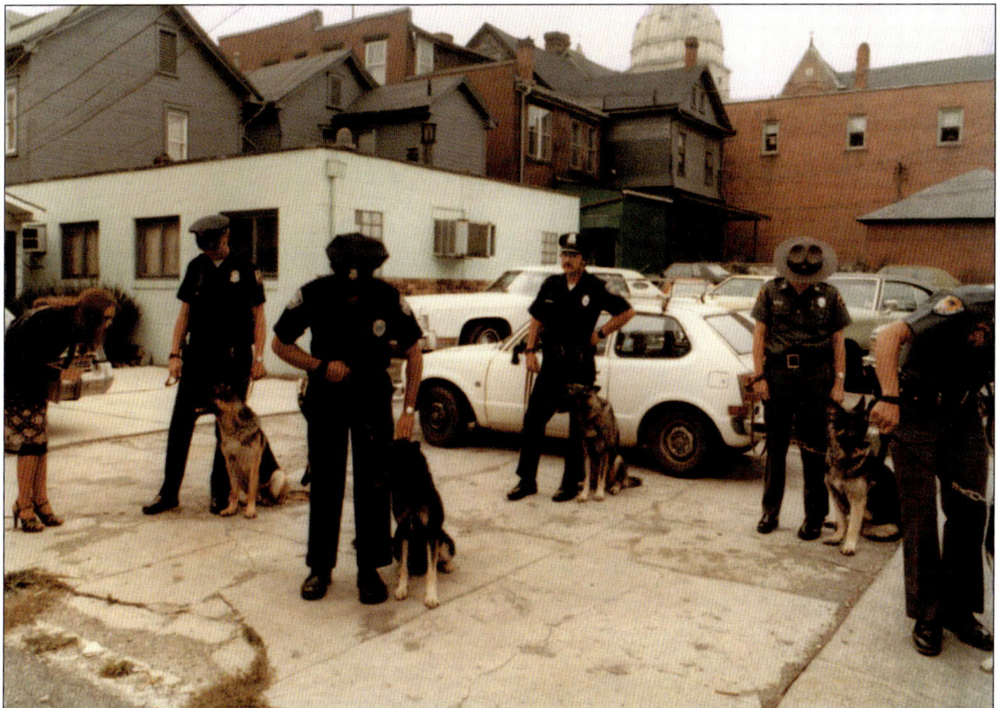

On September 20, 1978, the Altoona police and other regional law enforcement hosted a demonstration of their new police dogs outside city hall. The exhibition included a mock robbery in which the dogs pursued a thief. (Courtesy of APD.)

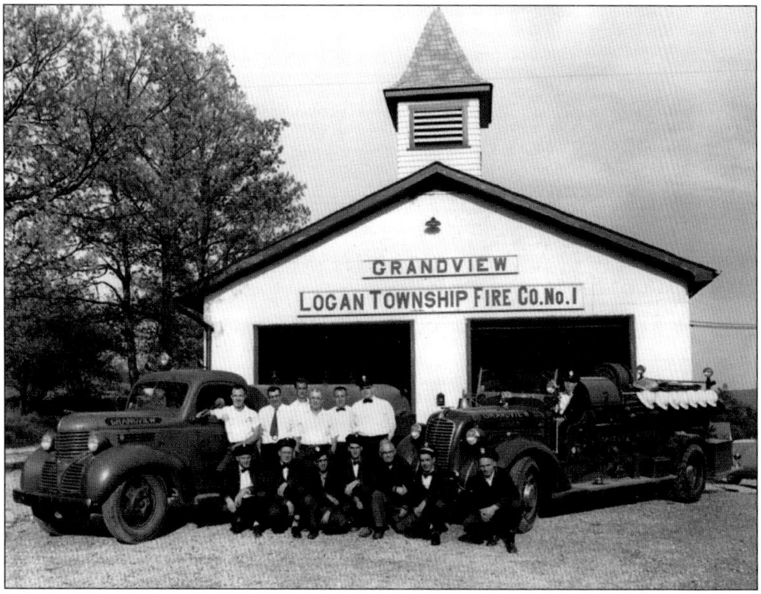

The Grandview Logan Township Fire Company was created in 1923. Located on the rural periphery of Altoona, the station was suited to fight brush fires. The new United Fire Department currently serves some 4,000 residents. The 1953 station seen here still stands, but it was replaced by a larger facility across Grandview Road. (Courtesy of AM.)

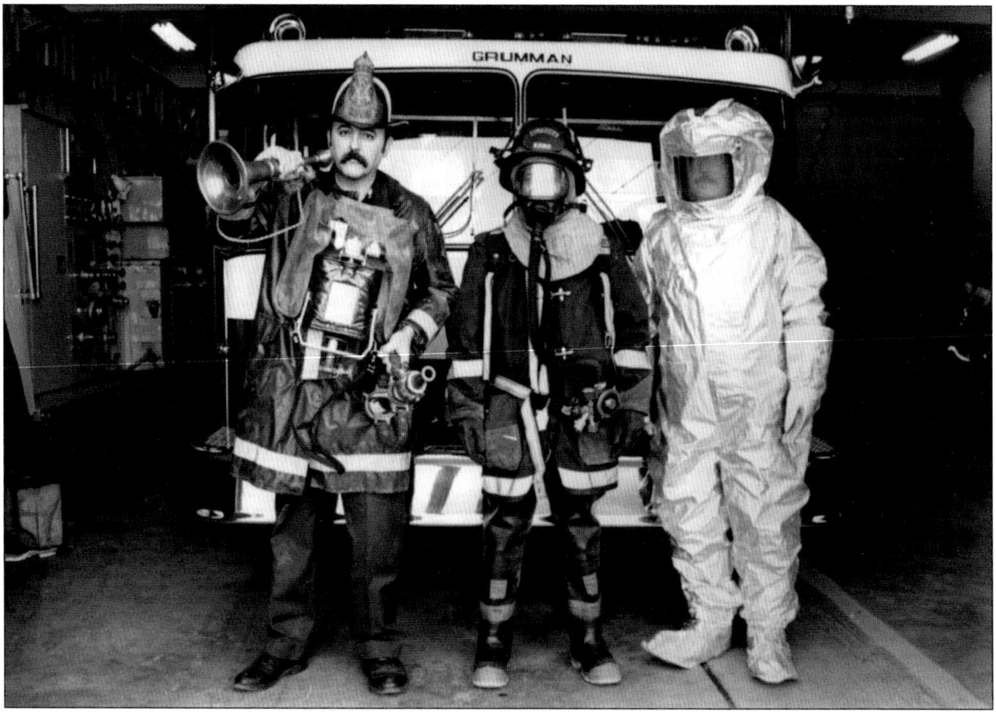

From left to right, Altoona firefighters Rick Weidlich, John Patton, and Ralph Campbell display a timeline of gear in this 1991 photograph. City firefighters responded to 1,119 calls in 1990 and saved $48 million in property. Deputy chief Ray Weimer noted, "There's a lot of challenge to firefighting," but "once it gets into your blood, it's there." (Courtesy of AM.)

Chief Renny Santone and public safety director Thomas Byrne discuss the Easter Sunday, April 3, 1988, blaze that engulfed Frank's Pizza, the Rent-A-Rabbit Costume Company, and other city dwellings. Frank's Pizza on Fourth Street was a popular keg spot among college students on Thursday nights. (Photograph by J.D. Cavrich, courtesy of AM.)

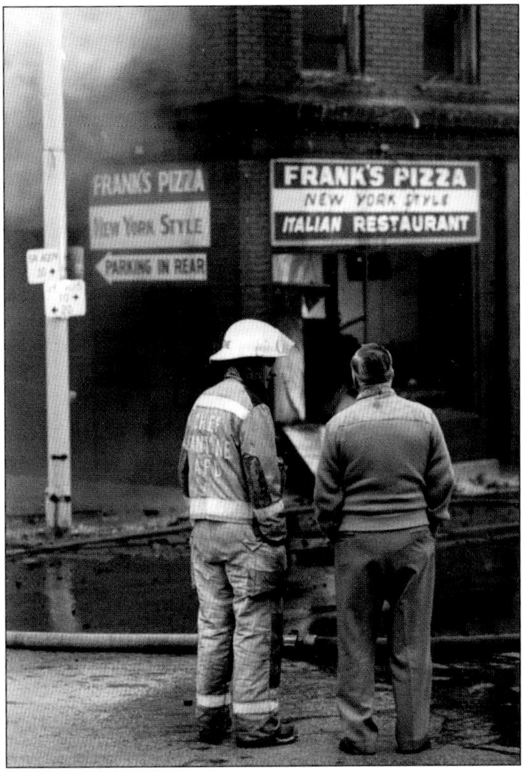

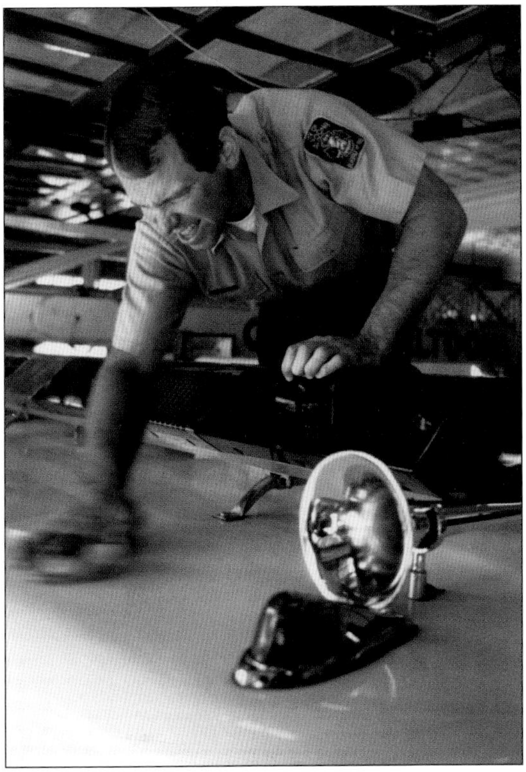

Firefighter Andy McDowell waxes the roof of a pumper at Station No. 1 in this 1991 photograph by J.D. Cavrich. McDowell briefly considered finding a new profession after colleague Ken Steel perished in a 1987 fire; however, his passion for his job persevered, and he retired two decades later as deputy chief. (Courtesy of AM.)

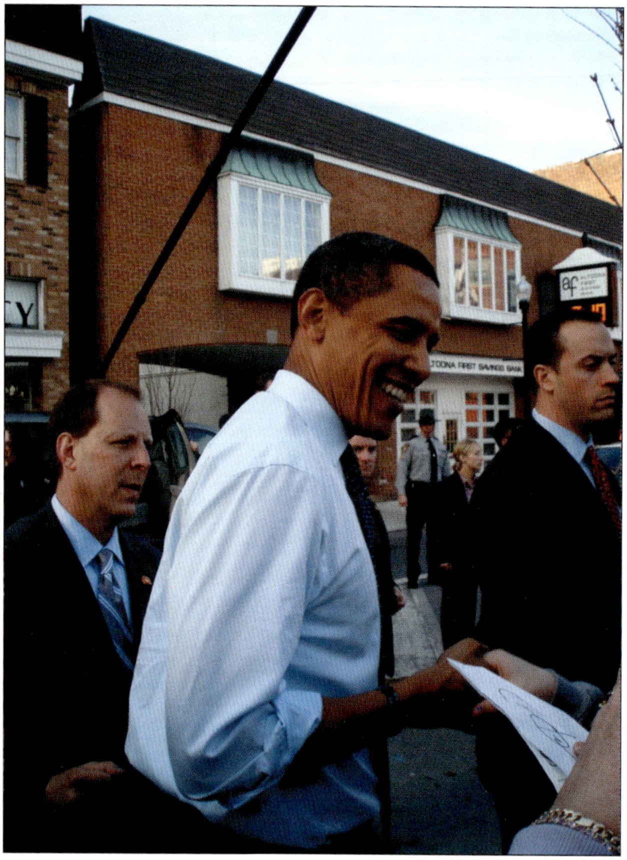

On March 30, 2008, presidential hopeful Barack Obama made a campaign stop in Altoona and paid a visit to Texas Hot Dogs. Proceeding afterward to Pleasant Valley Bowling, the candidate scored an abysmal 37. "My economic plan is better than my bowling," Obama laughed. "It has to be," a fellow bowler exclaimed. (Courtesy of Matt Michrina.)

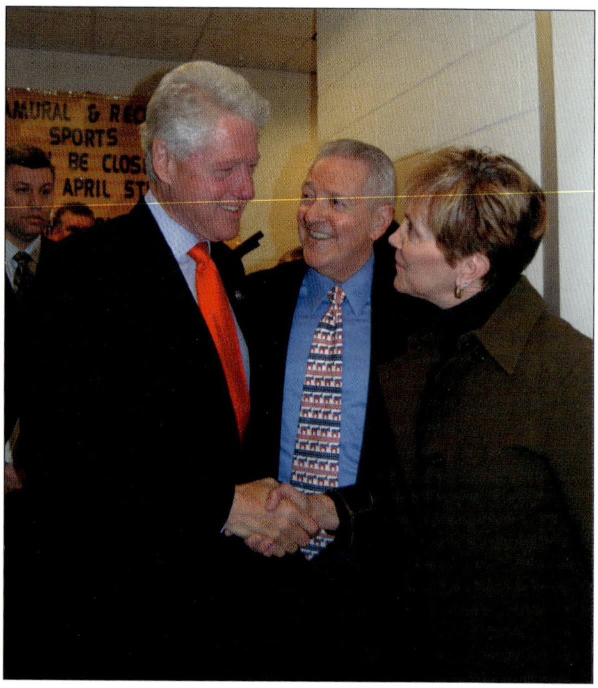

Frank and Ann Rosenhoover of the Blair County Democrats greet former president Bill Clinton on April 2, 2008, at Penn State Altoona's Adler Gymnasium. The former commander-in-chief helped secure wife Hillary's victory over Obama in the April 22 primary by a margin of 55 percent to 45 percent. (Courtesy of PSA.)

Two

Railroad City

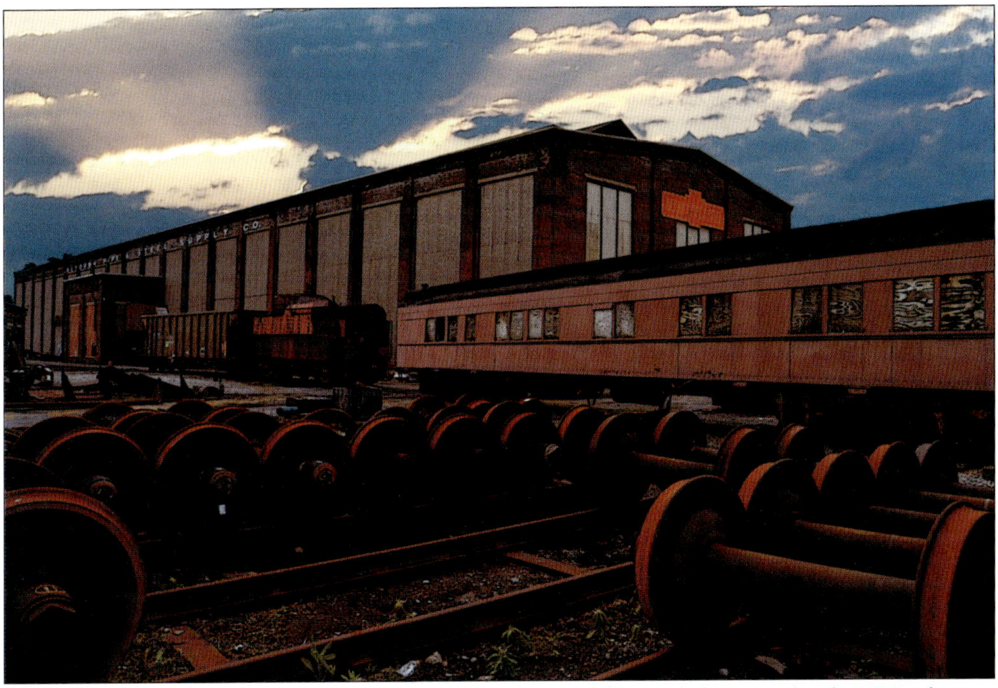

Altoona has long-prided itself on a rich railroading heritage. Founded in 1849 by the PRR, the city has gone through innumerable economic transformations since. Here, railroad relics of bygone days rust away near the Altoona Pipe & Steel Company. (Author's collection.)

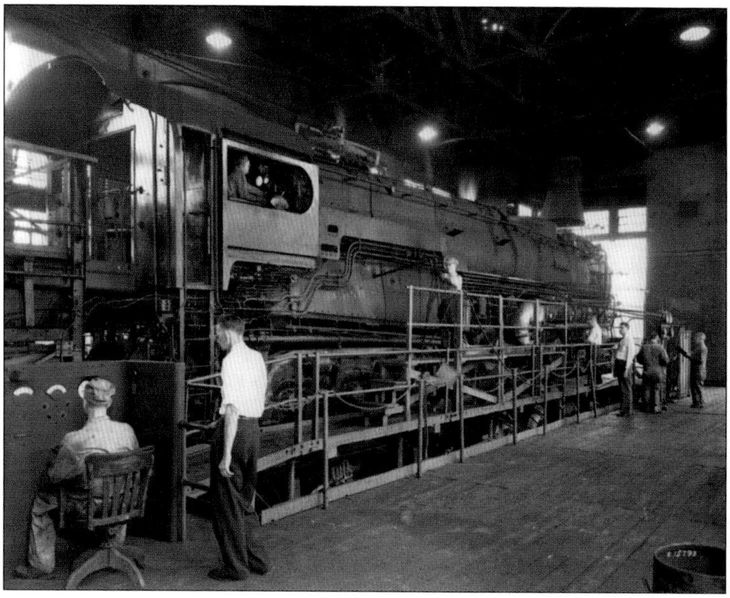

At the Twelfth Street Car Shop, locomotive machinery was tested in every conceivable manner. In one of only two such facilities in the western hemisphere, locomotives (including this 1940s S-2 steam turbine) were challenged on a massive treadmill to measure speed and endurance. (Courtesy of ARMM.)

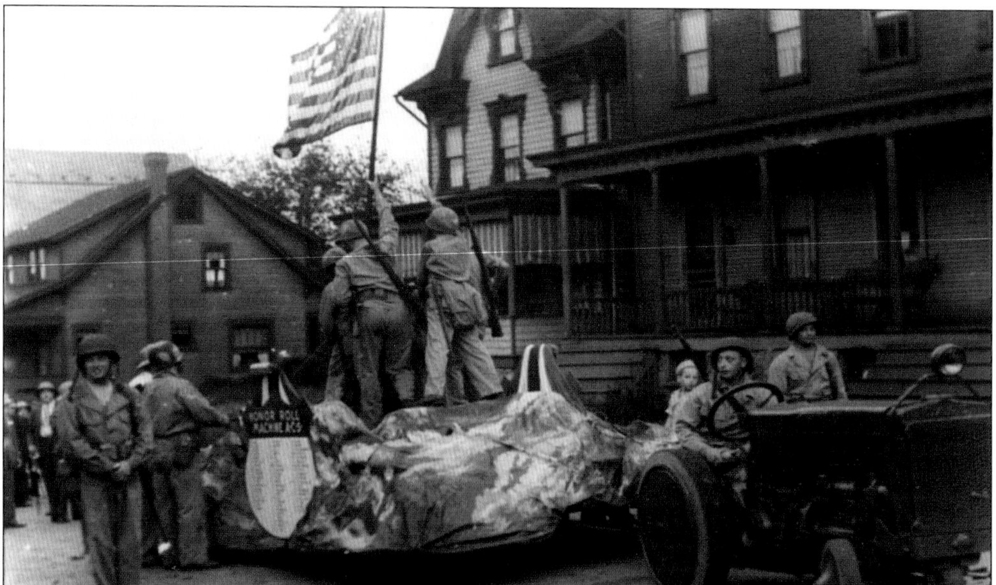

On October 25, 1945, the PRR hosted a parade in honor of 18,000 employees and war veterans. The procession was highlighted by Altoona Medal of Honor recipient Robert Laws and a tableau of Iwo Jima. The flag raisers were represented by E.W. Miller, C.J. Metzger, J.O. Blocherer, C.W. Wills, P.P. Apple, and P.L. Tomasetti. (Courtesy of David Seidel.)

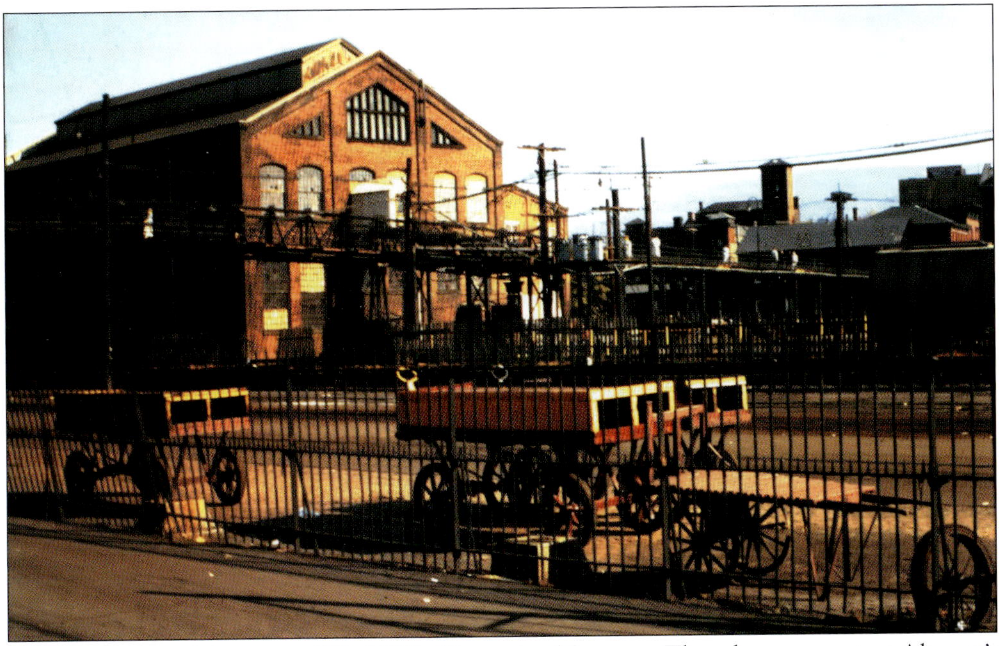

Grim reminders of the costs of World War II remained for years. These baggage carts at Altoona's Thirteenth Street station removed caskets from trains through the Vietnam War. Among those placed on these carriages was Chester Helsel on April 16, 1952. The 20-year-old Altoona private was killed on his first day of combat in Korea. (Courtesy of David Seidel.)

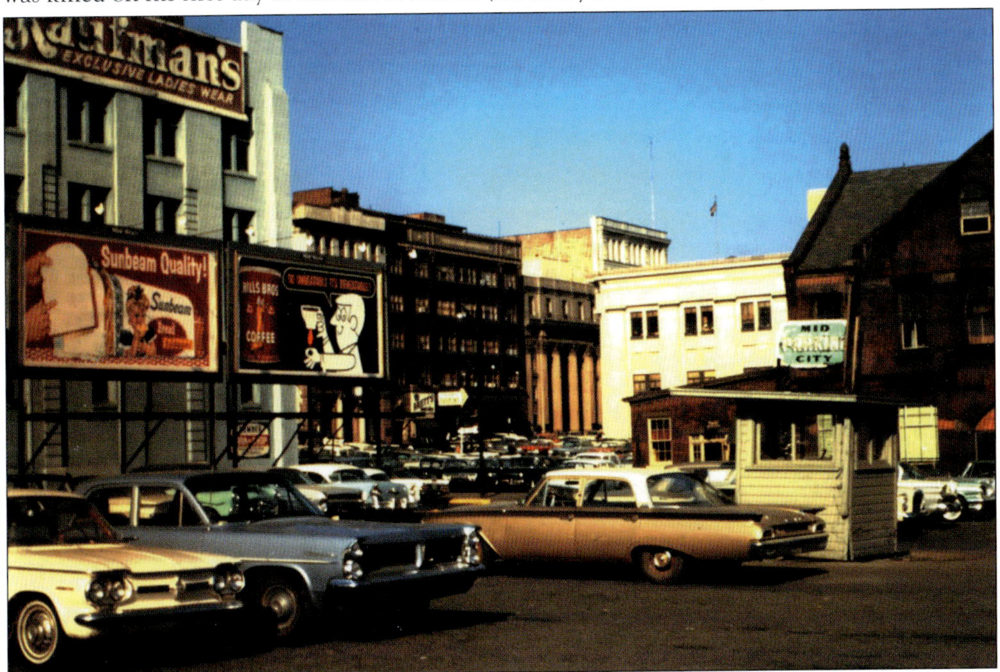

This mid-1960s view shows the city's weathered train station at right, near the post office. *Altoona Mirror* city editor Charles Rothrock regretted the station's 1971 demise, noting, "It's ironic that a parking garage, haven for automobiles that killed the passenger and commuter trains, is slated to rise in its place." (Courtesy of David Seidel.)

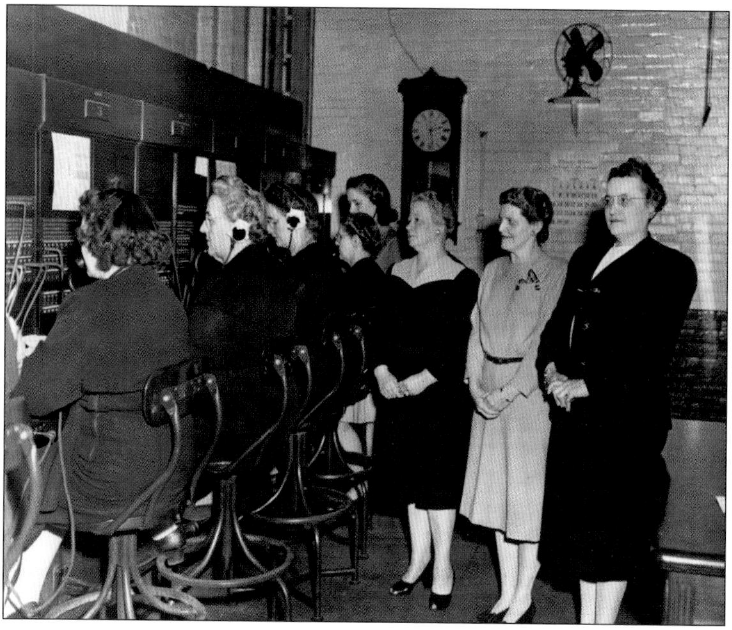

Pennsylvania Railroad switchboard operators connect calls at the Seventh Street office near Chestnut Avenue on May 27, 1946. Under the supervision of Dillie Seese, 17 operators worked various shifts. Paid generally lower wages than their male counterparts, these female operators nonetheless helped keep the PRR quite literally on track. (Courtesy of AM.)

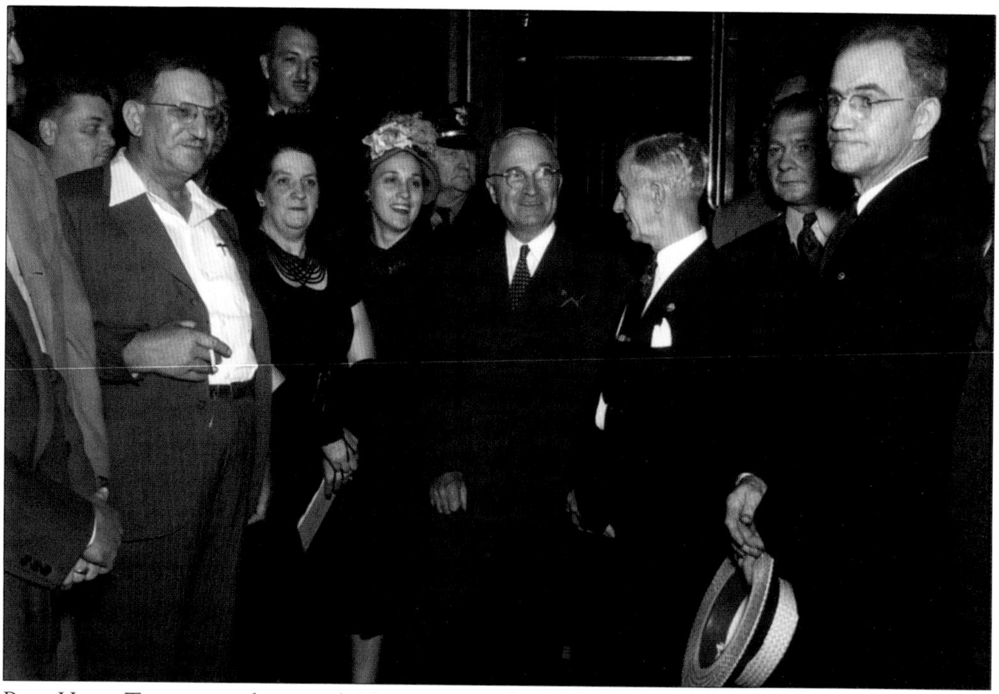

Pres. Harry Truman made several Altoona stops during his 1948 campaign. Between Ninth and Tenth Streets on September 5, Truman greeted local labor and political representatives, including county Democratic chair Beatrice Cochrane. The president then proceeded to Detroit, Michigan, where he criticized Republicans for their "pattern of aid for big business and attack on labor." (Photograph by Gelon Smith, courtesy of William Burket.)

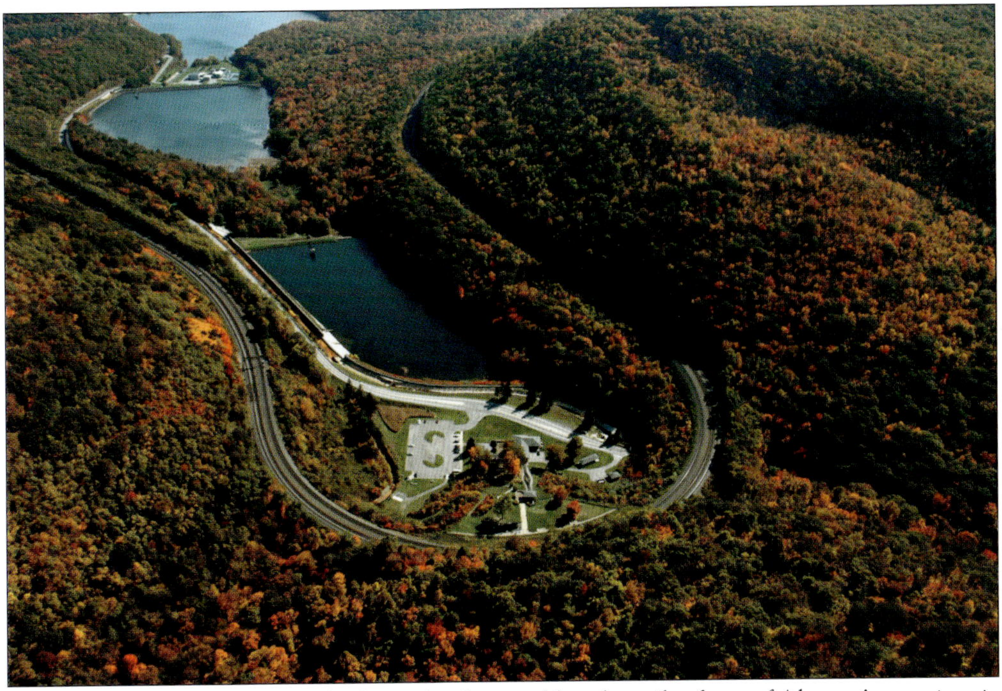

Many presidents and distinguished travelers have ridden the rails of one of Altoona's most iconic and visually stunning landmarks: the Horseshoe Curve. Completed in 1854 by Irish immigrants, the site remains a major railroad artery connecting east and west. (Courtesy of Explore Altoona.)

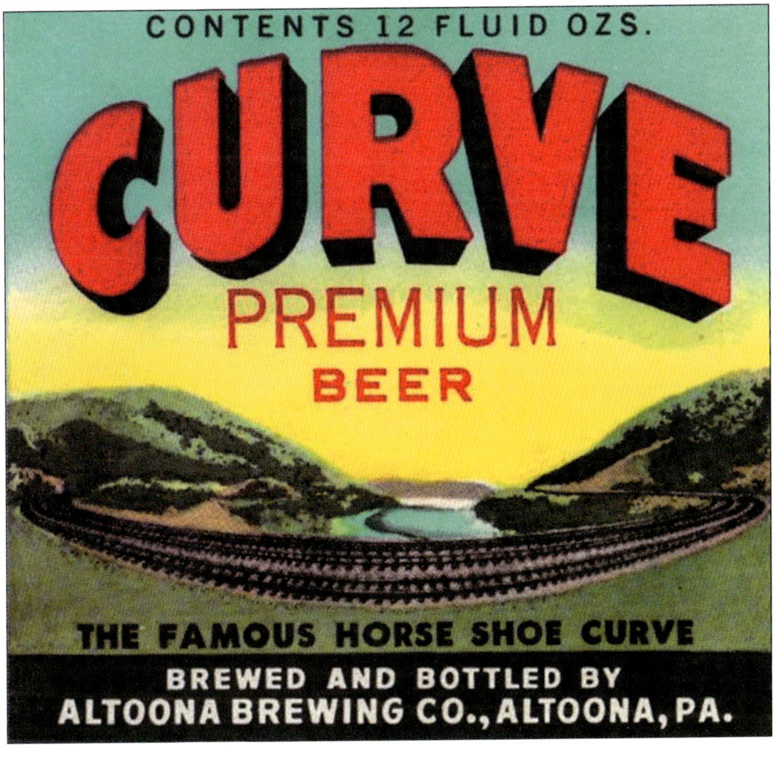

So iconic was the Horseshoe Curve that its likeness was featured on goods and souvenirs. Perhaps the most recognizable of these Rail City products was Curve Beer. First brewed in 1936 at Eighteenth Street and Ninth Avenue, the beverage was a staple of city pubs until the Altoona Brewing Company closed in 1974. (Courtesy of Scott Cessna.)

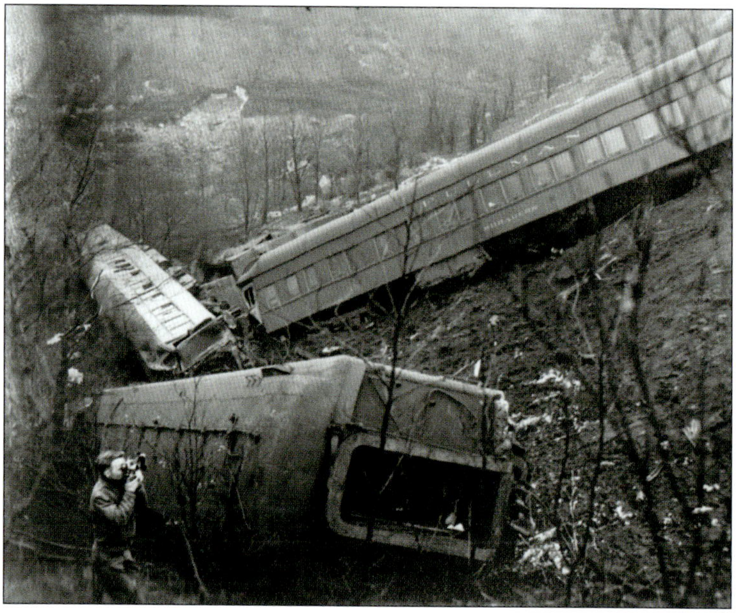

While 1940s rail travel is glamorized by popular imagination, inherent dangers persisted. On February 18, 1947, the speeding *Red Arrow* derailed on Bennington Curve and plummeted into a 150-foot ravine, killing 24 passengers and injuring 140 others. Additional safety measures were imposed on 19,000 miles of tracks the following year. (Courtesy of ARMM.)

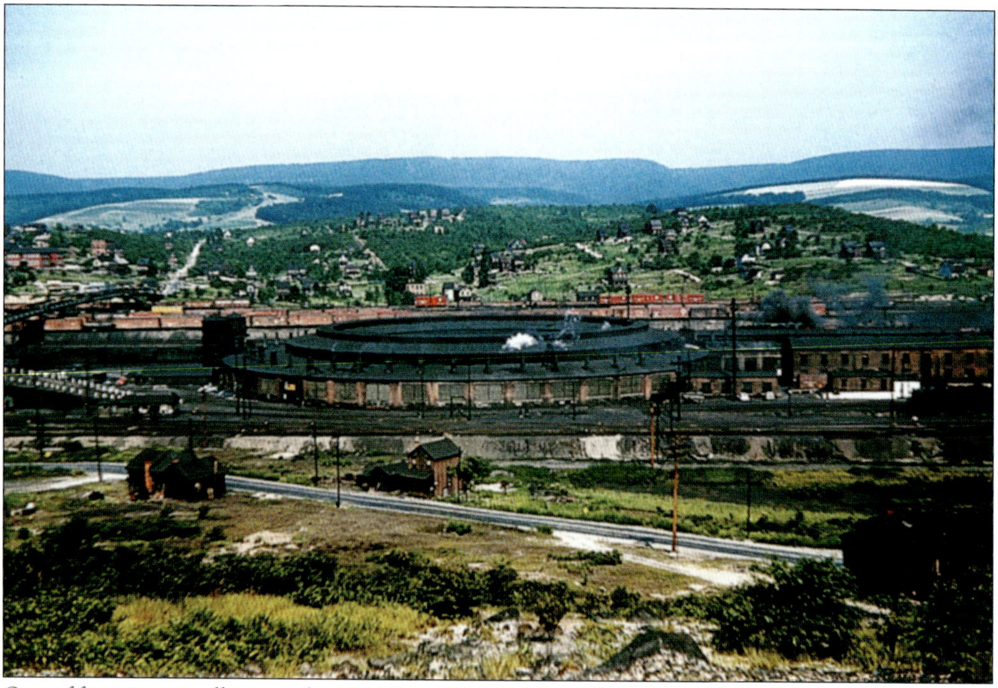

One of five city roundhouses, the 1904 East Altoona Roundhouse was the largest in the world, with a 395-foot diameter and 52 engine stalls. Located between North Fourth Avenue and Old Sixth Avenue Road (seen in foreground), the facility handled 300 locomotives daily. The roundhouse was demolished in 1968. Parts of the North Seventeenth Street Bridge at left stood until 2011. (Photograph by Mike Zollitsch, courtesy of William Burket.)

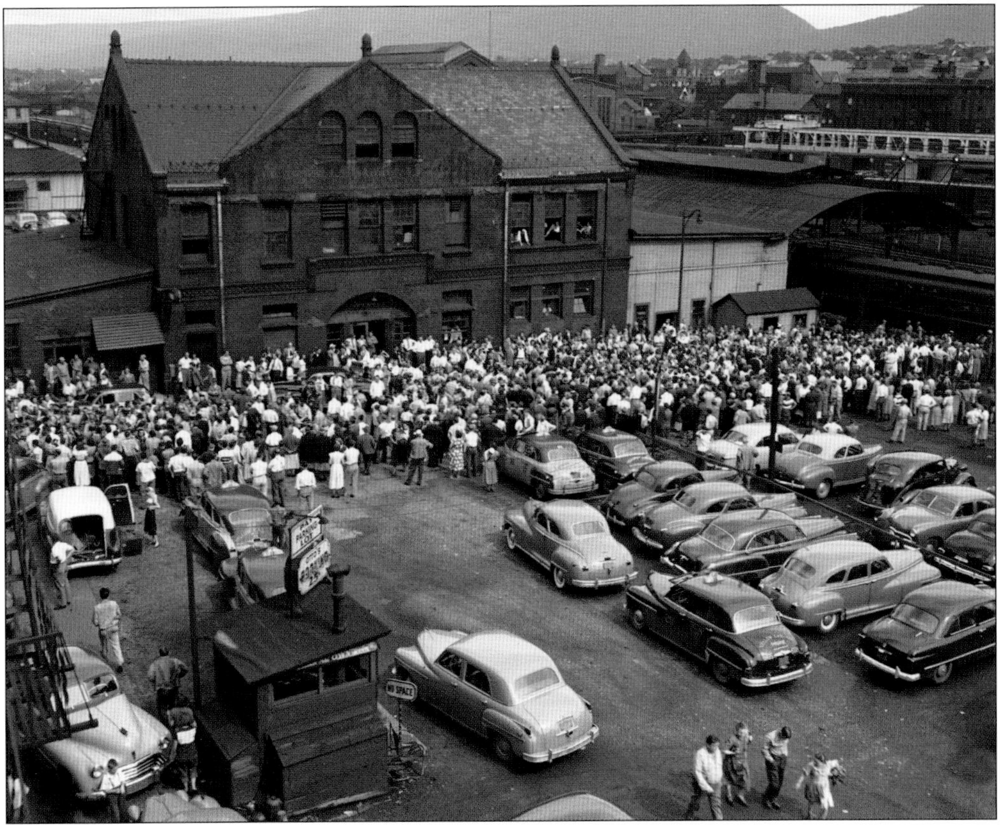

On September 10, 1950, the 110th Regiment of the 28th Division shipped out of Altoona for Camp Atterbury, Indiana. Those departing in uniform included three father and son pairs from throughout the county. Locals donated three new television sets for the regiment's enjoyment in camp. (Photograph by Gelon Smith, courtesy of William Burket.)

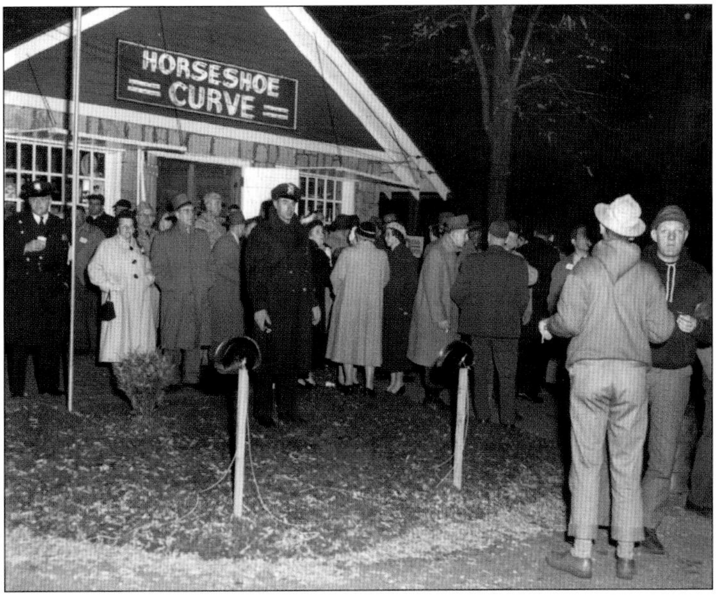

To mark the Horseshoe Curve's centennial, a colossal photoflash was carefully choreographed for October 20, 1954. Note the lights affixed to pie pans. Crowds began arriving at 6:00 a.m. the morning before. At right stand Sylvania Electric event supervisors John Zwald (back to camera) and Walter Trimby. (Courtesy of AM.)

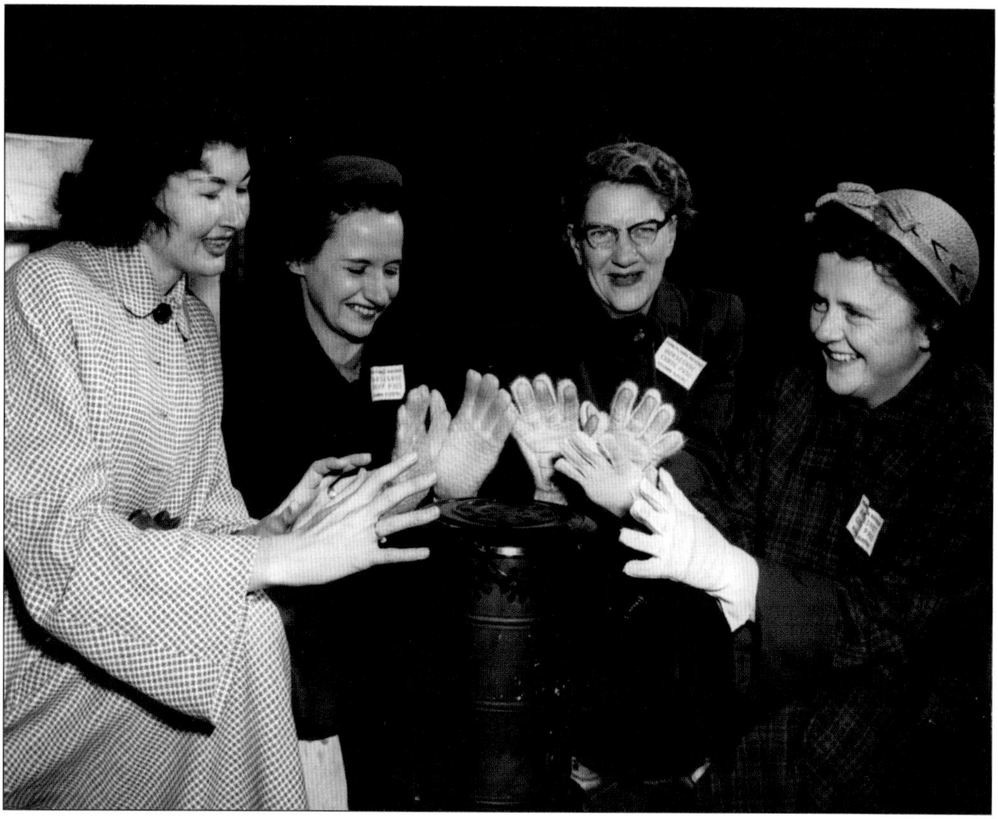

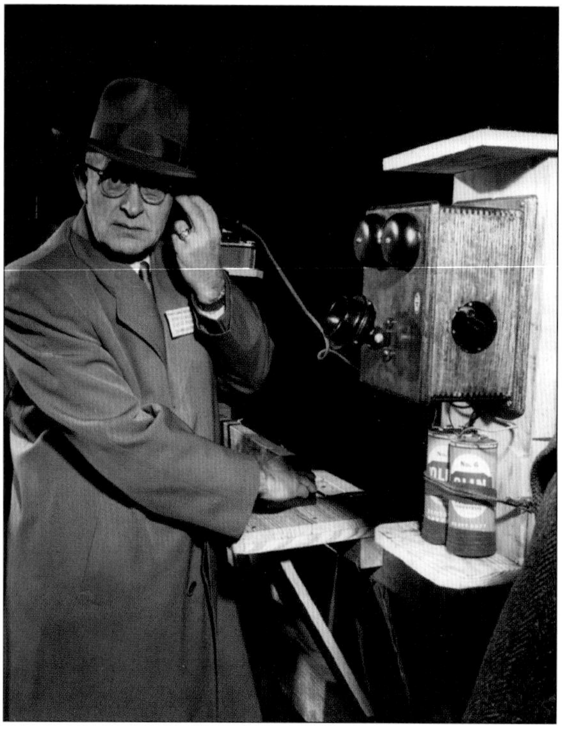

Wind howled through the mountains as spectators prepared for the Horseshoe Curve photoflash. Sgt. Ted Kettenheim of the PRR police provided an oil stove to the railroad wives. Pictured from left to right are Mrs. William Mutschmann, Mrs. Irvin Saylor, Mrs. C.F. Parvin, and Mrs. C.D. Herman. (Courtesy of AM.)

Altoona mayor Walter Grove stands attentively as he listens to the official countdown for the Horseshoe Curve centennial photoflash. With his hand resting steady over the heavy-duty button, the mayor soon after initiated one of the most memorable moments of the site's history. (Courtesy of AM.)

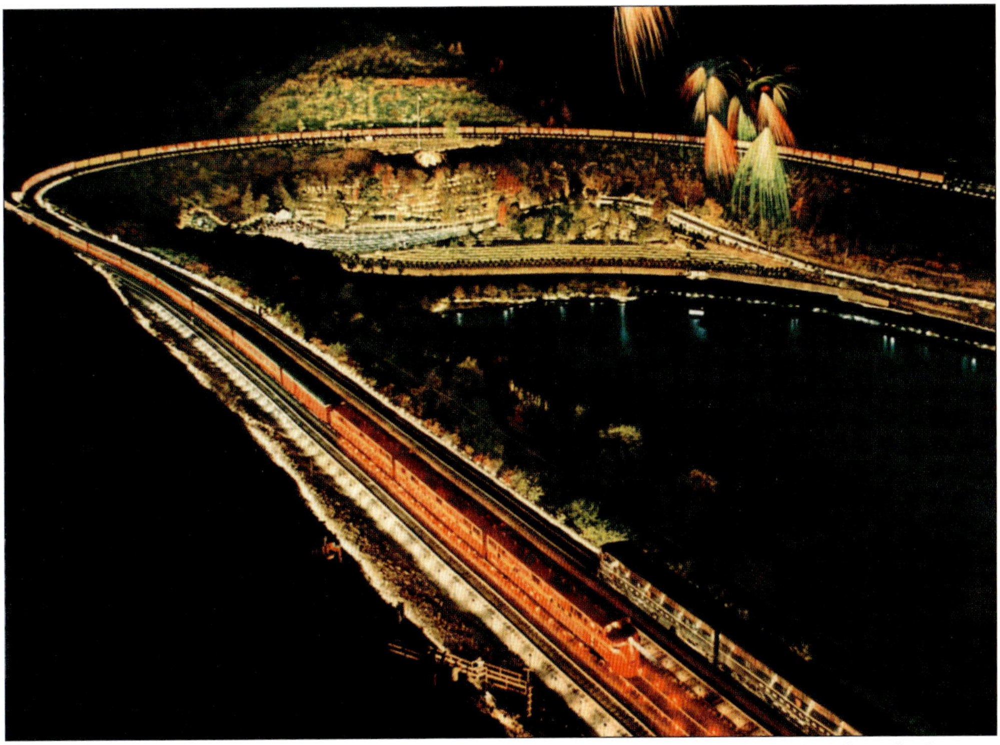

The first large-scale nighttime photograph of the Horseshoe Curve ever taken, the photoflash was a sight to behold: 30 miles of wire were attached to 6,000 flashbulbs over two million square feet. The flash at 10:50 p.m. lasted one-fifteenth of a second. Despite the cold and brevity of the attraction, "a recognizable esprit de corps permeated the entire crowd." (Courtesy of William Burket.)

The Horseshoe Curve remains a popular tourist destination—especially in the peak of fall foliage. Although closed for security reasons during World War II, the curve thrived with tourism afterward thanks to the rise of the automobile. It is seen here in the 1970s. (Photograph by Mike Schafer, courtesy of William Burket.)

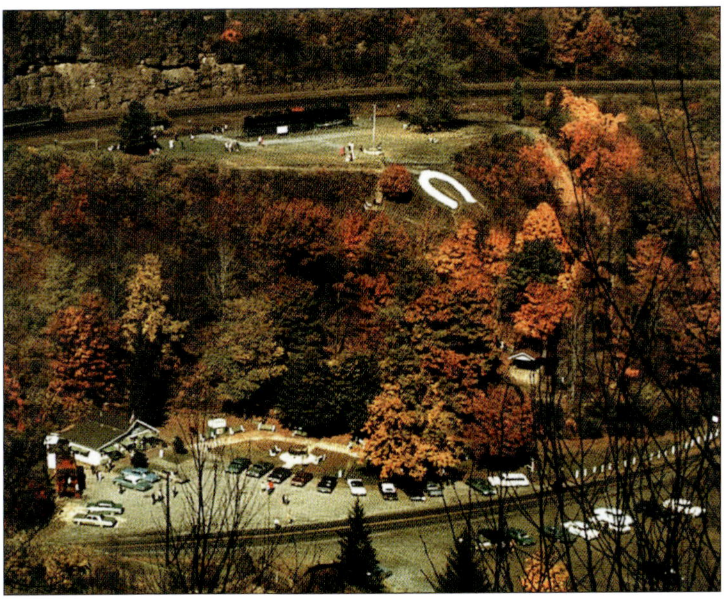

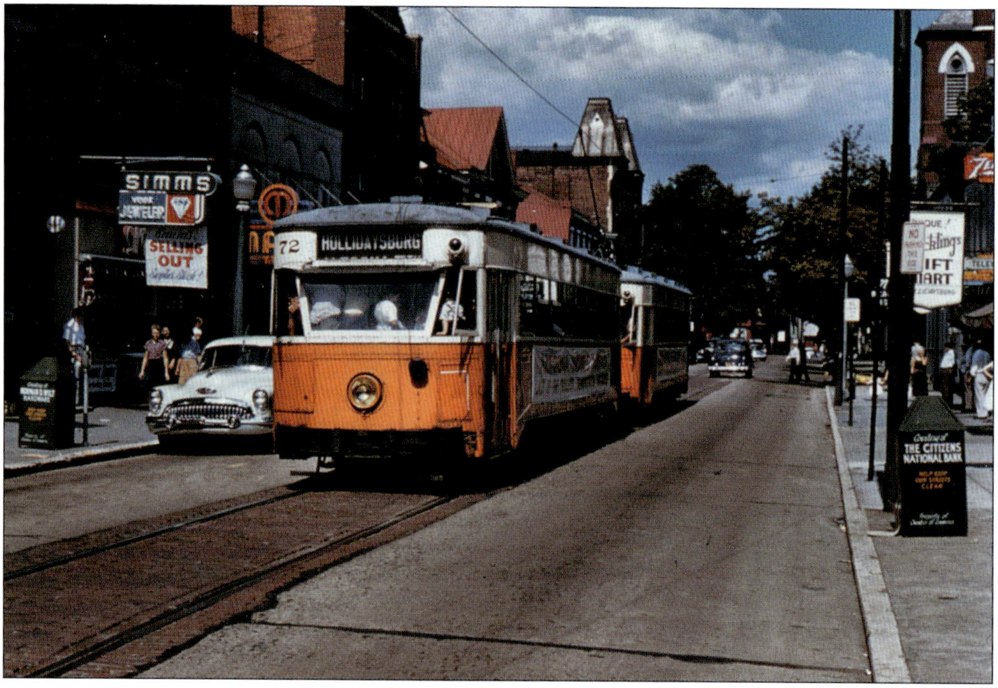

In conjunction with the decline of the railroad, local streetcar service also went out of vogue. Established in 1882, the Altoona & Logan Valley Electric Railway serviced over 11 million passengers annually. Converting to diesel buses, the company discontinued trolley operation in 1954. Here, trolley No. 72 glides down Allegheny Street in Hollidaysburg one last time on August 7, 1954. (Courtesy of William Burket.)

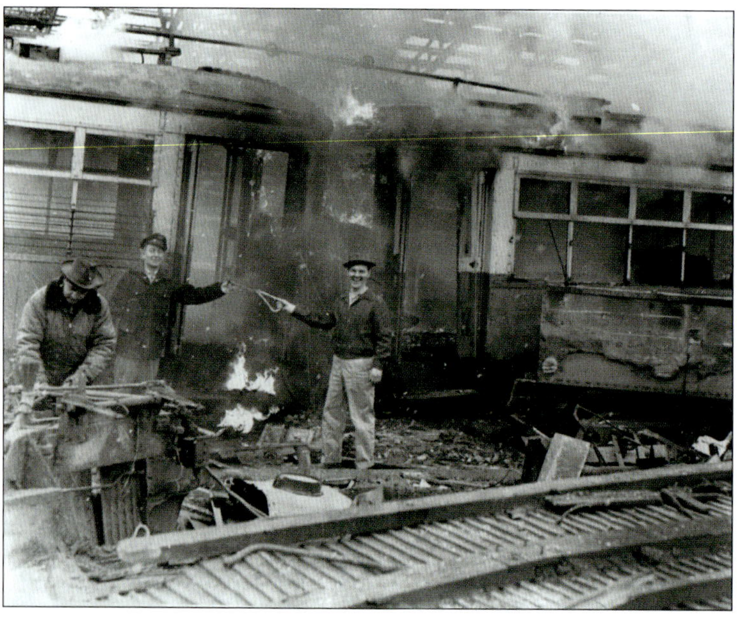

By the end of 1955, all of the Altoona & Logan Valley Electric Railway's trolleys ceased to exist. Junked at the company yards near Thirty-third Street and Fifth Avenue, the cars were set ablaze. In this highly symbolic photograph, laborers yank at a salvaged pulley chord. The era of the trolley was over. (Courtesy of David Seidel.)

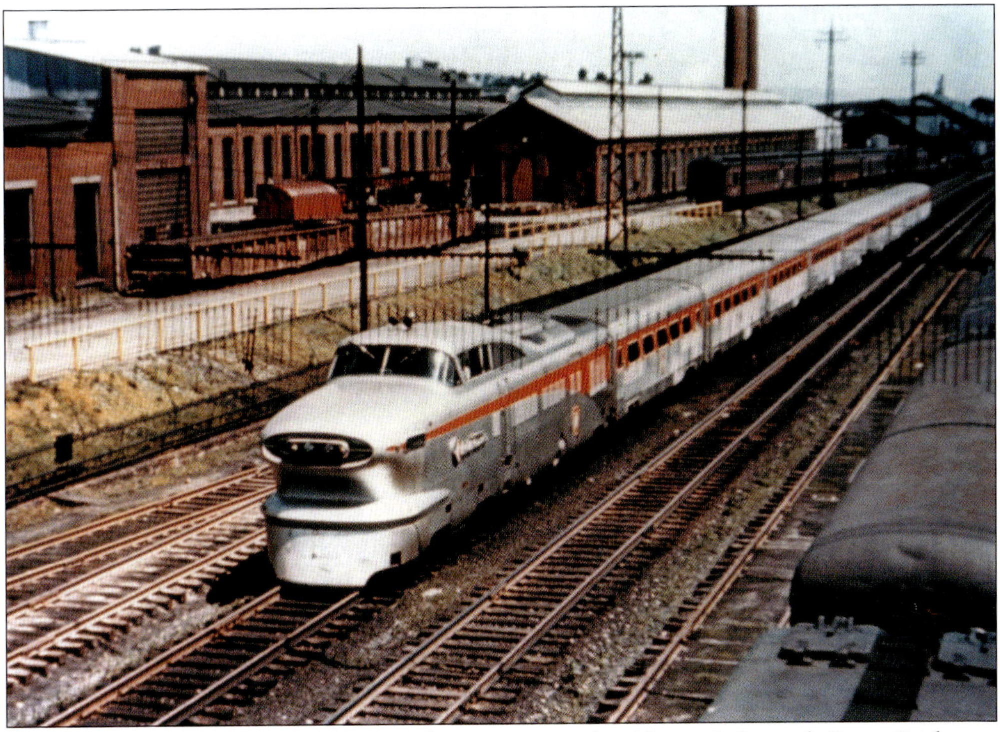

This sleek and rapid PRR Aerotrain is about to pass under Altoona's Seventh Street Bridge on July 18, 1956. Railroads invested $20 million in Aerotrain construction in 1956 alone, hoping to resurrect passenger service. Three days after this photograph was taken, the following appeared in the city newspaper: "Will you quit your car?" The answer "could determine one industry's future." (Courtesy of William Burket.)

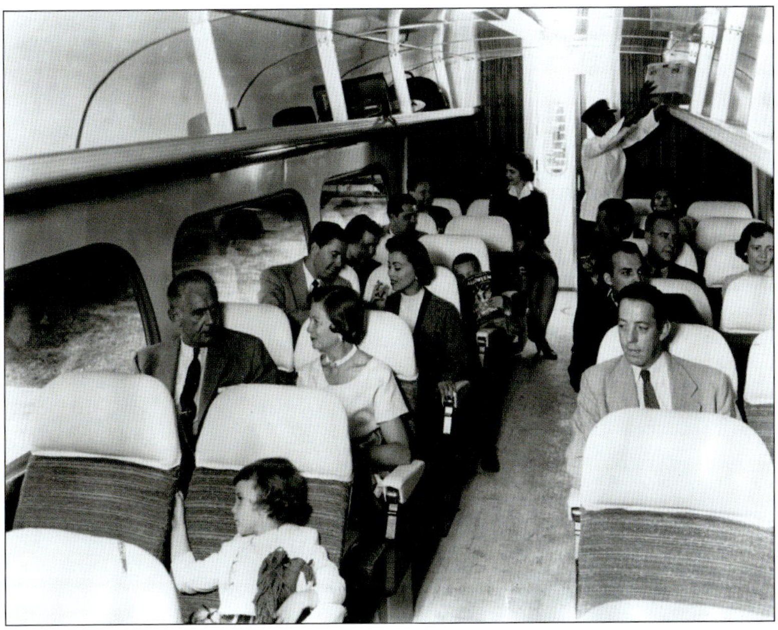

A PRR Aerotrain prepares to depart Altoona's station in 1957. Passenger train advocates touted the benefits of "long distance travel at coach rates with a high degree of luxury and scenic interests." Leisure aside, Americans chose highways over rails. (Courtesy of AM.)

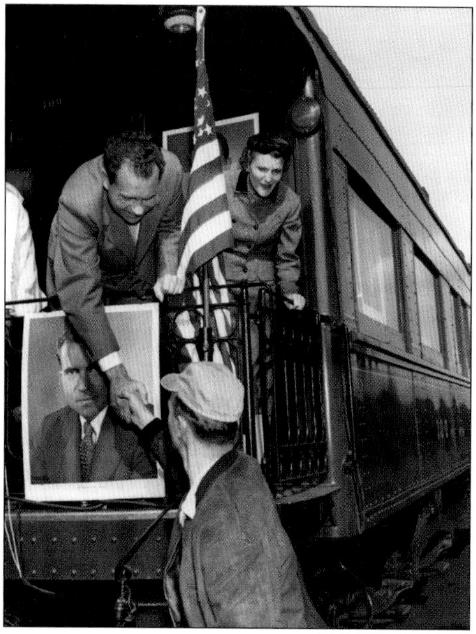

Vice Pres. Richard Nixon shakes hands with PRR worker Robert Focht as Pat Nixon looks on. Nixon's November 1, 1956, whistle stop along Tenth Avenue was greeted by thousands. Riding through rail and coal country, Nixon promoted "individual enterprise working in partnership with government when necessary." Five days later, the Eisenhower/Nixon ticket won 56 percent of Pennsylvania votes. (Courtesy of AM.)

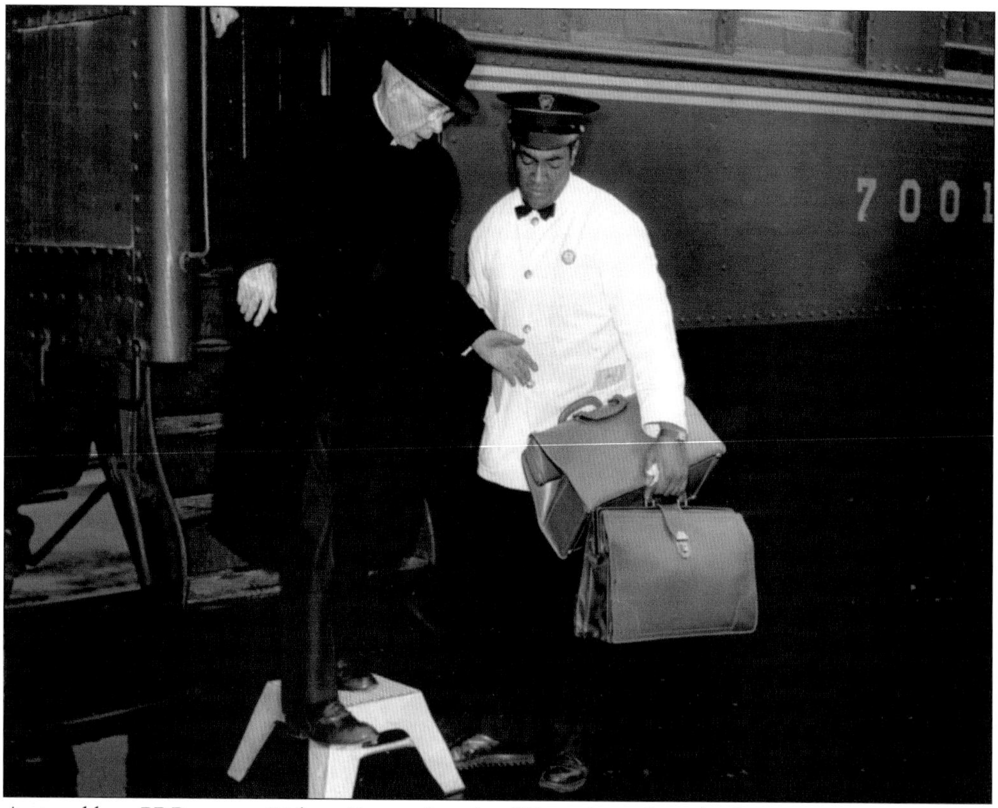

Assisted by a PRR porter, Bishop George Leech of Harrisburg disembarks a passenger car for the March 1960 Altoona funeral of Bishop Howard Carroll. Racial boundaries existed for African Americans in the PRR through the 1960s, but a job with the "Pennsy" offered upward mobility and the opportunity to disprove inaccurate racial assumptions. (Courtesy of AM.)

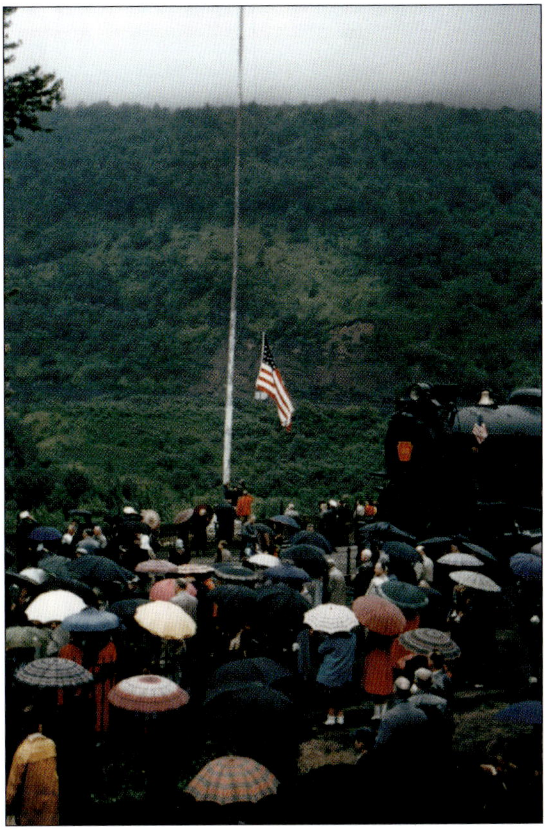

On the rainy day of June 8, 1957, the Altoona-made K-4 1361 was dedicated for display at Horseshoe Curve. The 1918 engine accumulated two million miles in its career. Replaced in 1985 by a vintage diesel, the locomotive ran excursions briefly before requiring major maintenance. Having undergone long-term restoration at Scranton's Steamtown and elsewhere, the locomotive may yet operate again. (Courtesy of ARMM.)

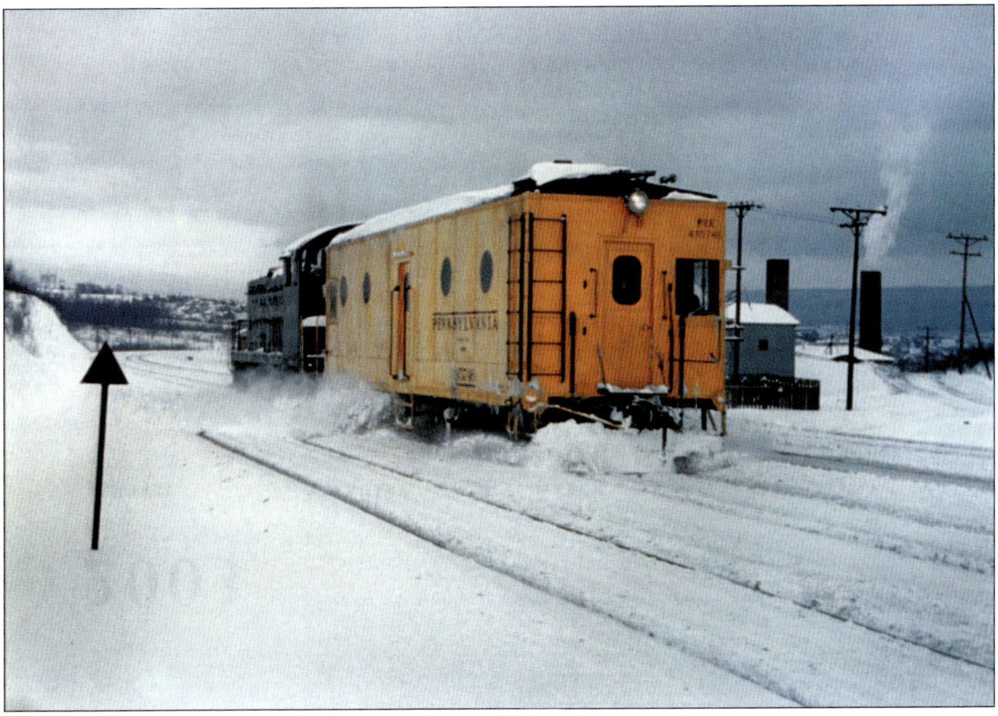

This rare March 1961 color photograph shows a Pennsylvania Railroad flanger car at Brickyard Crossing, west of the city. Responsible for removing snow and ice that other engines could not clear alone, flangers were essential to a railroad's safety, operation, and schedule during Pennsylvania's bitter winter months. (Photograph by Dave Sweetland, courtesy of William Burket.)

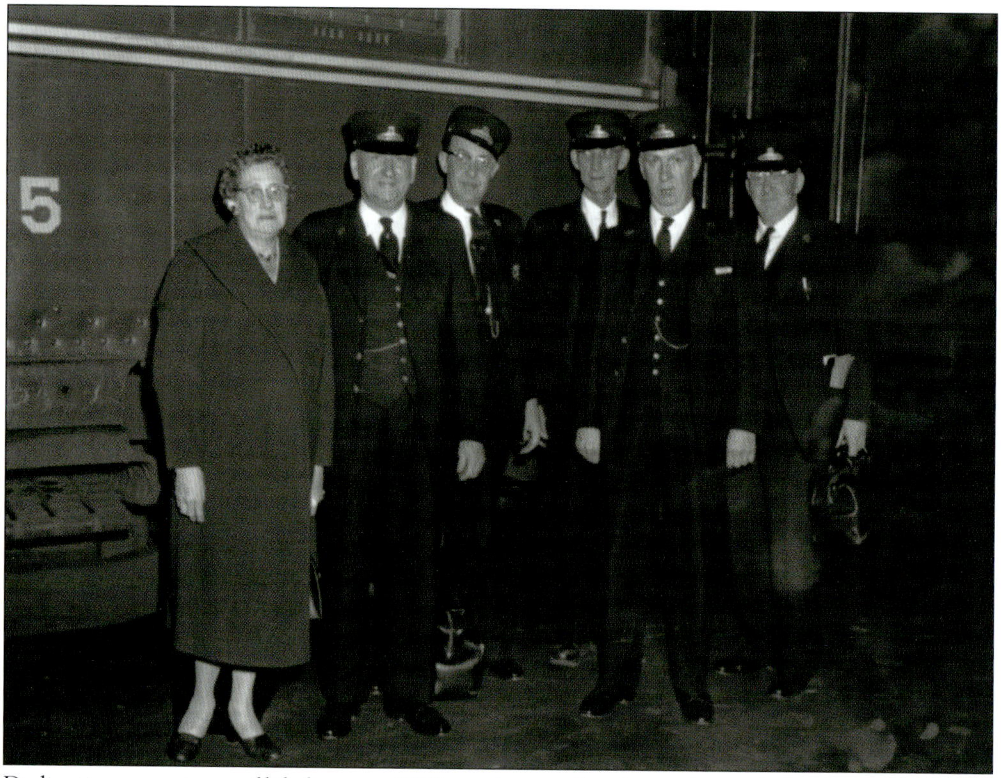

Dedication was a tenet of life for many PRR employees. Conductor James Geisinger (second from left) joined the company following service in World War I and retired 40 years later as a *Manhattan Limited* conductor. Seen here with his wife, Lorna, on his final Altoona return on October 29, 1960, Geisinger is joined by colleagues, from left to right, H.A. Filson, C.E. McCartney, E.S. Helsel, and J.G. Reichel. (Courtesy of ARMM.)

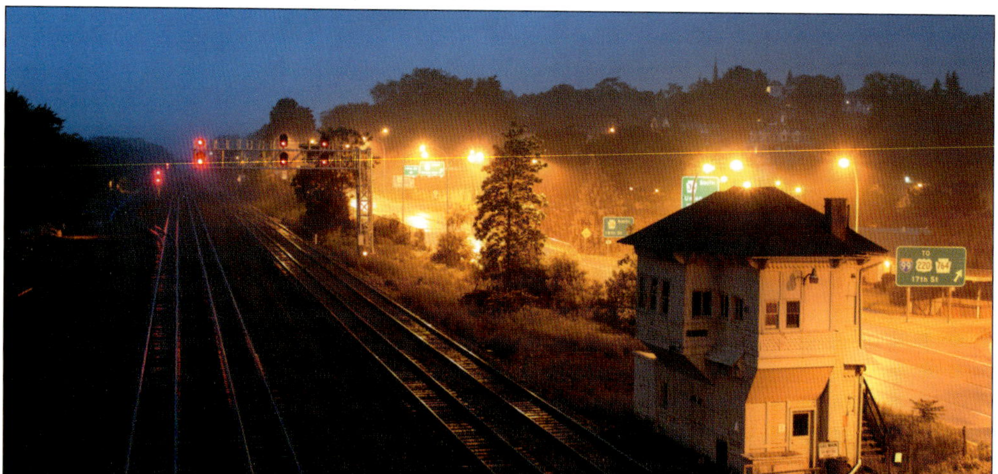

Built in 1915, the iconic Alto Tower along Tenth Avenue controlled a five-mile sector of the Pennsylvania Main Line for nearly a century. The valuable relic of the steam age closed on June 16, 2012, after operations were relocated to Pittsburgh. This nostalgic photograph was taken three days prior to the tower's shutdown. (Photograph by Dustin Faust.)

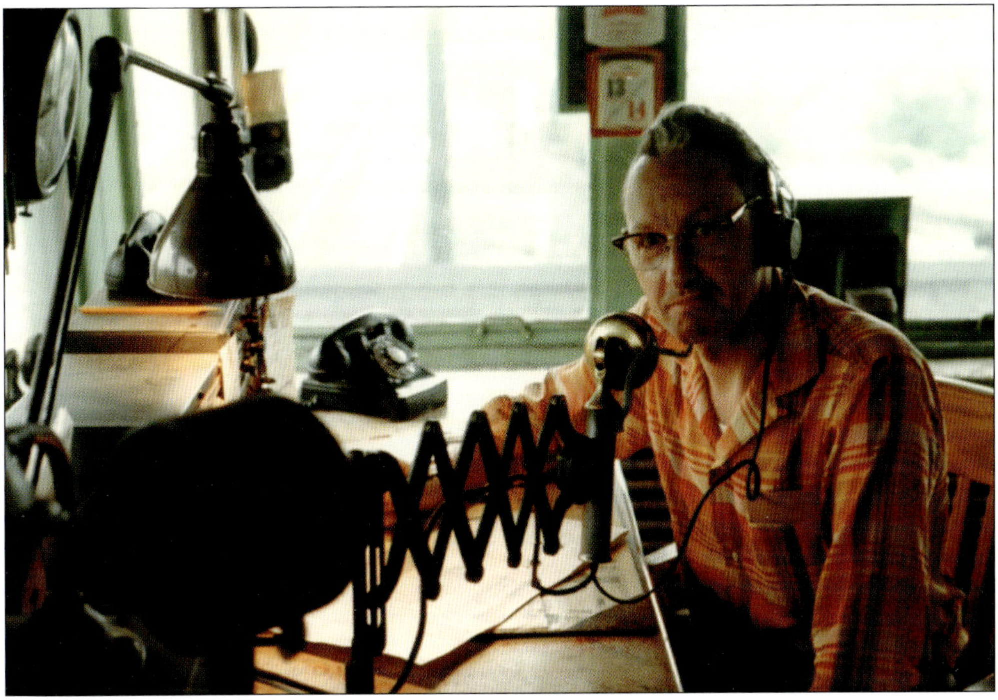

The Alto Tower's interior included 42 manually controlled switches that determined the routes of individual trains. This August 1966 photograph shows tower operator Glen Fink hard at work. Despite the determination of employees, the days of the PRR were few. (Photograph by Julius Westheimer, courtesy of ARMM.)

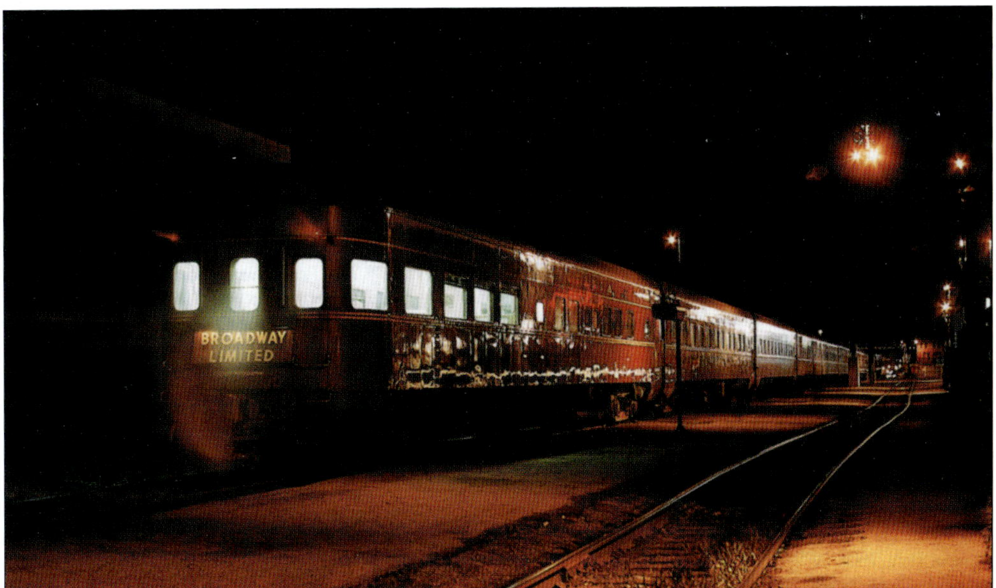

The *Broadway Limited* rolls into Altoona in October 1966. Connecting New York and Chicago, Illinois, on a daily basis, the *Limited* was the essence of luxury. Regardless of service, the PRR could no longer overcome the changes of the times. After 122 years of business, the PRR ceased to exist in 1968. (Photograph by David Seidel, courtesy of William Burket.)

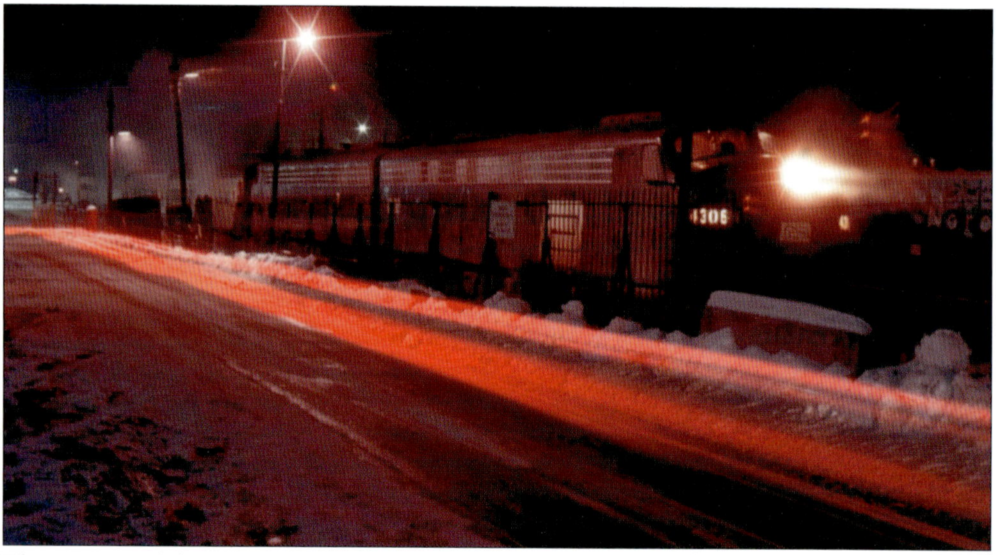

The merging of the PRR and New York Central Transportation on February 1, 1968, resulted in the creation of Penn Central. In this 1970s photograph, a westbound passenger train, with class EMD E-8 locomotives, awaits passengers in the snowy cold of night. To the consternation of Altoonans, Penn Central lasted less than a decade. (Courtesy of David Seidel.)

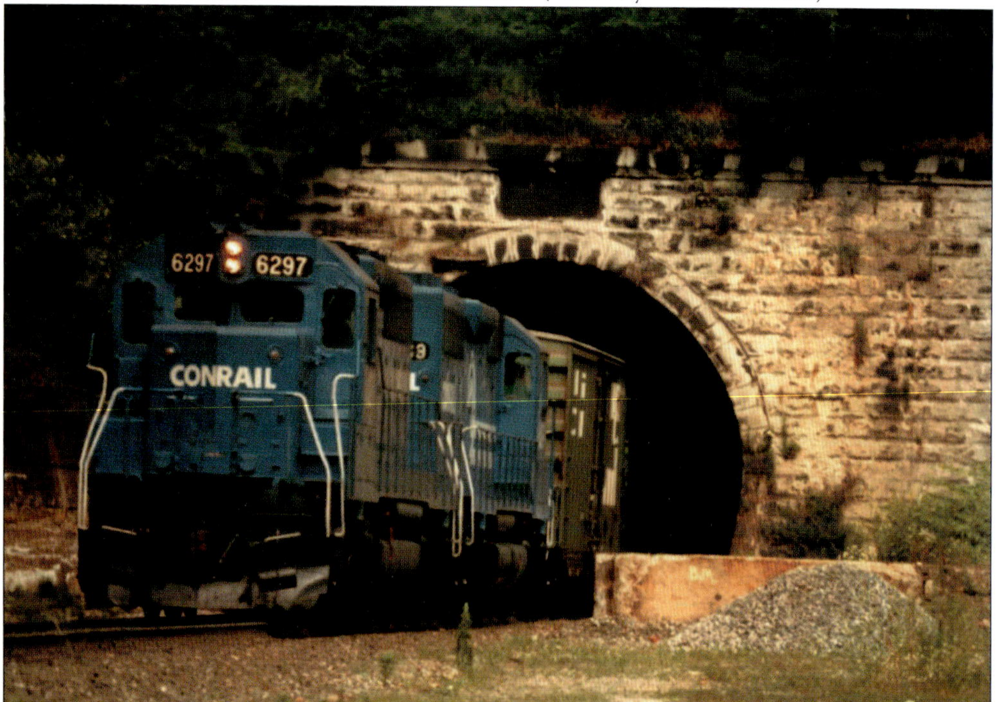

In 1976, the federal government consolidated the collapsed Penn Central with six other financially unstable railroads to create Conrail. For two decades, Conrail thrived—ultimately leading to its buyout between CSX and Norfolk Southern in 1999. In this 1988 photograph, a Conrail engine emerges from the famous Gallitzin Tunnels, built in the 1850s. (Photograph by Julius Westheimer, courtesy of ARMM.)

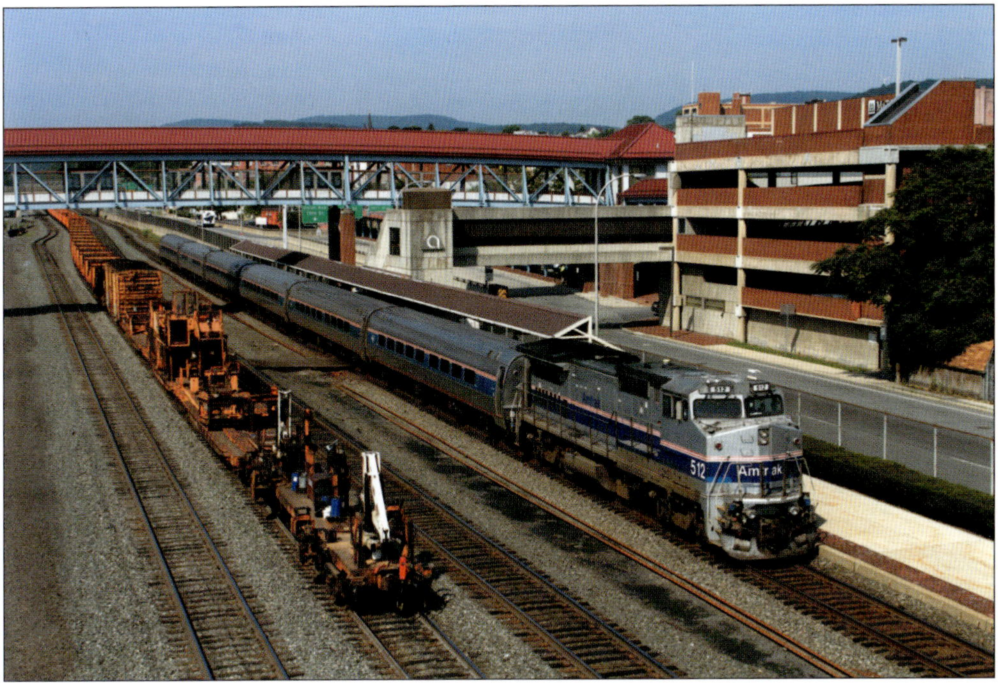

Pictured here along the Tenth Avenue Expressway in 2013, Amtrak filled the passenger service gap left by the PRR. Few expected the semi-public corporation, established under the Nixon administration in 1971, to endure. The *Altoona Mirror* reported that Amtrak offered a "renewal of hope for an industry the nation must have." (Photograph by Dustin Faust.)

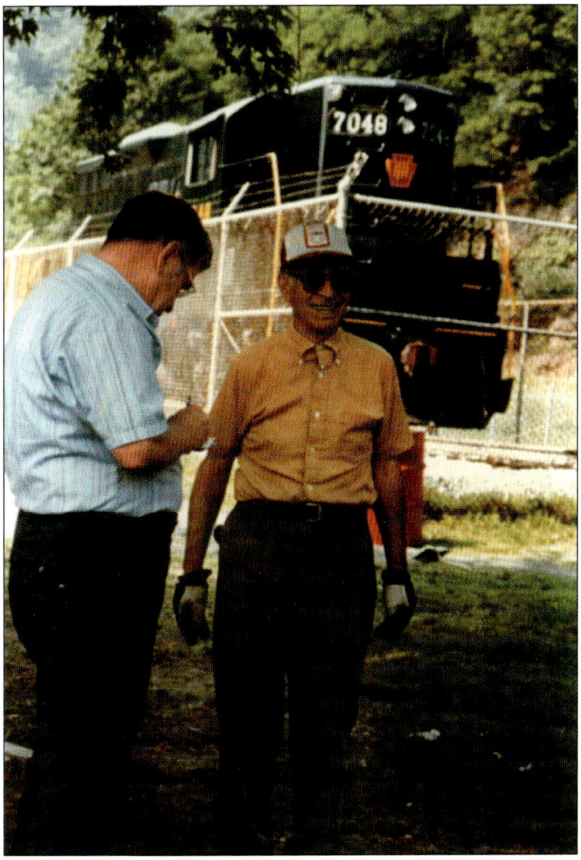

Italian-born Oscar Salpino (at right) began his career with the PRR carrying railroad ties at age 13. Serving as foreman at the Horseshoe Curve for decades, he became the beloved groundskeeper following his 1969 retirement. After Salpino's 1988 passing, railroad fan Ken Heyl lamented that the curve "won't be the same" without him. (Courtesy of ARMM.)

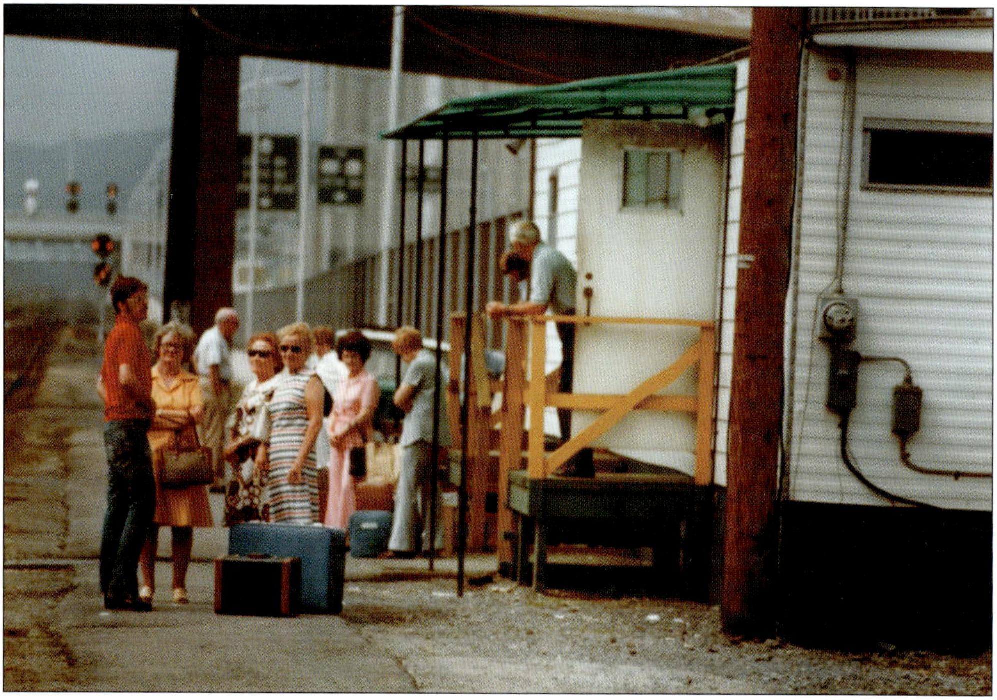

Perhaps the greatest indicator of Altoona's decline as a railroading powerhouse was its replacement train station. From 1971 until the opening of the Altoona Transportation Center in 1986, passengers waited at this wholly inadequate trailer, pictured here about 1975. (Photograph by Julius Westheimer, courtesy of ARMM.)

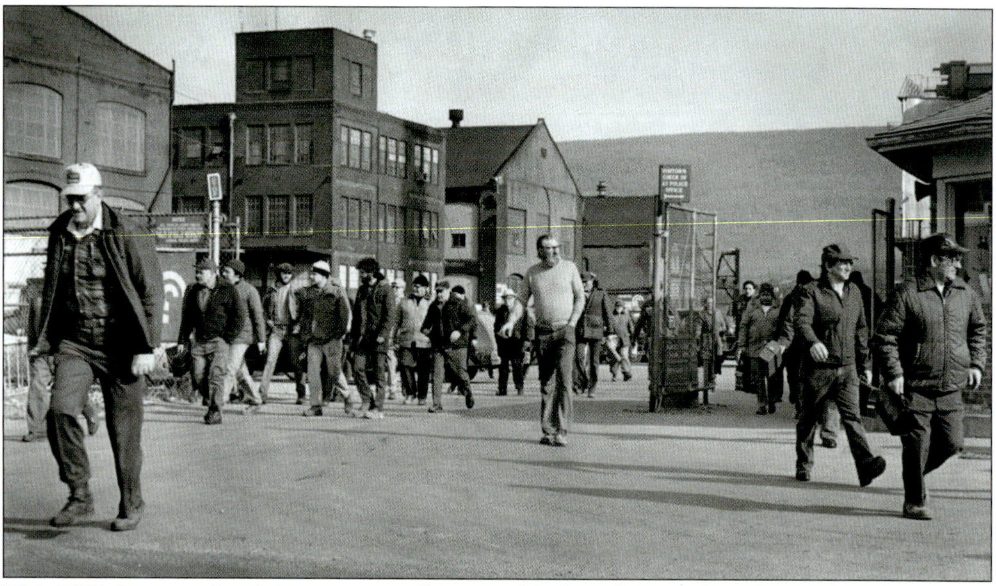

This 1980 photograph exhibits a scene still repeated daily as shop workers depart their shift at 3:30 p.m. Having worked for three different railroads in only a dozen years, many Conrail employees had grave uncertainties about the future. Nonetheless, their days were bookended by the shop whistle that bellowed above Juniata daily. (Courtesy of AM.)

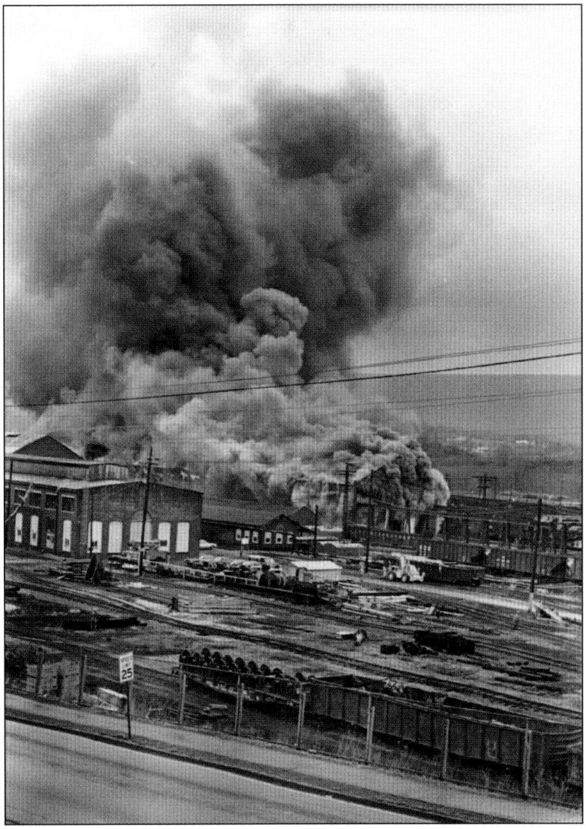

On April 9, 1981, 35 Conrail workers barely escaped an inferno that engulfed Juniata's Miscellaneous Shop No. 1 when paint thinner, oil, and gas erupted in explosive fury. Conrail workers watched helplessly as the 1889 structure collapsed. "There goes my job," one brooded. (Courtesy of AM.)

The dangers of the railroad were not reserved solely for its employees. In the hope of raising public awareness to railroad perils, Conrail joined a nationwide education safety campaign entitled Operation Lifesaver. In this April 1990 photograph, Rudy Bilka instructs local students about railroad crossings. (Courtesy of AM.)

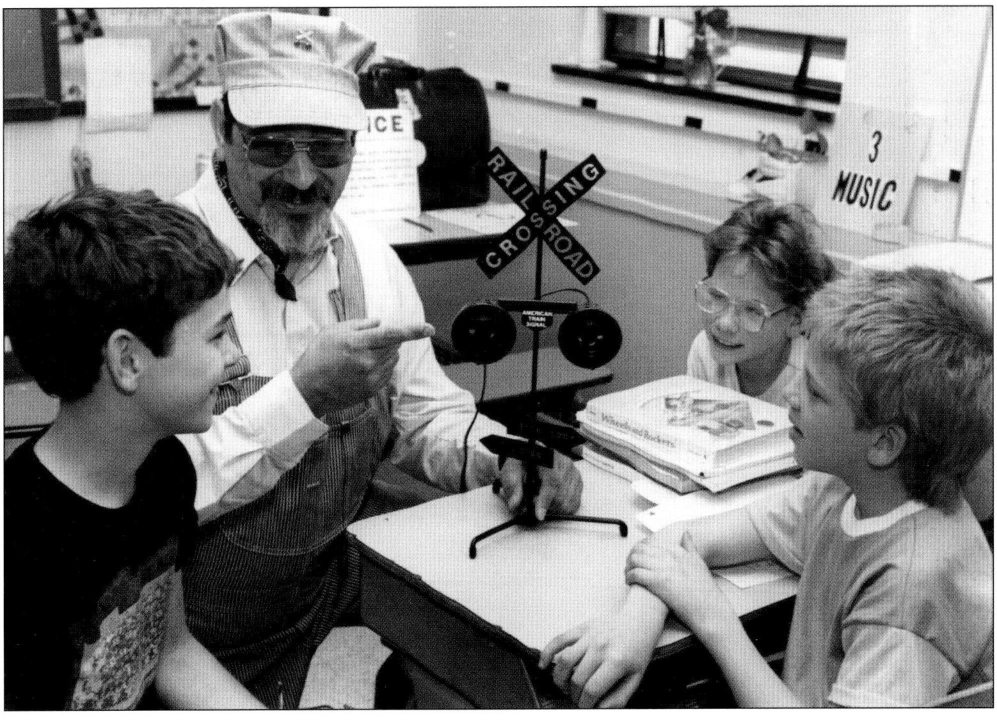

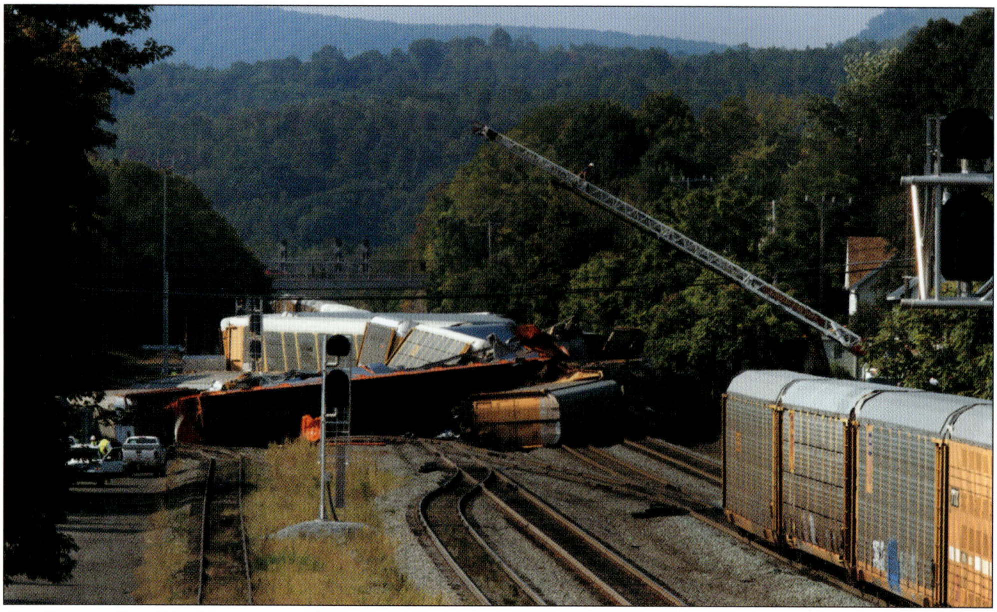

On September 20, 2014, more than two dozen cars derailed from an eastbound train near Twenty-first Street and Tenth Avenue. Brand-new automobiles onboard were flattened amidst the wreckage, and some train cars were hurled only feet away from nearby homes. (Courtesy of Dustin Faust.)

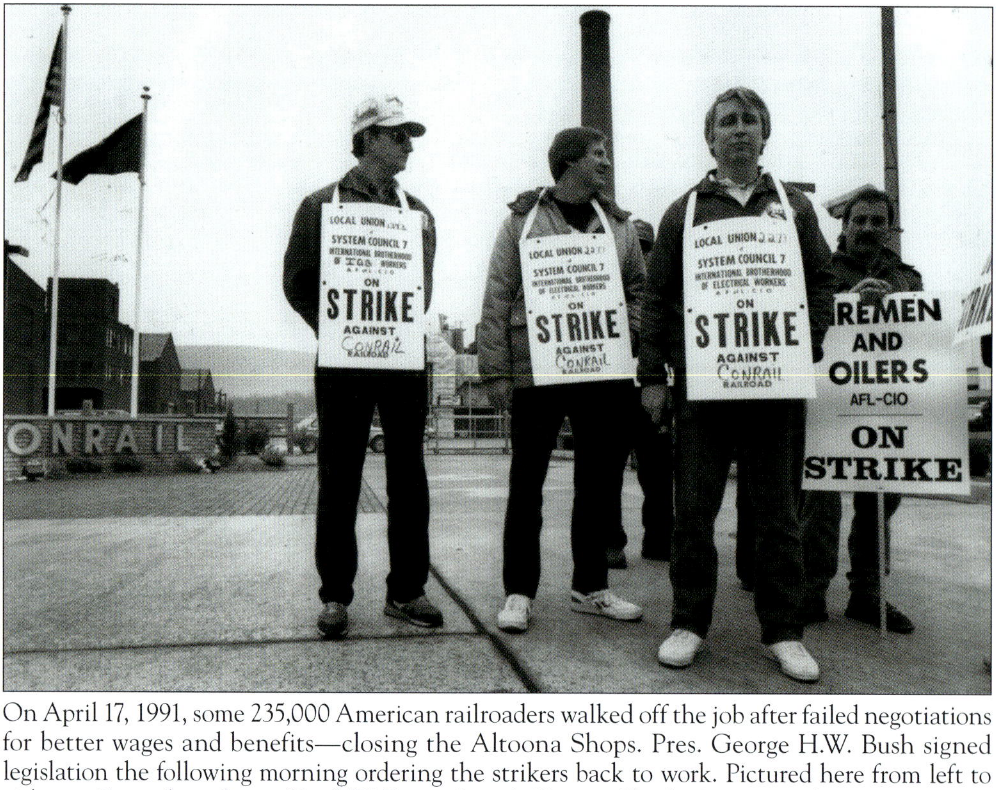

On April 17, 1991, some 235,000 American railroaders walked off the job after failed negotiations for better wages and benefits—closing the Altoona Shops. Pres. George H.W. Bush signed legislation the following morning ordering the strikers back to work. Pictured here from left to right are Conrail employees Hank Williams, Joseph Hogan, Charles Hogan, and Victor Fiochetta Jr. (Courtesy of AM.)

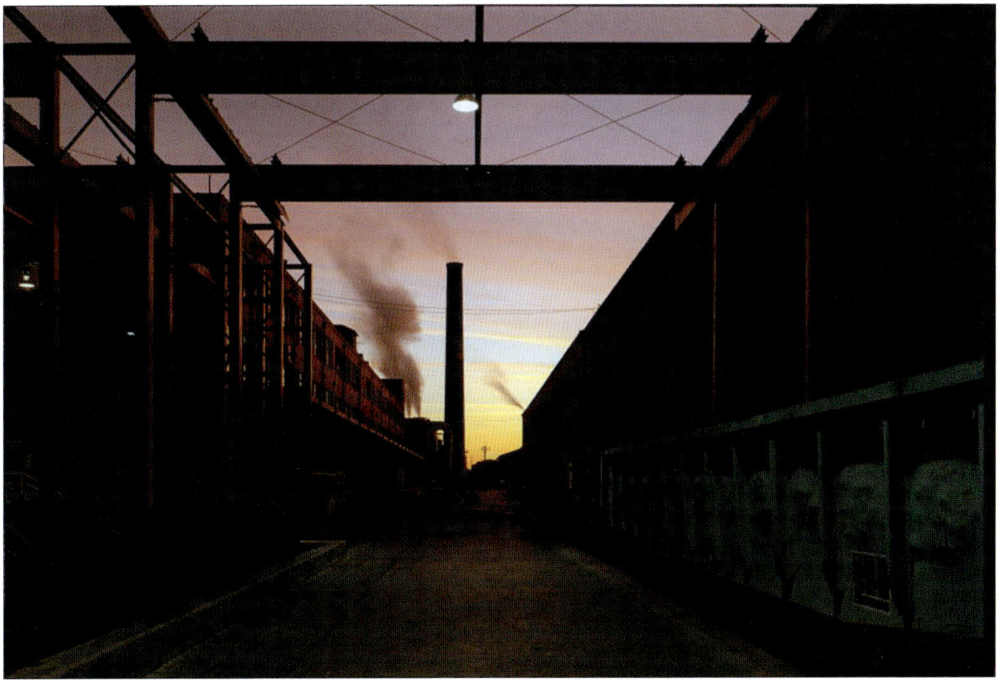

This 1988 sunrise vista of Juniata's machine shop and storehouse was taken by Jack Boucher for the federal government's Historic American Buildings Survey. The Altoona railroading facilities were deemed noteworthy for their contribution to the nation's industrial heritage. (Courtesy of the Library of Congress.)

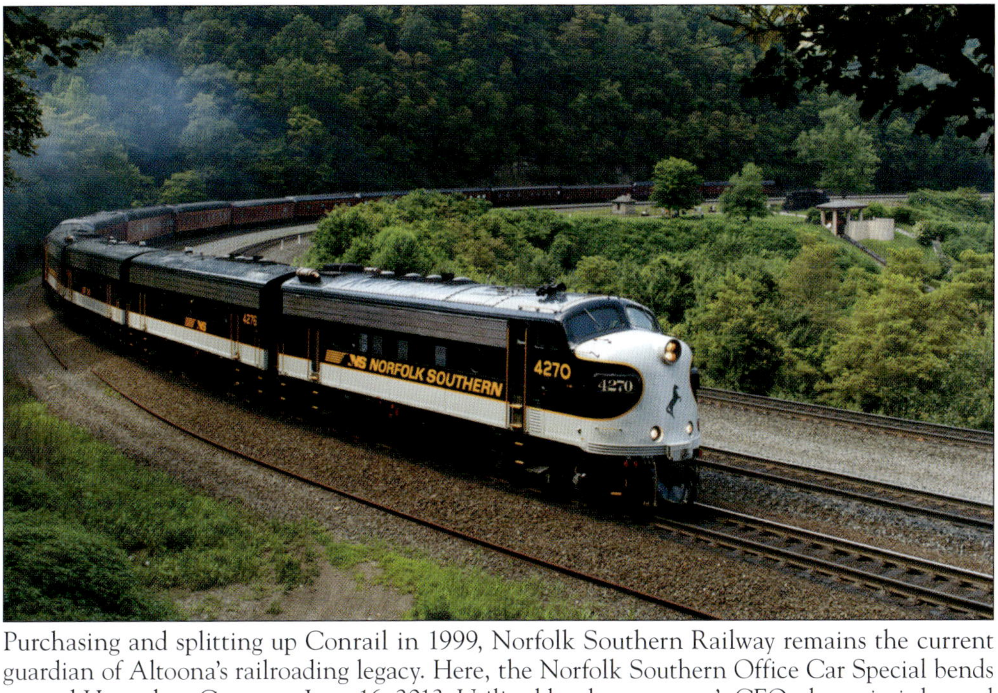

Purchasing and splitting up Conrail in 1999, Norfolk Southern Railway remains the current guardian of Altoona's railroading legacy. Here, the Norfolk Southern Office Car Special bends around Horseshoe Curve on June 16, 2013. Utilized by the company's CEO, the train is housed and maintained in Altoona. (Photograph by Dustin Faust.)

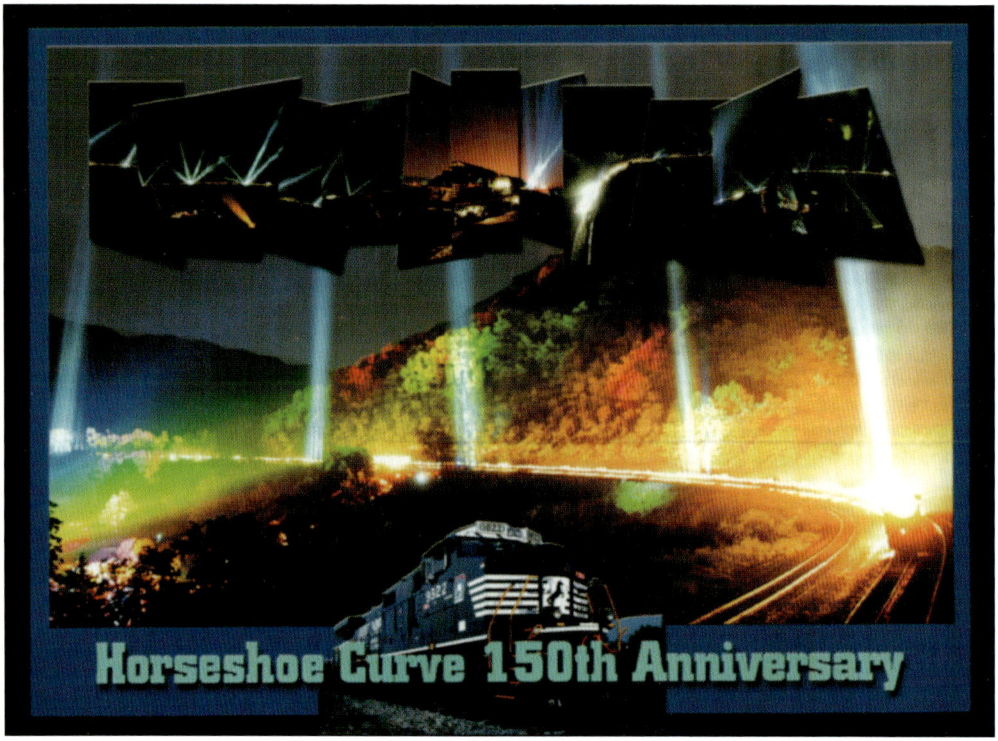

Thousands attended the vibrant light show commemorating the 150th anniversary of the Horseshoe Curve on Independence Day 2004. Norfolk Southern and Osram-Sylvania partnered to produce a majestic display of spotlights and fireworks. Heavy rains prior to the show generated a foggy aura that enhanced the glow of the spectacle. (Courtesy of ARMM.)

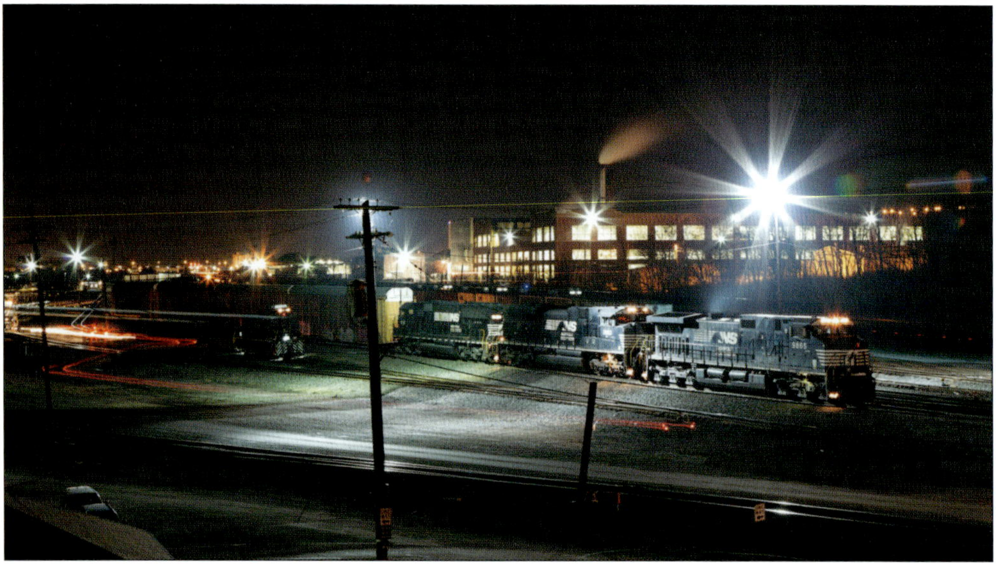

Taken on March 27, 2014, this view of Norfolk Southern's Rose Yard demonstrates that a railroad never sleeps. The Juniata Shops employ over 1,000 workers and have the capacity to rebuild entire locomotives in less than one week. Even 70 years after the golden age of steam, the yards remain an impressive sight. (Photograph by Dustin Faust.)

Three

Pillars of a Community

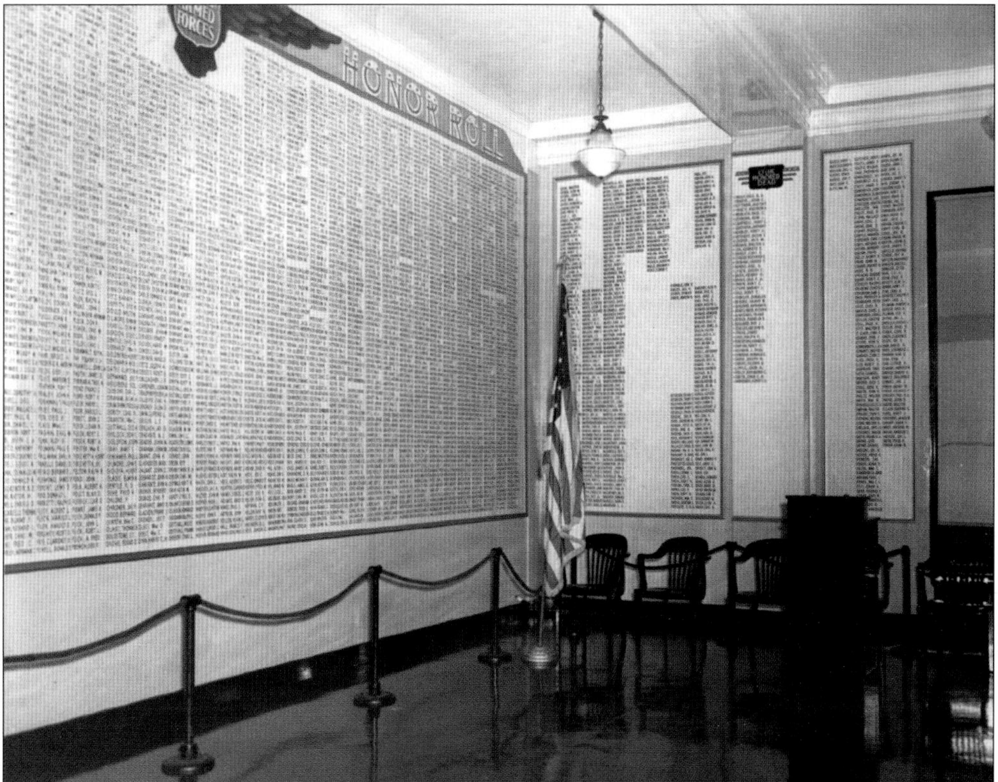

One cannot truly understand modern Altoona without first acknowledging the dramatic shift it underwent during World War II. This transformation was evident at the dedication of the Honor Room in city hall on Memorial Day 1943. Thousands gathered to see the names of Altoona service members. "I have never seen anything that moves me so deeply," one visitor noted. The memorial was removed during a postwar renovation. (Courtesy of AM.)

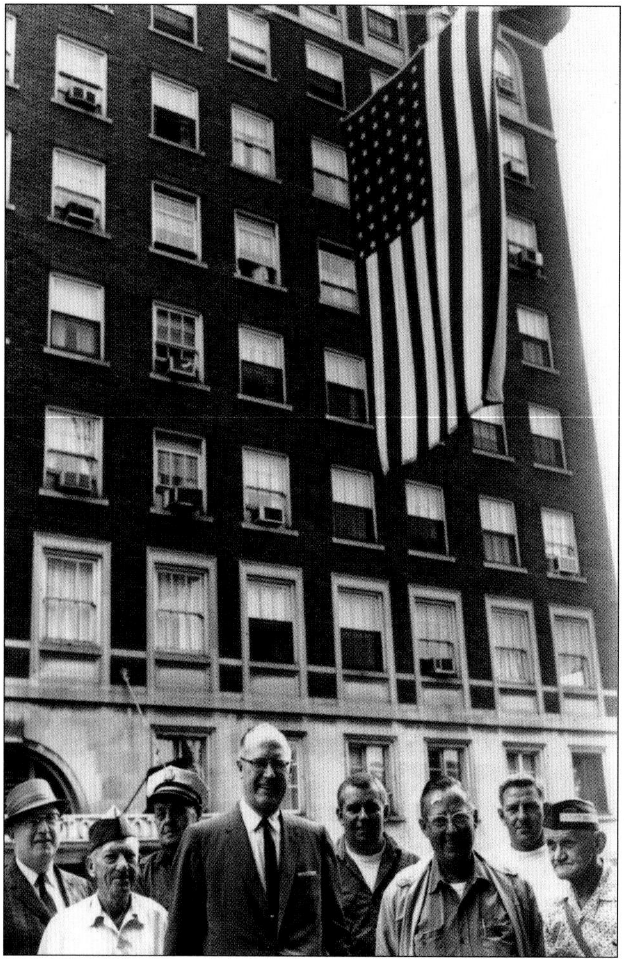

Over 800 Pennsylvanian World War I veterans gathered for a convention at the Penn Alto on July 26, 1962. The 48-star flag carried in Altoona's original Armistice Day parade flutters from the hotel. Pictured here from left to right are Bruce Crumm, Wayne O'Shell, J.W. Pearson, hotel manager Herbert Hanson, James Vaughn, George Fockler, Peter Ciaverella, and Chester Troutman. (Courtesy of David Seidel.)

Built in 1930, the Jaffa Mosque was once the largest convention hall in central Pennsylvania. Seen here in a humorously coincidental twist, the Jaffa was advertising the forthcoming show *Ice Vogues of 1951* when the devastating ice storm of November 25, 1950, struck. "The unintentional publicity stunt lasted for several days," wrote the *Altoona Mirror*. (Courtesy of AM.)

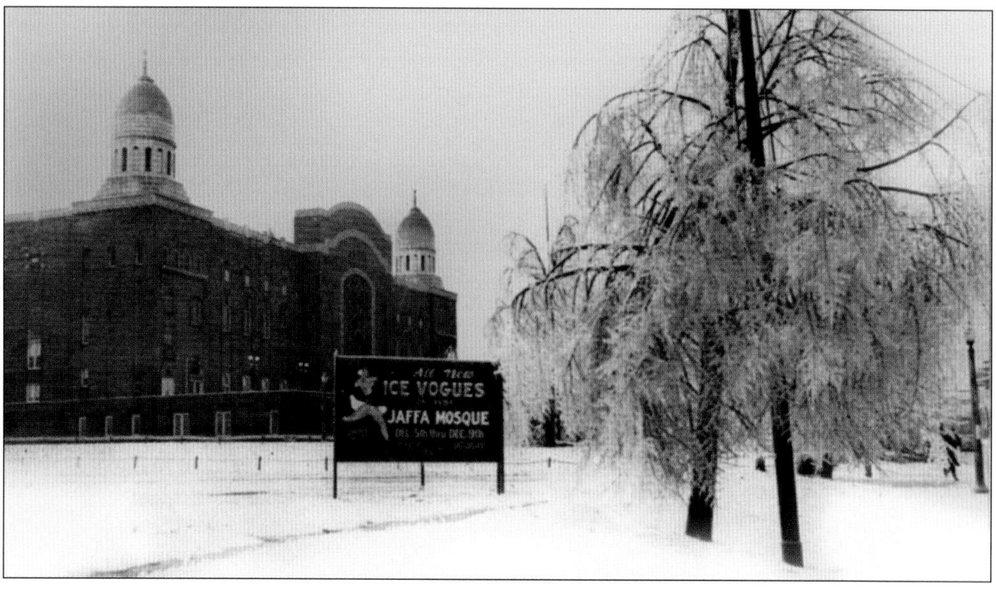

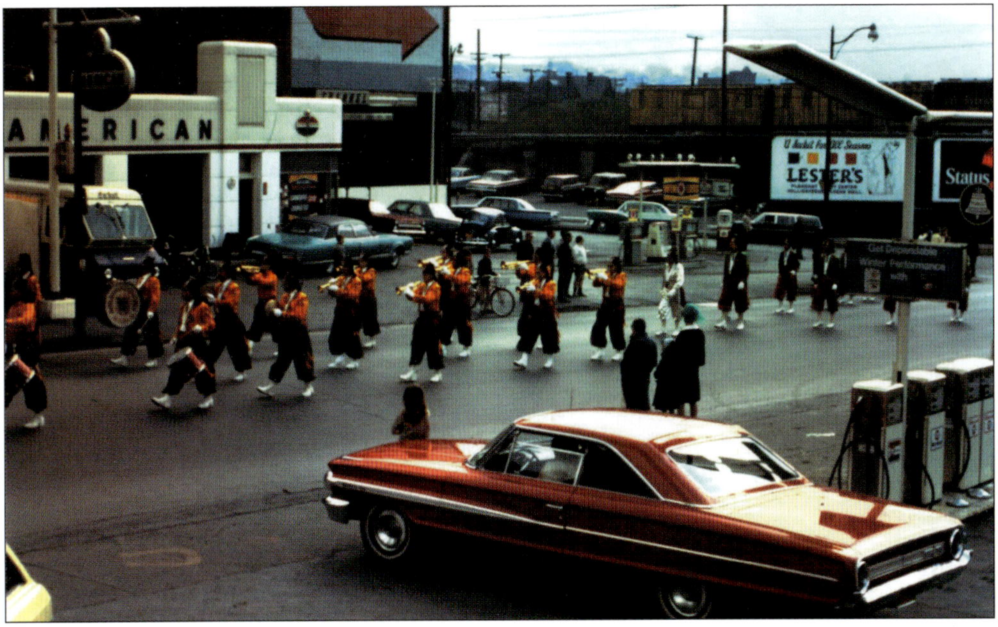

Formed in 1909, the Jaffa Shrine Band is seen here marching in a mid-1960s procession along Eighteenth Street. Whether riding on horseback, driving go-carts, steering mini-motorcycles, or wearing clown makeup, Shriners have always served as one of the liveliest components of Altoona parades. (Courtesy of David Seidel.)

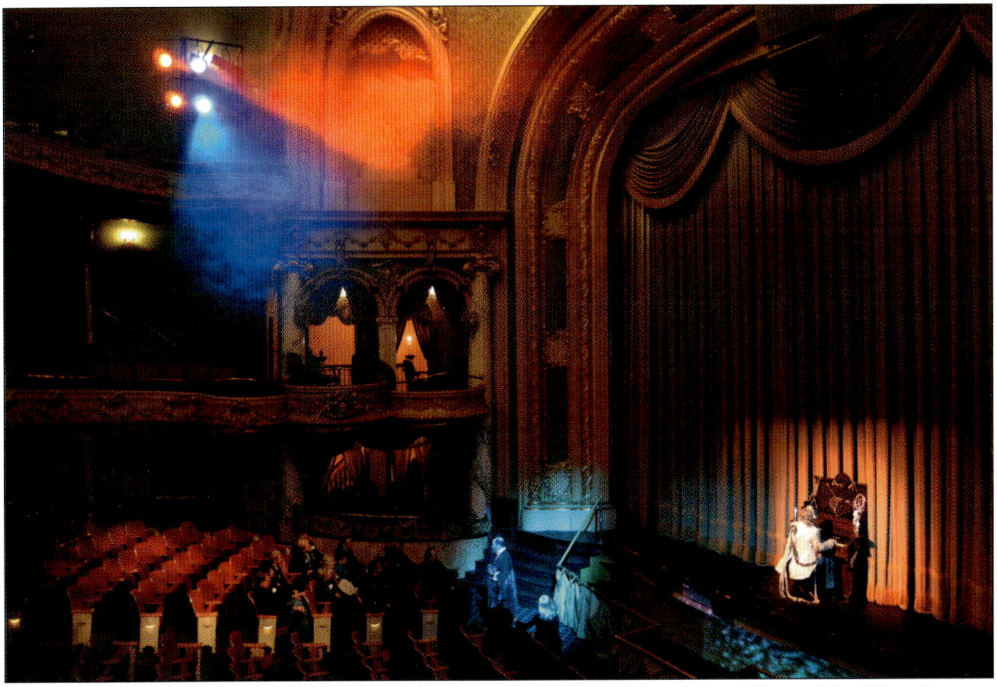

Nearly bulldozed, the historical Mishler Theatre was saved by the valiant efforts of the Blair County Arts Foundation and the Altoona Community Theatre. The cultural gem reopened in 1969 with *The Sound of Music*. Restored extensively since that time, the 1906 playhouse remains a vibrant center for the arts. Here, patrons enjoy ghost tours on Halloween in 2014. (Author's collection.)

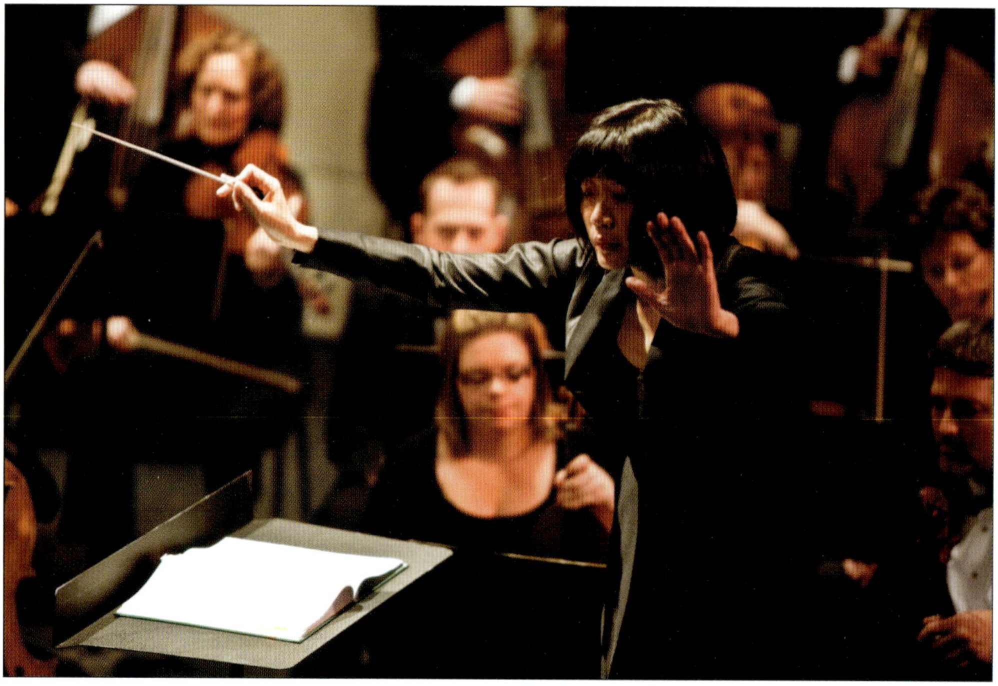

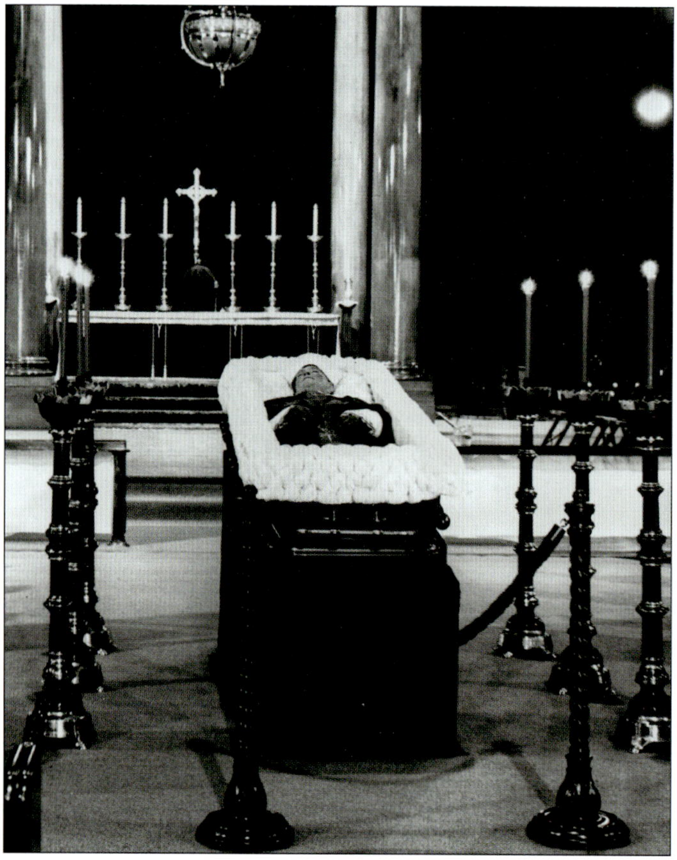

The Altoona Symphony Orchestra has shared the wonders of music since 1928. Teresa Cheung is seen here conducting a 2010 performance at the Mishler Theatre. (Courtesy of the Altoona Symphony Orchestra.)

One of the longest-serving bishops of the Altoona-Johnstown Diocese, Richard Guilfoyle served in that capacity from 1936 until his death. The ever-jovial Guilfoyle guided his churchgoers through years of depression and war. He passed away on June 10, 1957, and his remains laid in state prior to burial in the cathedral's crypt. (Courtesy of AM.)

Four years after Bishop Guilfoyle's passing, the new building for Altoona Catholic High School on Pleasant Valley Boulevard was named in his honor. This 1968 view shows seniors making use of the library. Pictured from left to right are Rayanna Williams, Bob Eger, Weldon Wirick, and Judy Maddas. The school's 1967 state championship basketball sits above, while the magazines attest to the momentous social issues of 1968. (Photograph by Tom Lynam, courtesy of BGHS.)

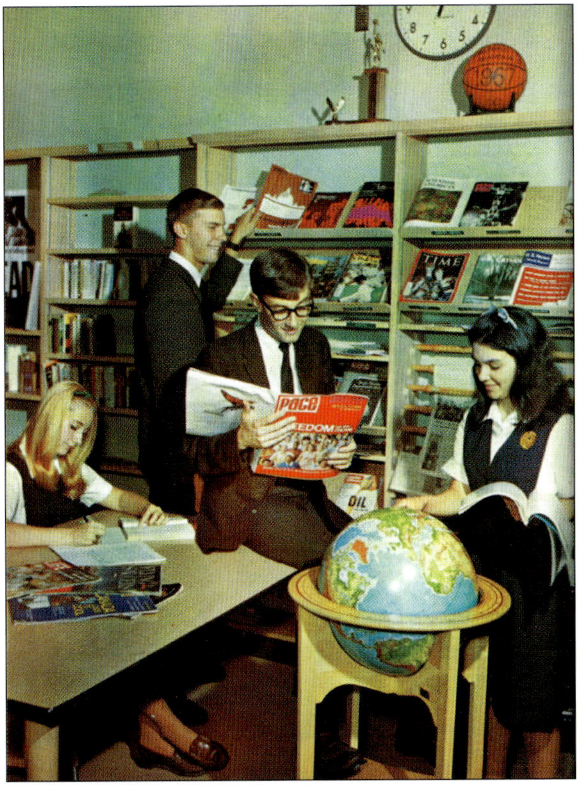

On September 9, 2012, members of local firefighting, police, and emergency agencies participated in the Blue and White Mass at the Cathedral of the Blessed Sacrament to remember the 9/11 attacks and to pay tribute to first responders. (Courtesy of Tony DeGol.)

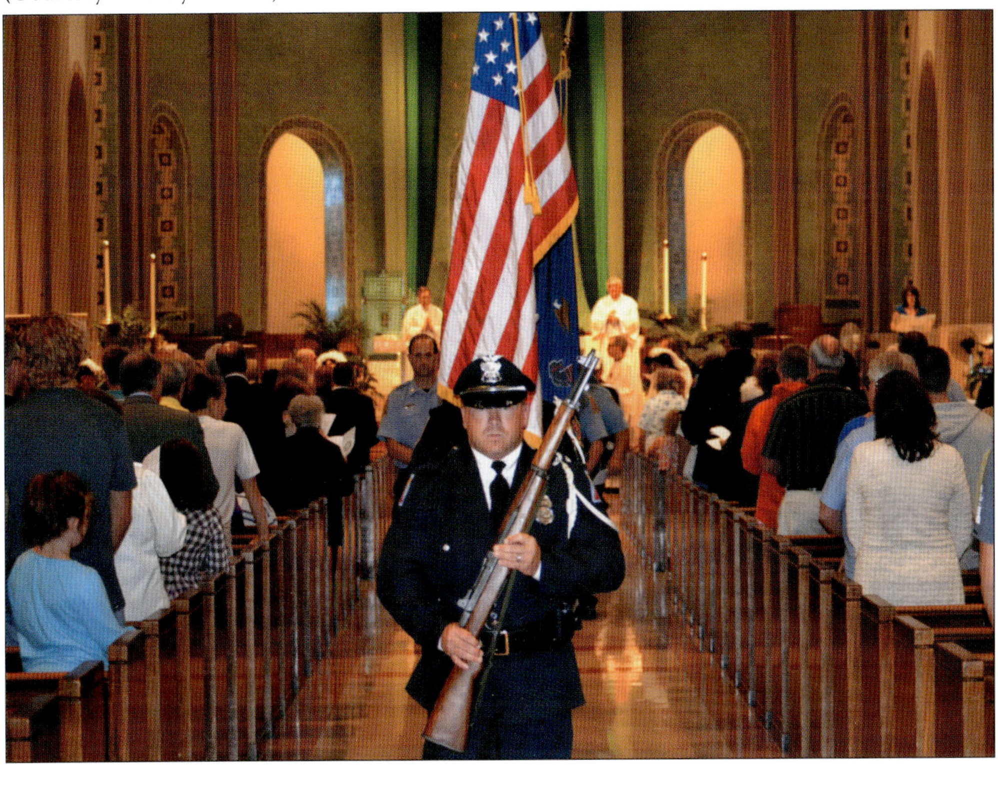

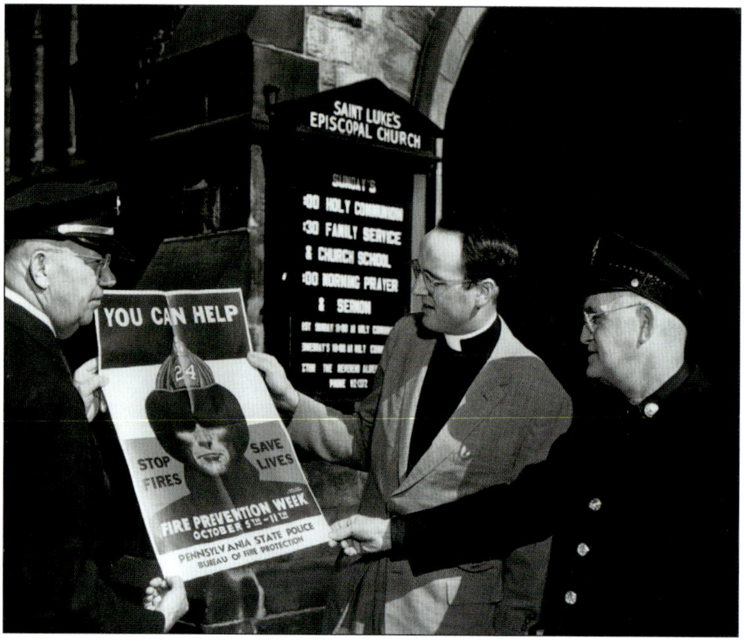

October 5–11, 1964, marked the annual Fire Prevention Week in Altoona. Often consisting of firemen school visits and parades featuring Smokey the Bear, the initiative also reached out to congregations. Here, Rev. Harry Hart of St. Luke's Episcopal Church on Thirteenth Street accepts a poster from firefighters. (Courtesy of BCCC.)

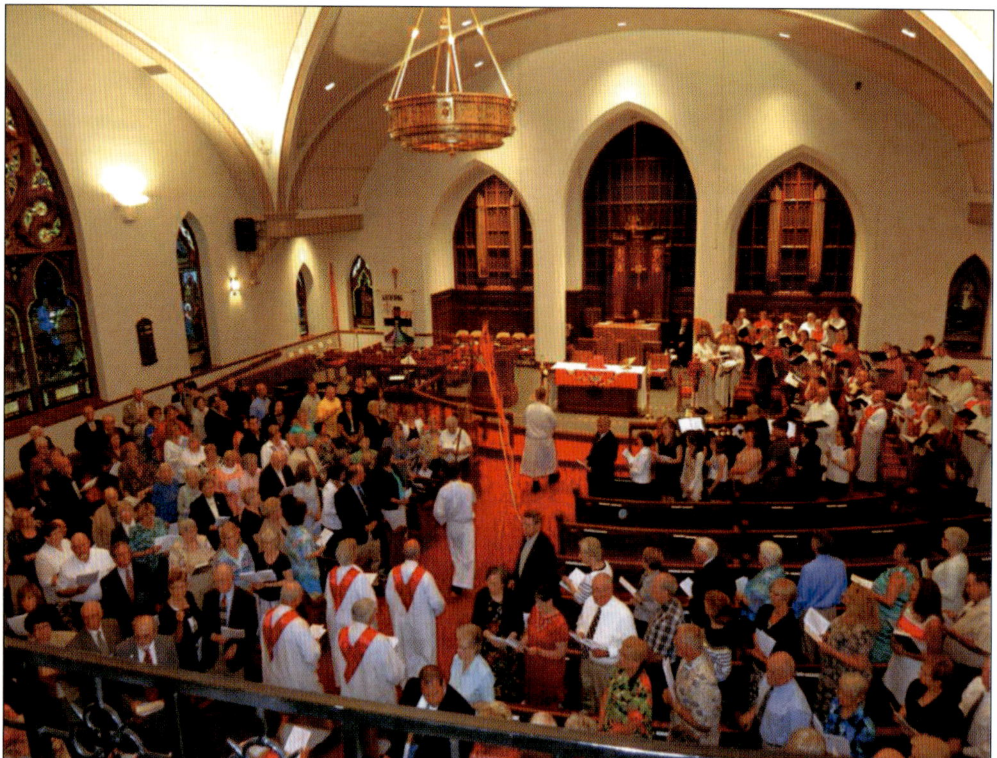

The First Evangelical Lutheran Church on Twelfth Avenue, built in 1896, suffered widespread damage due to an electrical fire on September 11, 1997. In the following years, however, the congregation rebuilt and flourished. Here, the church is hosting the opening worship for the Allegheny Synod Convention on June 5, 2014. (Courtesy of Steve Ellis.)

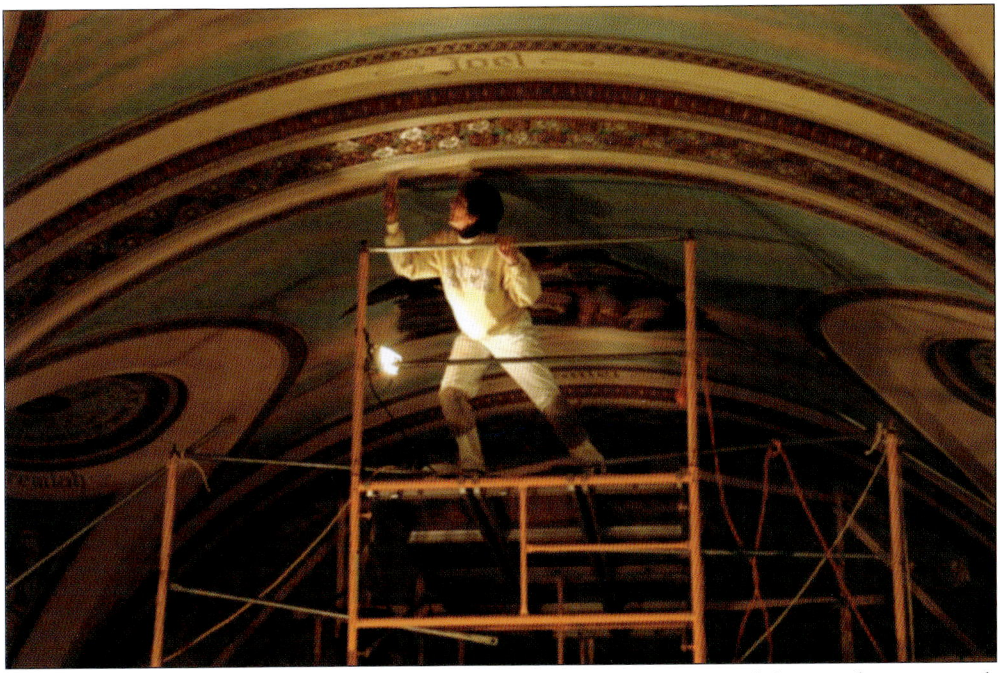

Our Lady of Mount Carmel was established in 1905. In anticipation of the parish centennial, an exhaustive restoration was undertaken to maintain the church's ornate features. Guided by Franciscan priests since 1910, the church remains a cornerstone of Altoona's Little Italy. (Courtesy of Our Lady of Mount Carmel.)

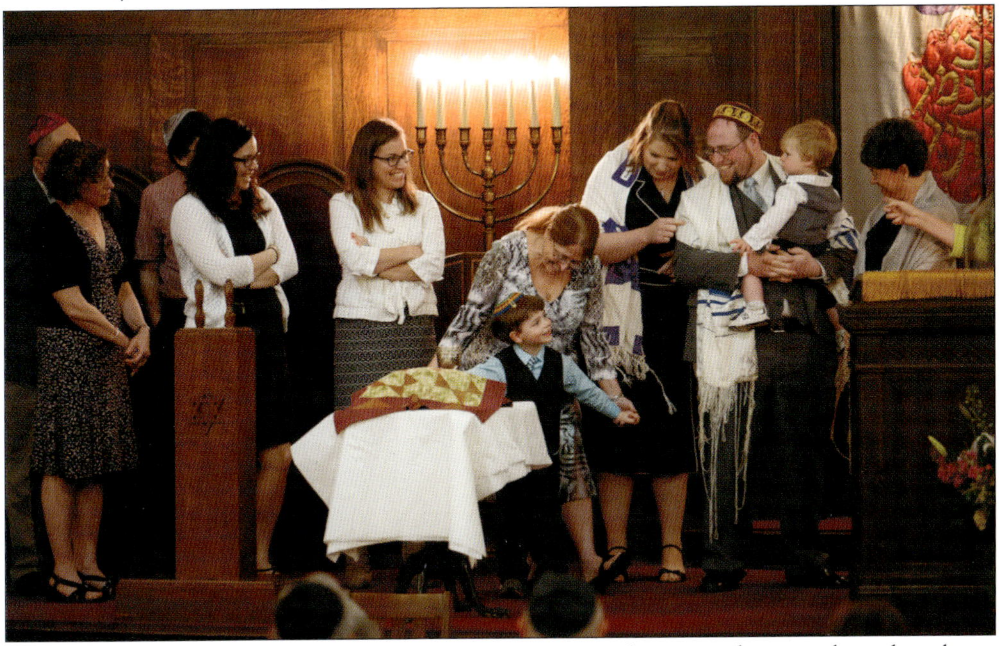

Open since 1927, Temple Beth Israel on Union Avenue stands as an architectural gem but also as a testament to Altoona's spiritual diversity. Here, family and friends gather for the 85th birthday Shabbat celebration of Norma Sevel (not pictured) at the temple on May 24, 2014. (Courtesy of Jon Beightol.)

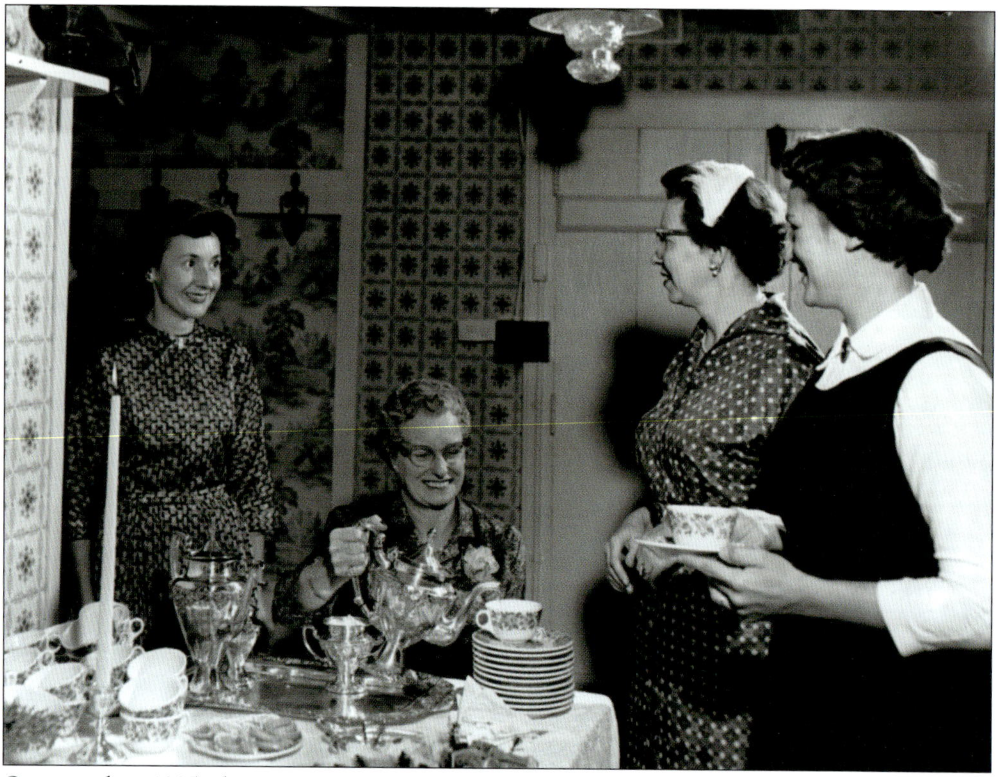

Organized in 1935, the Women's Club of Altoona seeks to promote "educational and social betterment." In this early 1960s photograph, club members welcome teachers to a tea in observation of American Education Week. From left to right are Mrs. Robert Johnson, Mrs. James Smiley, Lois Metzler, and Jean Gates. (Courtesy of the Women's Club.)

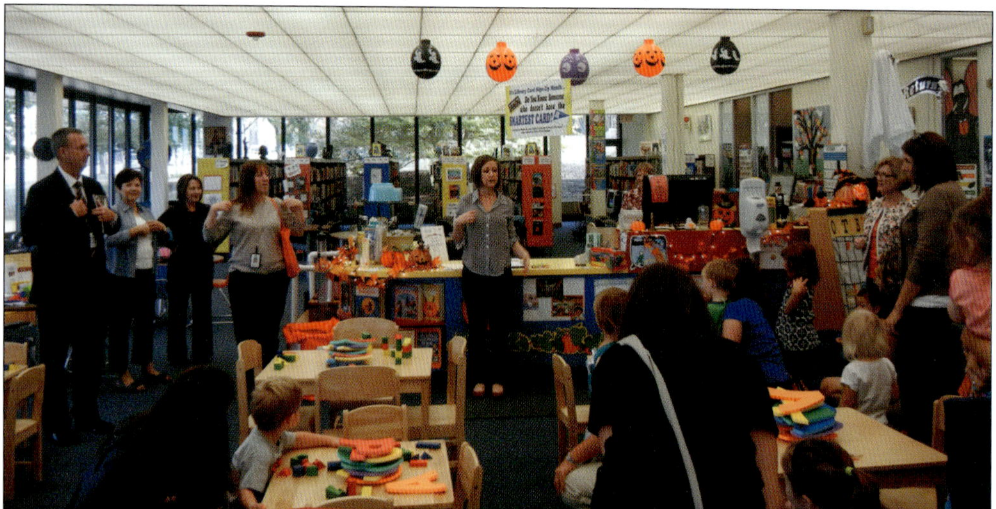

The Altoona Area Public Library has its roots in the PRR's Mechanics' Library. Finding its next home in Roosevelt Junior High in the 1920s, the library remained there until the dedication of the current Fifth Avenue facility (pictured) in 1969. Here, children's services supervisor Adrienne Brown directs the opening poem before story time on October 2, 2013. (Courtesy of the Altoona Library.)

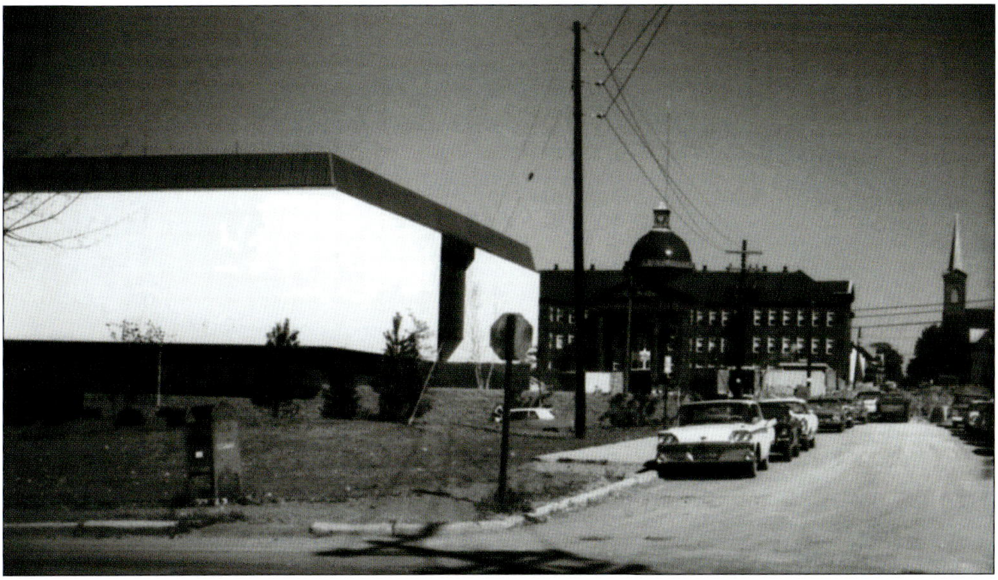

The location of the new Altoona Library was conveniently adjacent to Altoona High School. An initial portion of the library's $1.7 million cost was delivered by the Appalachian Regional Redevelopment Act. William Schmidt of the Appalachian Regional Commission praised Altoonans in his dedication speech "for taking advantage" of the forthcoming community asset. (Courtesy of David Seidel.)

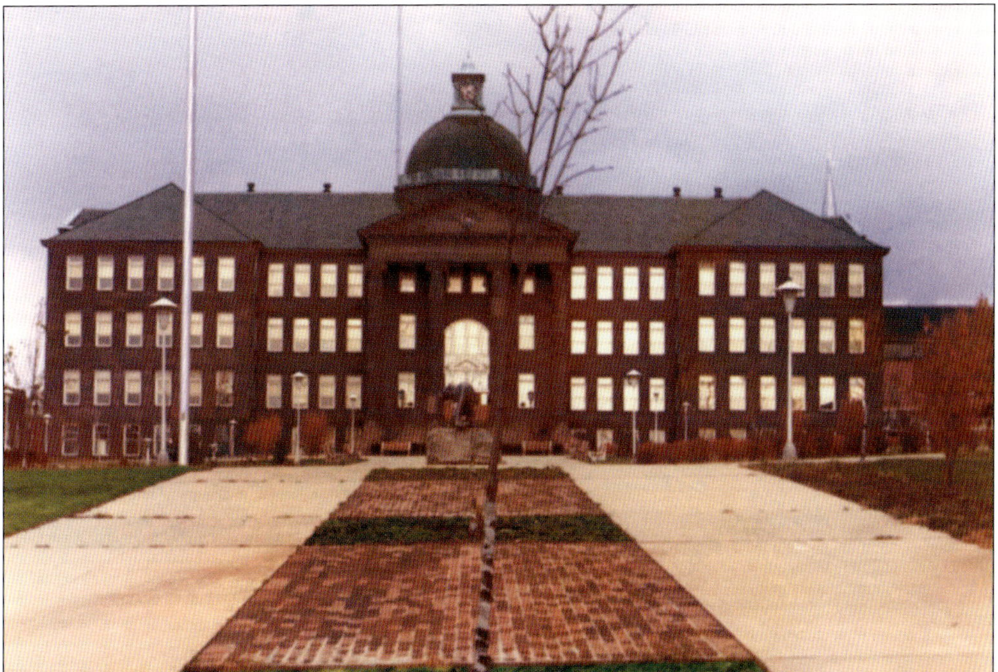

Constructed in 1905, Altoona High School between Fifth and Sixth Avenues was a "Cathedral of Learning." Built of Hummelstown brownstone, the school was capped with a stately dome. By the late 1960s, school officials deemed the structure inefficient and called for its demolition. (Courtesy of David Seidel.)

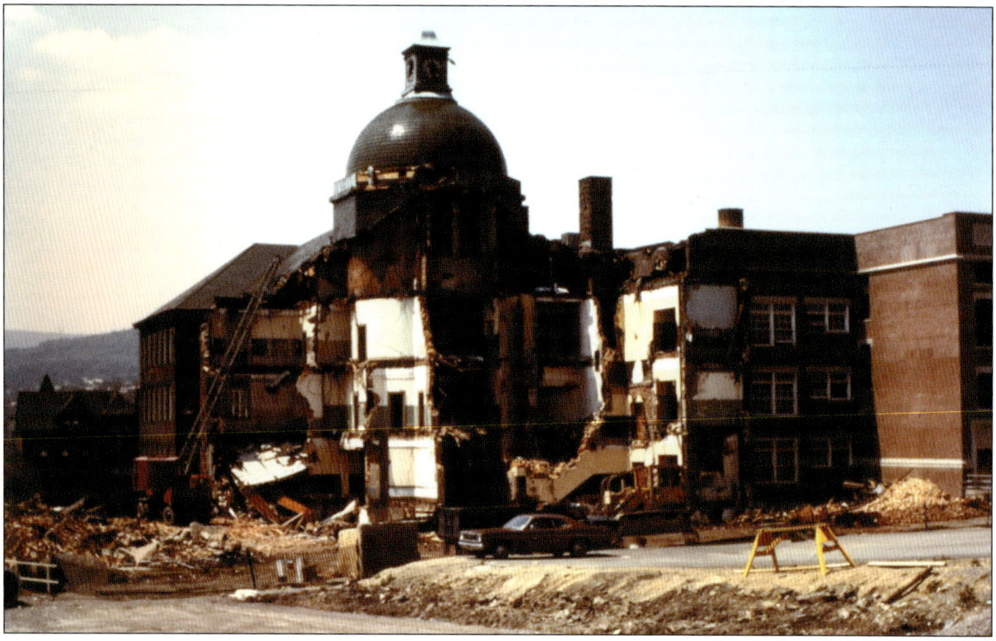

Preservationists under the auspices of Blair County Heritage, Inc. attempted legal action to prevent the original high school's destruction—they were too late. Demolition of "Old Brownie" was initiated on June 17, 1974. School board member Nadine Heiss called the annihilation of the structure "disgusting." By summer's end, the brownstone was gone forever. (Courtesy of David Seidel.)

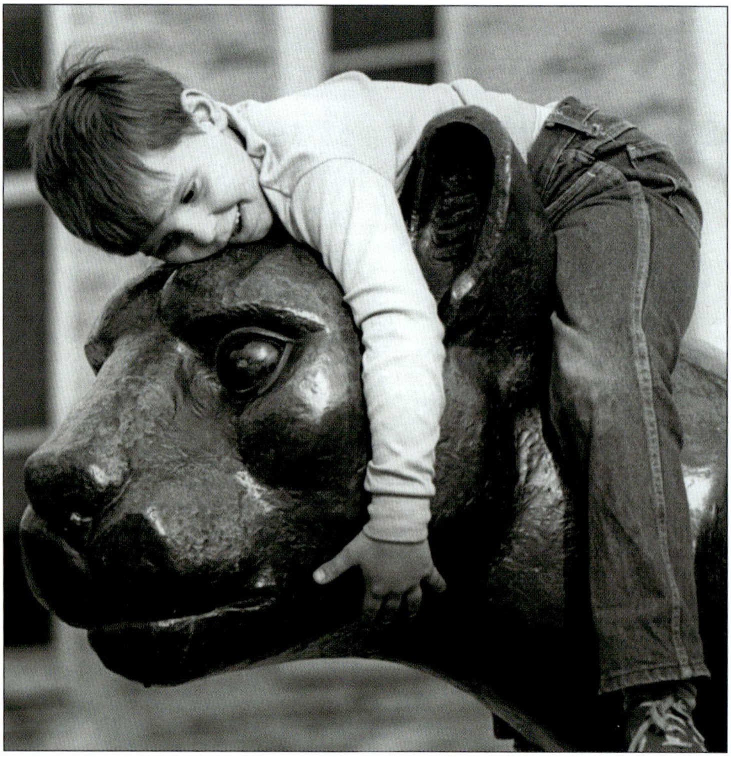

With Brownie flattened, annexes were added to the 1926 wing of Altoona High. Some $11 million was spent in the creation of new offices, classrooms, and a sports complex. Two years prior, the sculpture *Altoona Mountain Lion* by Heinz Warneke was dedicated as a feature of the grounds. Here, Allen Geist offers the copper statue some affection around 1987. (Courtesy of AM.)

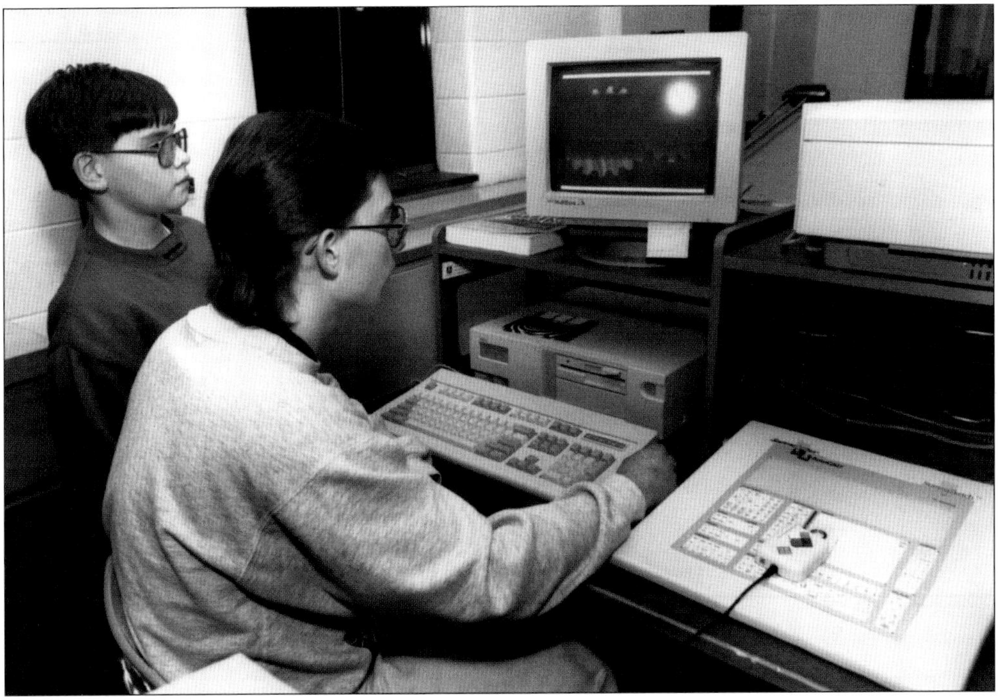

Constructed in 1970 between the high school and library, the Altoona Area Vocational-Technical High School served students coming of age in an era of rapid scientific advancement. Now known as the Greater Altoona Career & Technology Center, the school offers superlative technical education. Here, Michael McCoy (left) watches his brother Jason work on the Auto-Cad computer during a 1991 open house. (Courtesy of AM.)

On February 2, 1991, Genevieve Kabello, Rev. Anna Daugherty, and Pauline Johnson tied over 100 yellow ribbons on trees at Trinity United Church of Christ on Seventh Avenue in honor of Americans fighting in the Persian Gulf War. The day before, 25 US troops were killed in the Battle of Khafji. (Courtesy of AM.)

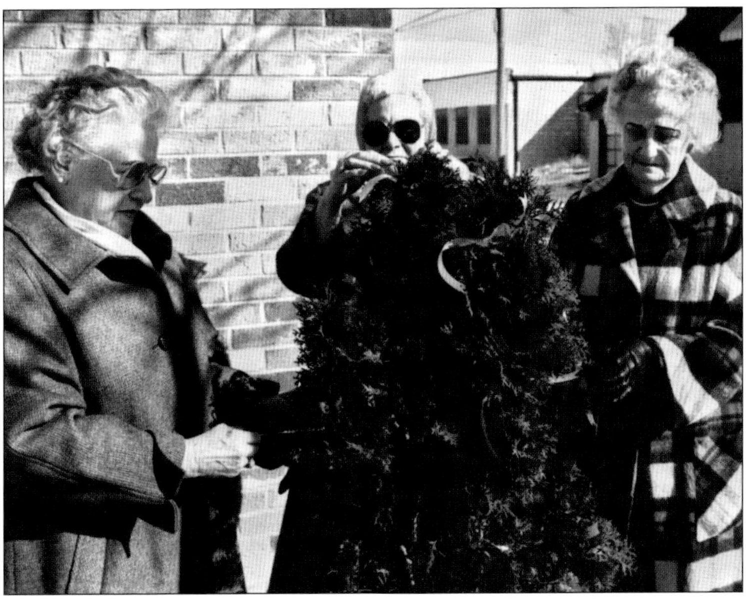

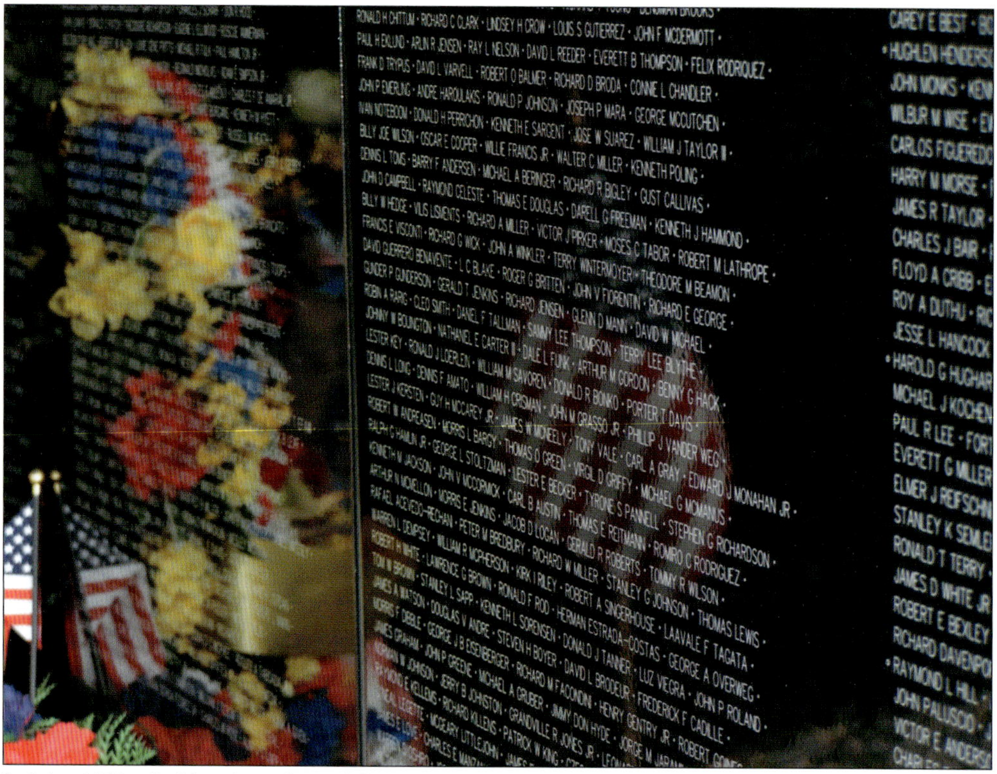

In May 1999, a half-scale replica of the Vietnam Veterans' Memorial was exhibited on the grounds of Altoona's Van Zandt VA Medical Center. Locals subsequently purchased the memorial for permanent display. The 58,000 names on the wall include Altoonan Nicholas Cancilla, killed on a night patrol on March 26, 1969. He was 22 years old. (Author's collection.)

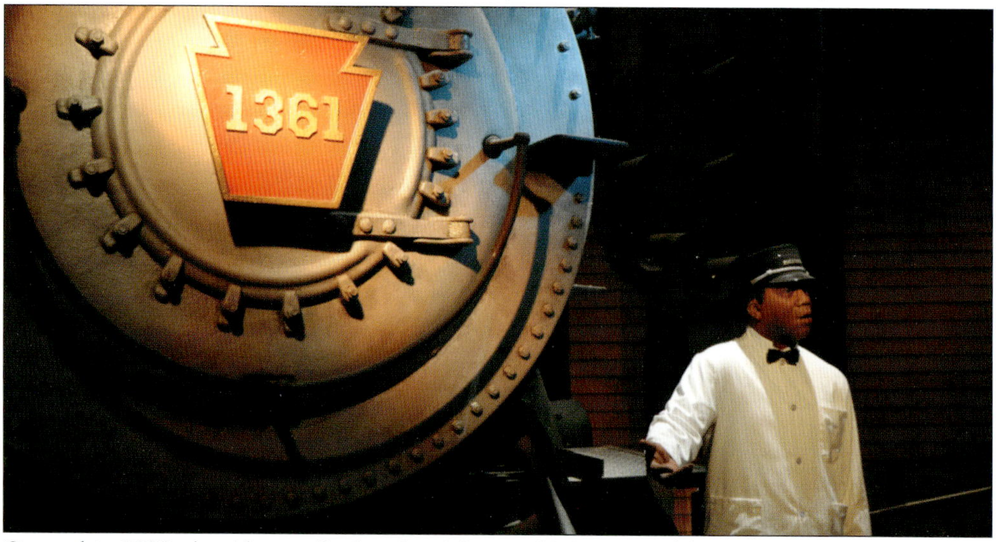

Opened in 1980, the Altoona Railroaders Memorial Museum celebrates the experiences of the town that built some 6,000 steam locomotives in its heyday. The museum expanded into the historic 1882 Master Mechanics Building in 1998. This exhibit features the story of PRR porter Jim Corbett with an impressive multimedia display. (Courtesy of Mark Frederick.)

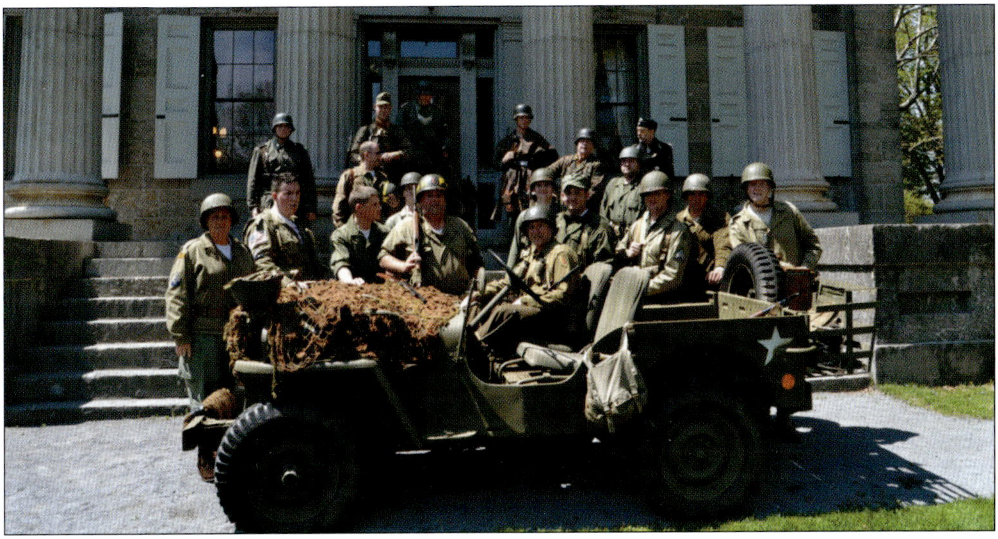

Completed in 1849, Baker Mansion, near Logan Boulevard, was the property of elite ironmaster Elias Baker, who once owned much of what is modern Altoona. Now the home of the Blair County Historical Society, the site hosts numerous exhibits and events, including the World War II History Weekend in May 2014. (Courtesy of Bob Airhart.)

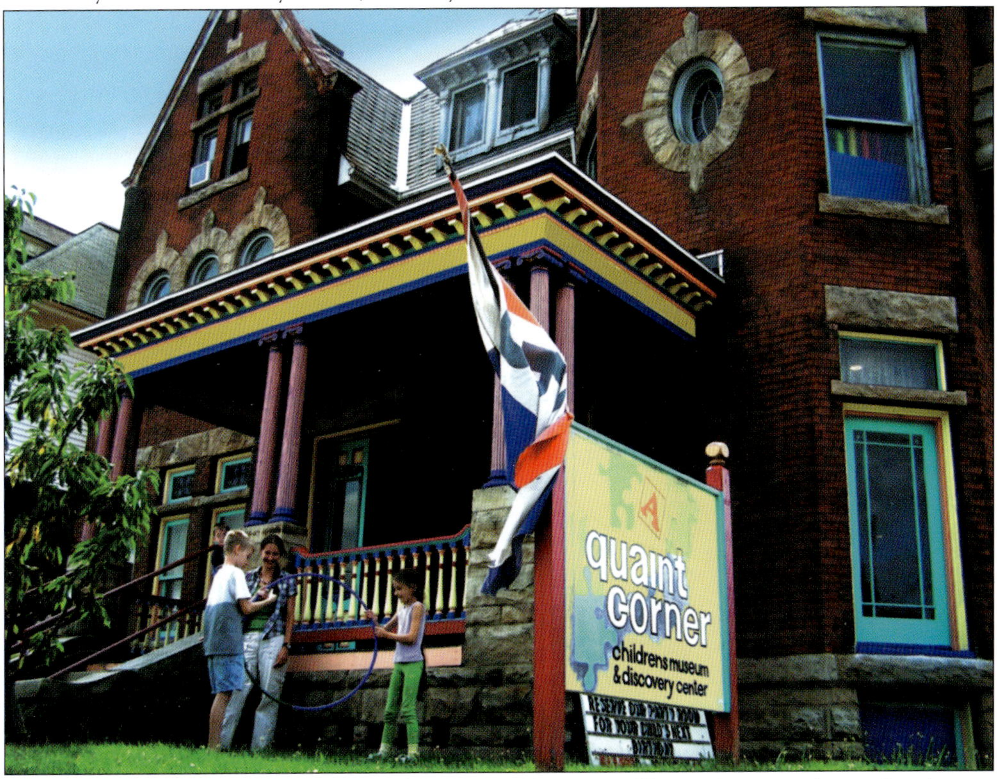

Quaint Corner Children's Museum and Discovery Center on Union Avenue is located within an ornate 1893 Victorian structure. In 1986, the museum was established "to promote creative thought in children" by raising cultural awareness. This August 15, 2014, photograph shows Benjamin Kletzing and Chaya Detrich playing as Coreena Detrich looks on. (Author's collection.)

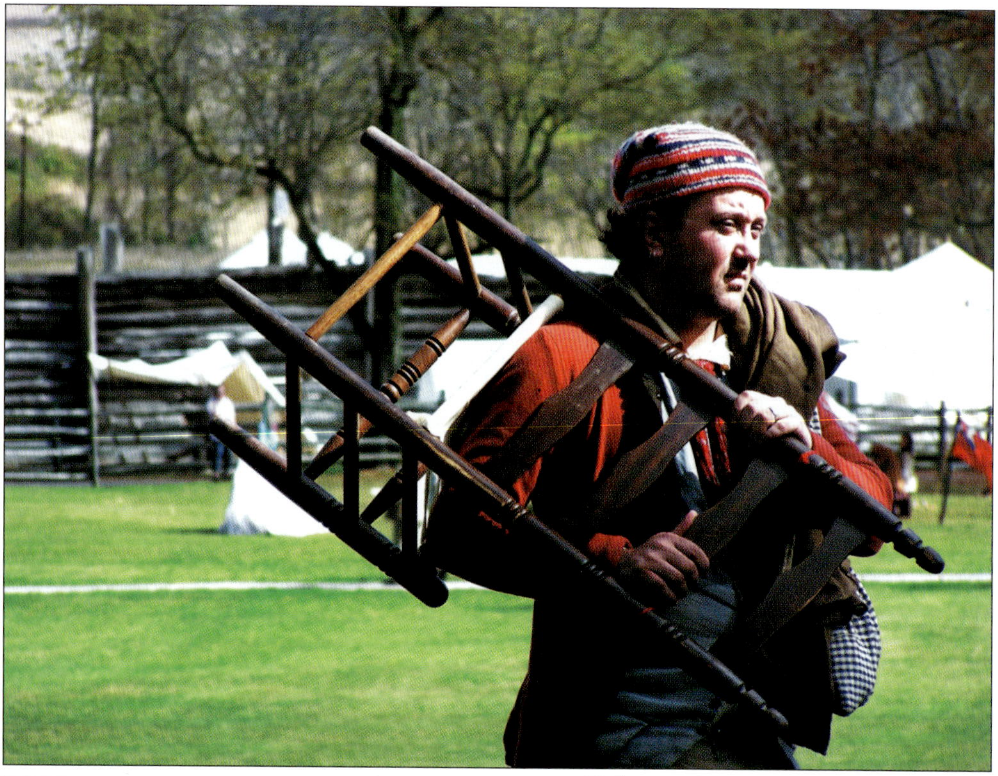

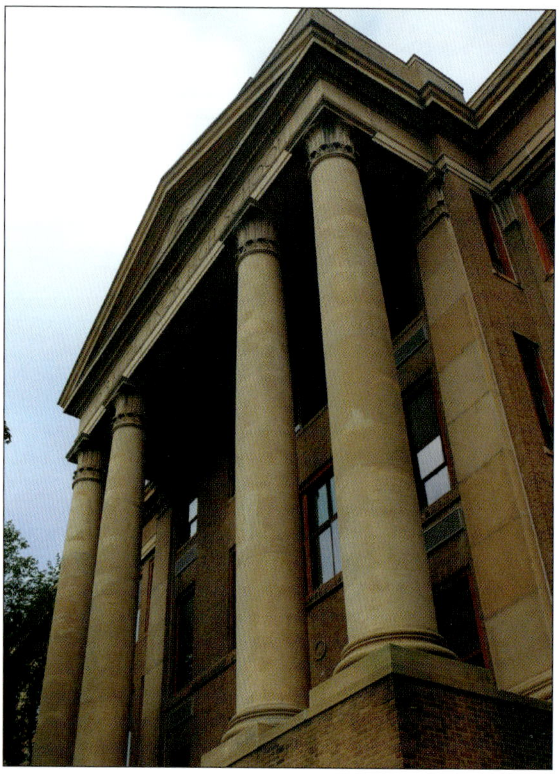

To honor the nation's 1976 bicentennial, Blair County oversaw the reconstruction of Fort Roberdeau in Sinking Valley. The original Continental outpost was established in 1778 to mine lead and protect frontier families. In this October 2013 photograph, reenactor Nate Killbuck portrays a trader at the fort's 18th-century Marketfaire. (Author's collection.)

The former Keith Junior High School stands dominantly on its Calvert Hills bluff on Nineteenth Avenue. Constructed at the onset of the Great Depression, the sandstone and brick Classical Revival structure symbolized perseverance and opportunity to its first generation of students. Home of the Rams, the school was closed in 2008 as part of a junior high school consolidation. The building now houses apartments. (Courtesy of David Seidel.)

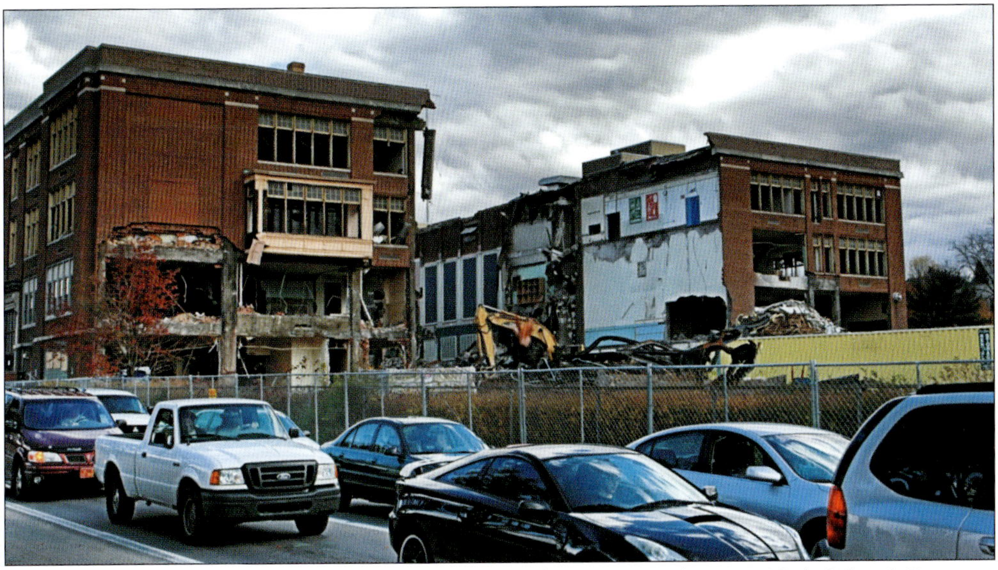

Closed in conjunction with Keith Junior High School was Roosevelt Junior High School. Opening in 1924, the school was known for its elaborate auditorium. The home of the Rough Riders was demolished in the fall of 2008. On the last day of school that year, student Marlena Nash-Persad was asked if she was glad. She answered no, "They're tearing the building down. It holds a lot of history," she said. (Courtesy of Bob Airhart.)

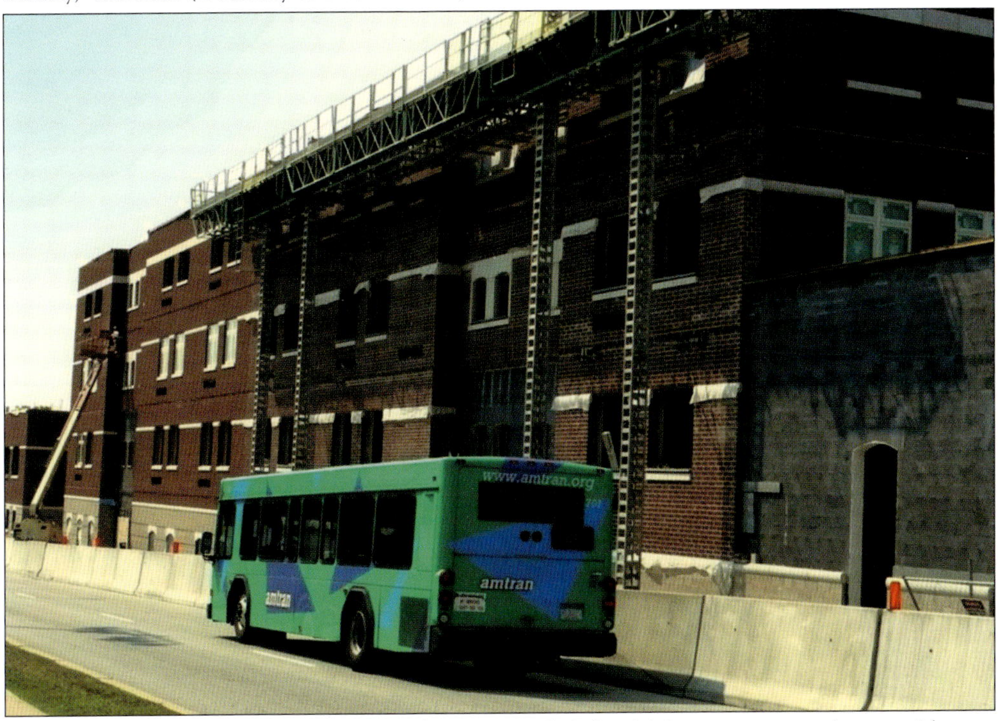

Rising in the wake of Keith and Roosevelt Junior High Schools' destruction was the new Altoona Area Junior High School along Seventh Avenue. The site offered expanded facilities, technology centers, and athletic complexes. This view shows an Amtran bus rolling past the empty shell of the junior high during its 2007 construction. (Courtesy of David Seidel.)

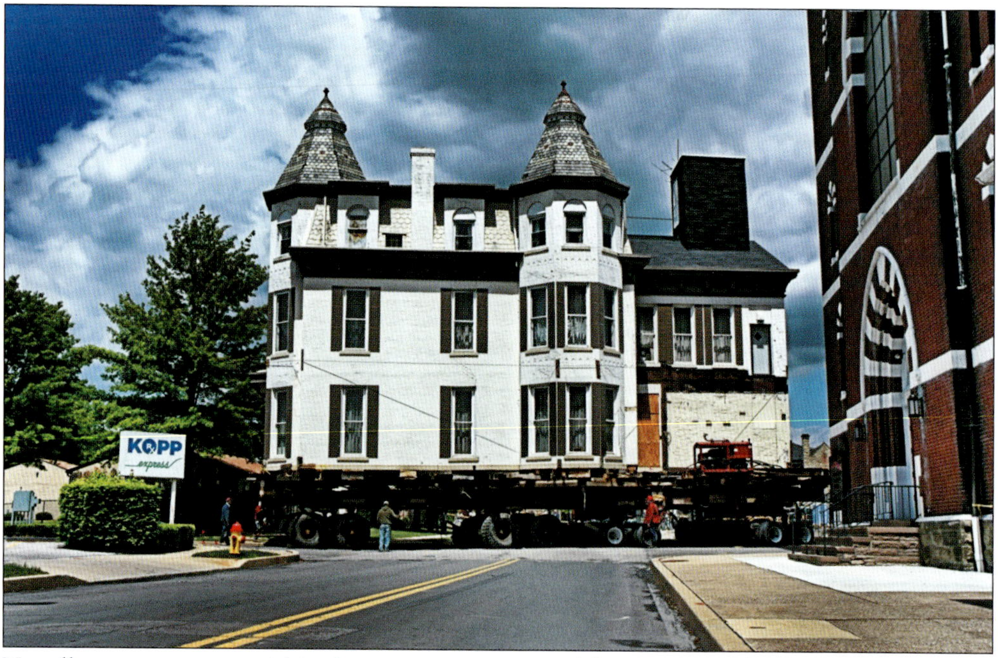

Not all property owners within the construction zone of the new junior high wanted to see their culturally valuable real estate lost in the name of progress. In May 2006, the 1888 Gilden Barton Funeral Home on Eighth Avenue was delicately relocated a block away. The spectacle was recorded by the History Channel's *Mega Movers*. (Courtesy of Bob Airhart.)

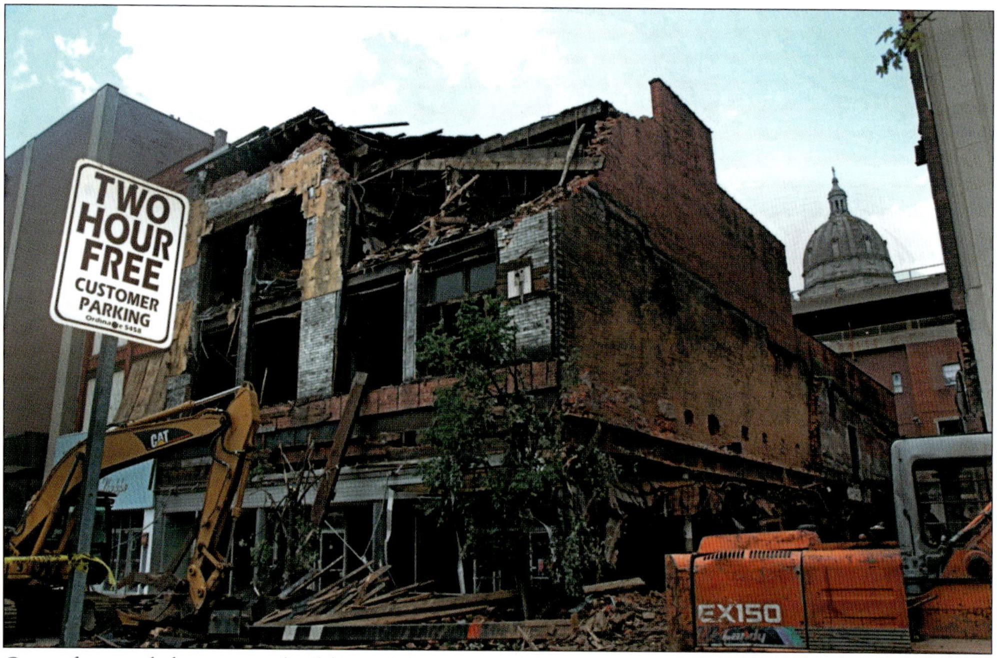

One of several downtown buildings left to languish over time, the F.W. Woolworth Building on Eleventh Avenue was open for 84 years prior to its 1994 closing. The five-and-dime store also included a popular lunch counter. Condemned by the city, it was demolished in June 2009. (Courtesy of Bob Airhart.)

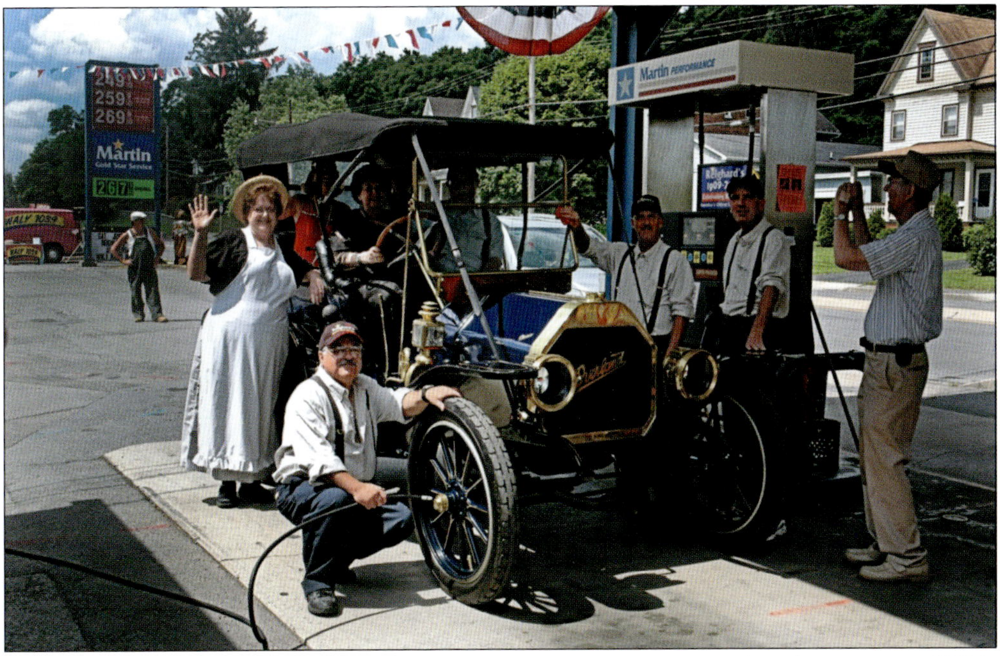

Reighard's Gas Station on Sixth Avenue commemorated its centennial in the summer of 2009. Known as America's oldest gas station, Reighard's still serves motorists with uniformed attendants. Customer Larry McKee noted, "They are friendly and you get that old-fashioned service. That is a rarity these days." (Courtesy of Bob Airhart.)

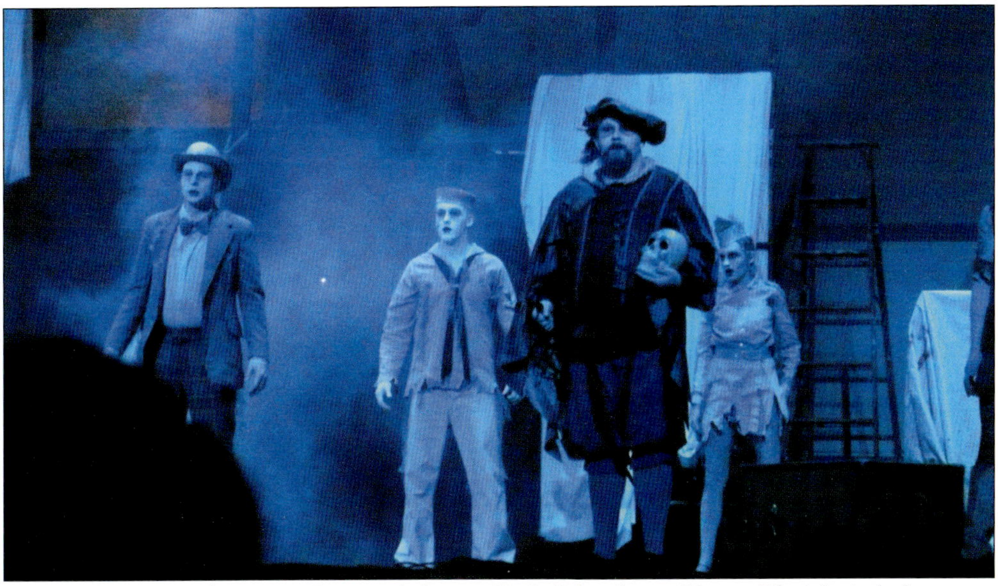

The final stage production at Roosevelt Junior High School was *Ghosts: The Musical*, shown on October 25, 2007. The play's plot dealt with apparitions attempting to save their historical theater from destruction. The symbolism of the moment struck a chord with emotional audience members who realized that the junior high's theater would be demolished within the year. (Courtesy of David Seidel.)

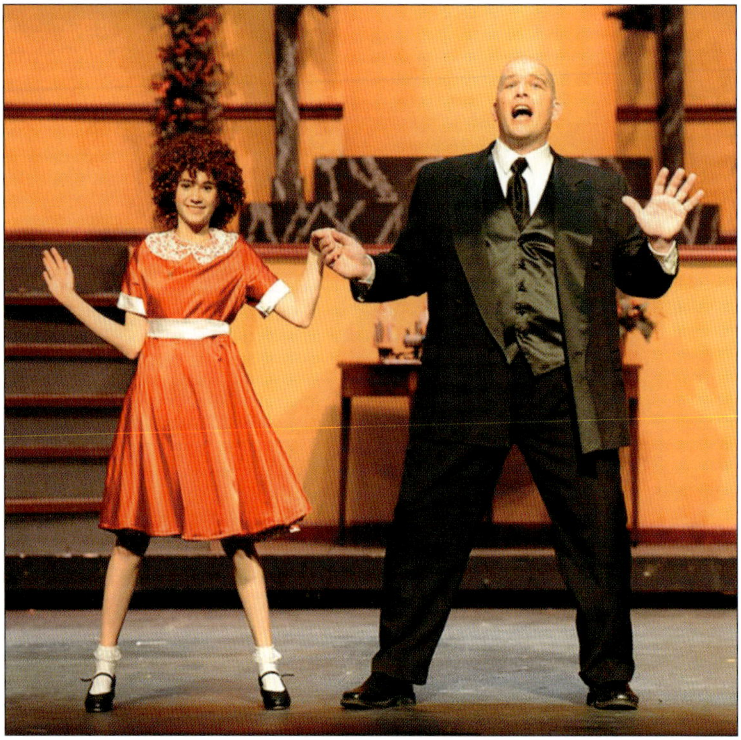

Delivering acclaimed performances since 1948, the Altoona Community Theatre was one of the original organizations that helped save the historic Mishler Theatre in the late 1960s. Here, Felicia Devorris and Doug Rosenberry act in a November 2013 rendition of *Annie*. (Courtesy of Altoona Community Theatre.)

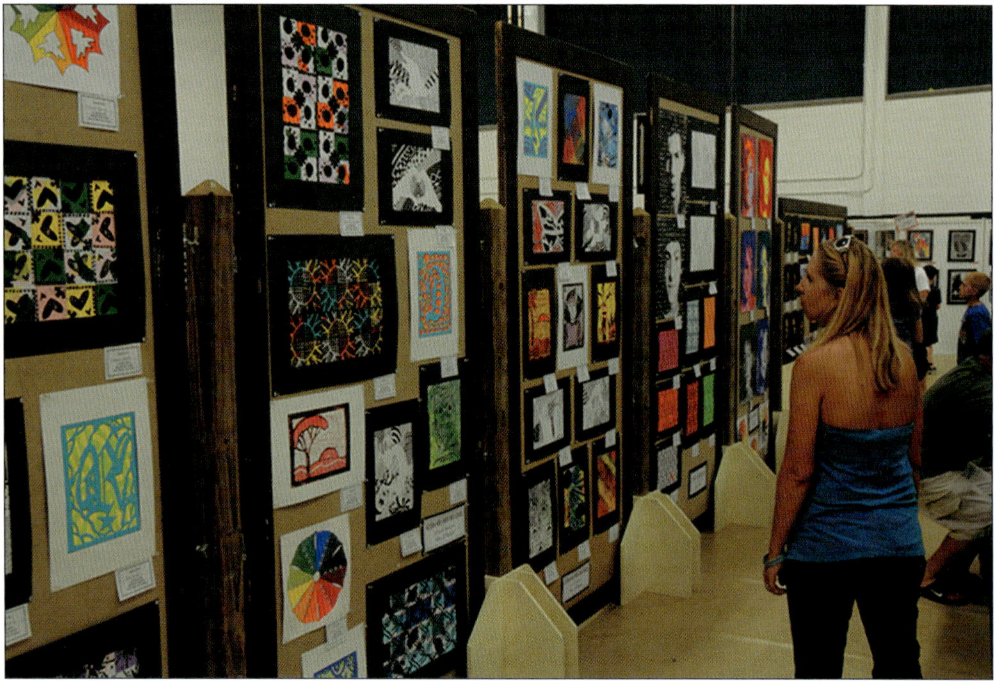

First taking place in the late 1960s, the Blair County Arts Festival has become a beloved spring tradition among central Pennsylvanians. The event includes artistic exhibitions and a rich carnival atmosphere. The annual event at Penn State Altoona attracts some 9,000 visitors. (Courtesy of BCAF.)

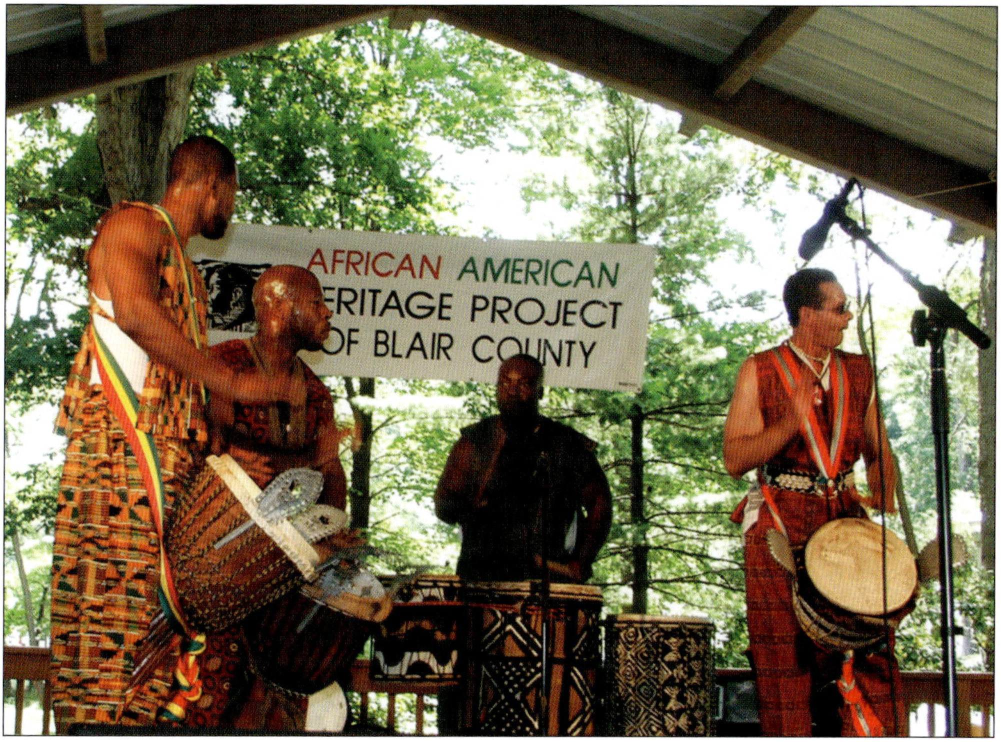

Since 1993, the African American Heritage Festival has been a community-wide event that shares the wide breadth of music, cuisine, and culture from the African American experience. Organized by the African American Heritage Project of Blair County, the event takes place at Penn State Altoona every summer. (Courtesy of PSA.)

Penn State Altoona was established in 1939 at the former Webster School downtown. Barely surviving the student exodus during World War II, the campus enjoyed a postwar resurgence. The college found its new home at the abandoned Ivyside amusement park. This 1950s photograph shows instructor Jack Zubrod teaching anatomy. (Courtesy of PSA.)

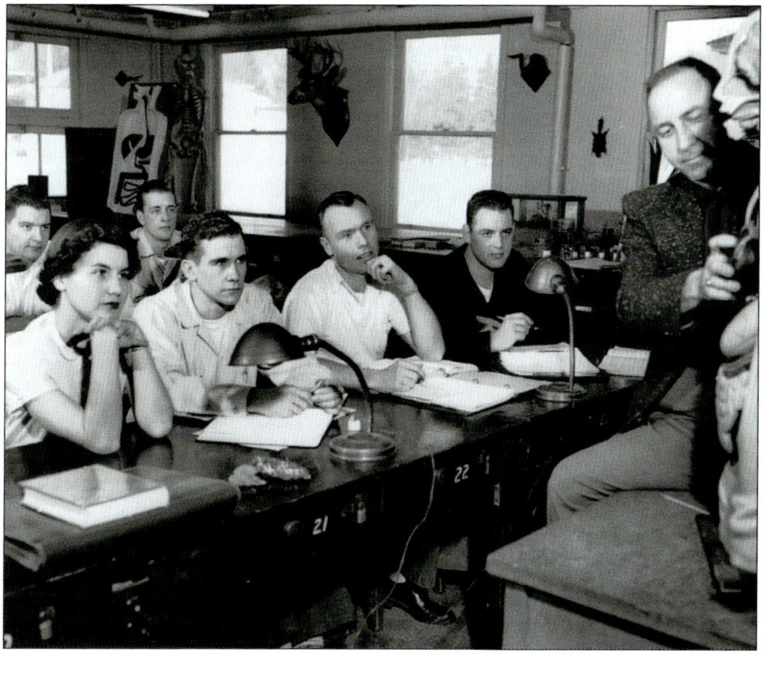

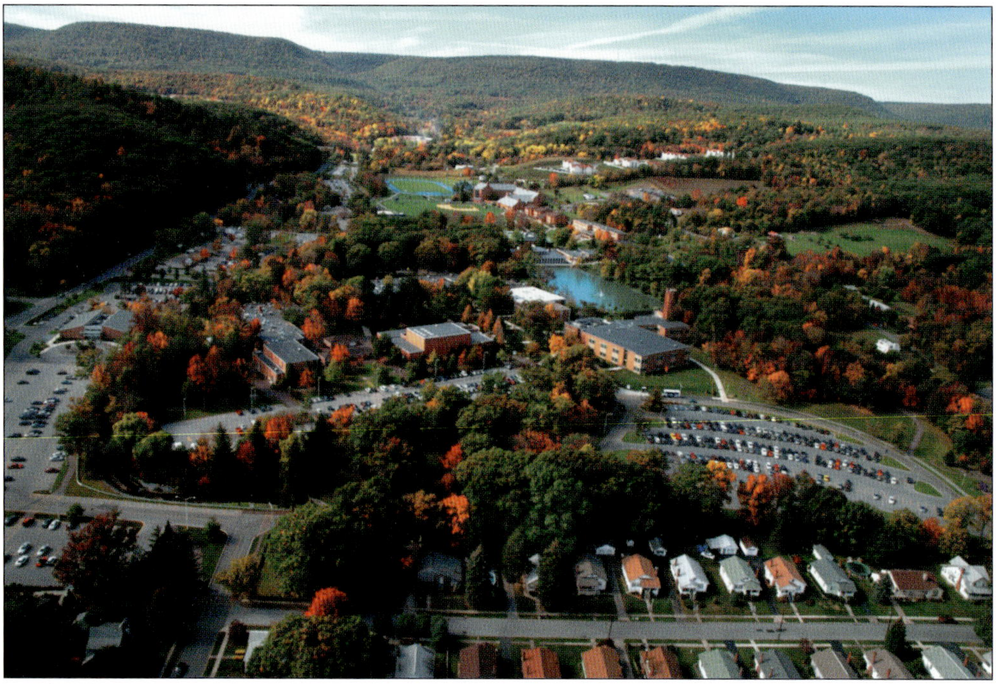

In what began as a humble endeavor with 119 students in 1939, Penn State Altoona served some 4,000 pupils during its 75th anniversary in 2014. Offering 25 different baccalaureate degrees, the campus has grown to one of the largest and most successful within the commonwealth. (Courtesy of PSA.)

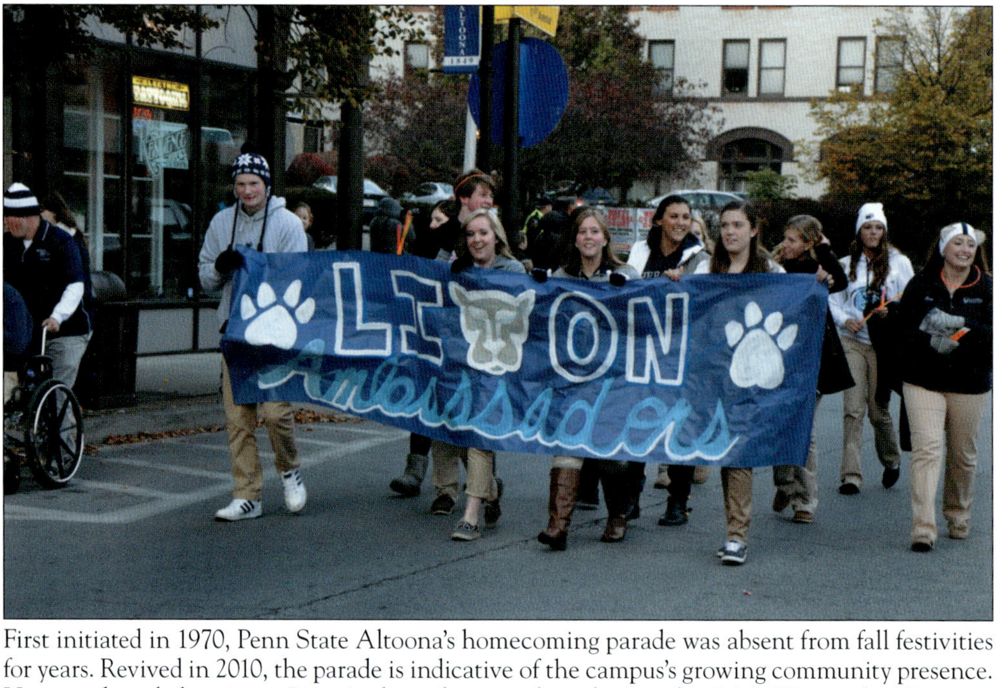

First initiated in 1970, Penn State Altoona's homecoming parade was absent from fall festivities for years. Revived in 2010, the parade is indicative of the campus's growing community presence. Here, students belonging to Lion Ambassadors march in the October 24, 2013, parade. (Courtesy of PSA.)

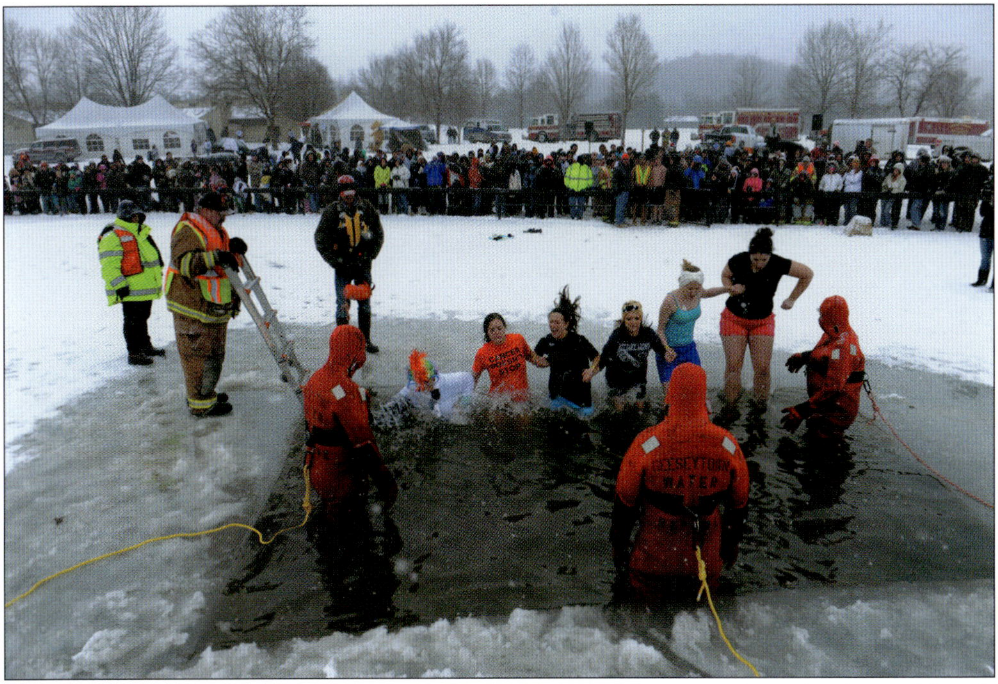

"Buoyed by the spirit of philanthropy," over 100 Penn State Altoona students, faculty, and friends dove into Canoe Creek State Park for the second annual Winter Plunge on January 26, 2014. Despite temperatures in the 20s, the frigid fundraiser garnered over $50,000 to fight pediatric cancer as part of the university's THON initiative. (Courtesy of PSA.)

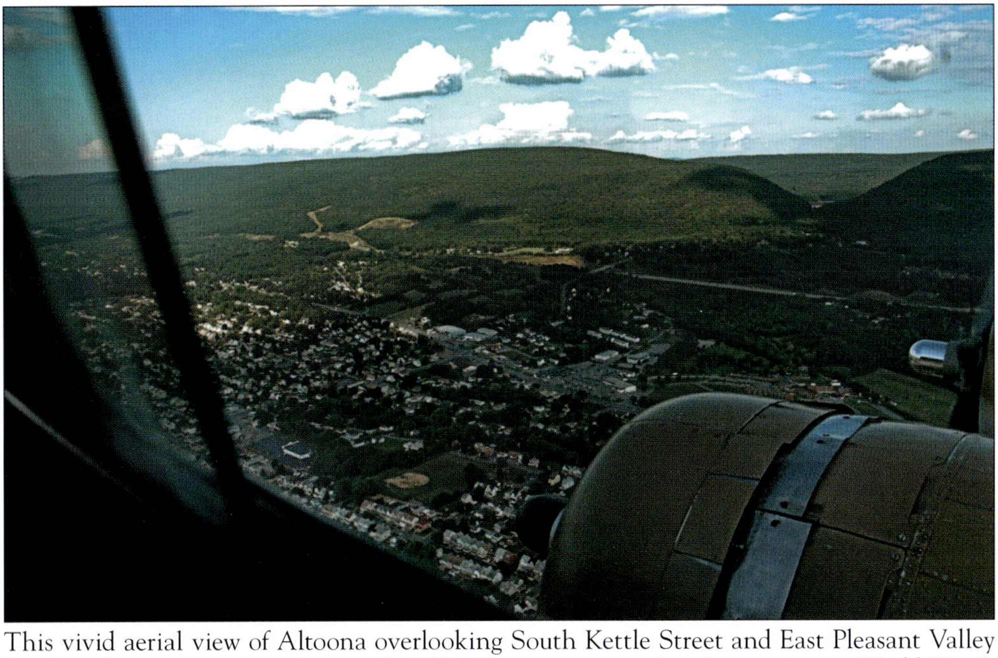

This vivid aerial view of Altoona overlooking South Kettle Street and East Pleasant Valley Boulevard was captured on August 13, 2009. The image was taken from a vintage World War II Boeing B-17G Flying Fortress named the *Nine O Nine*. Such a photograph exhibits the majesty of the Allegheny Mountains towering over the city. (Photograph by Bob Airhart.)

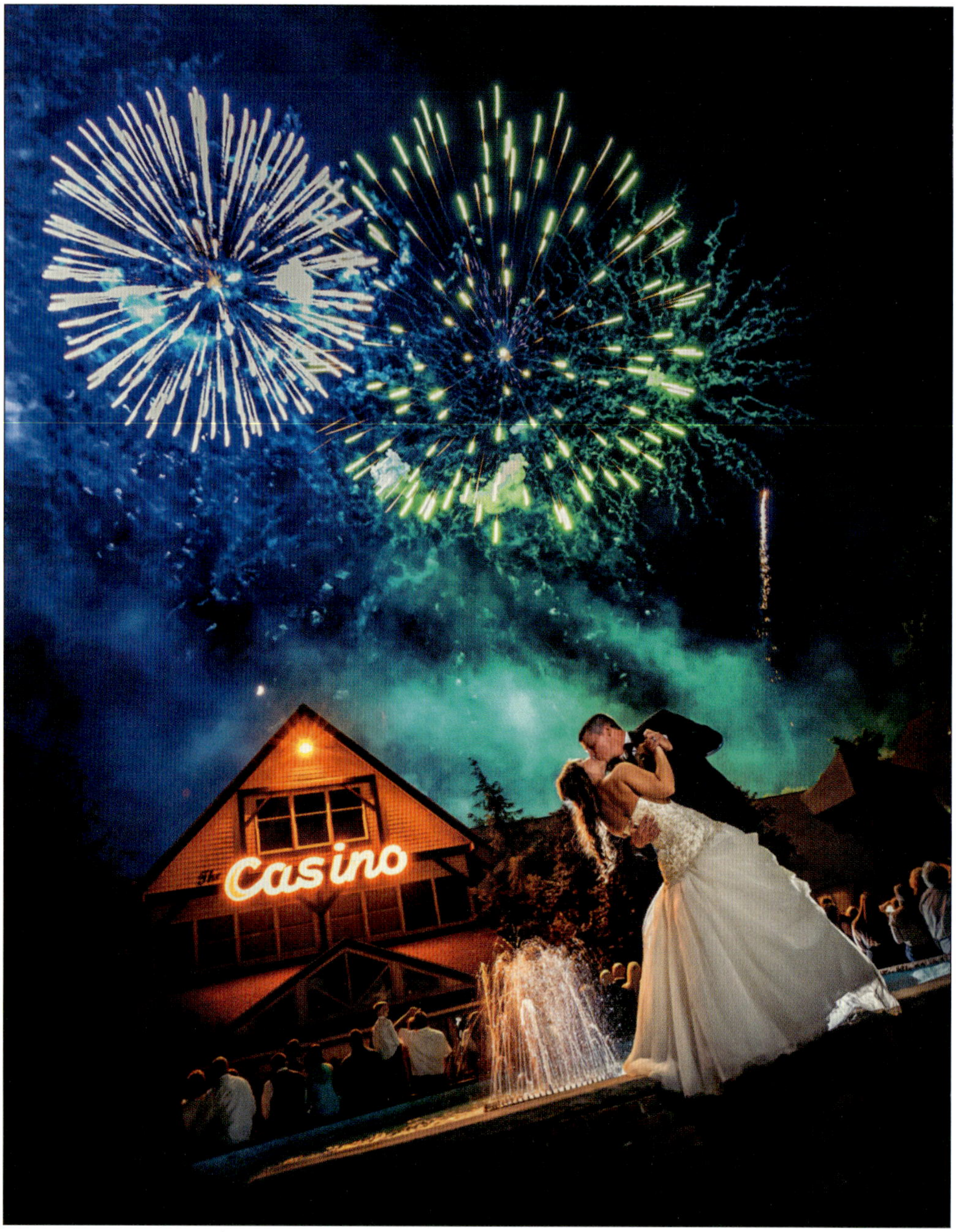

Built in 1890, the Casino in Lakemont is a festive reception hall that has hosted business gatherings, swing dances, church banquets, and school proms in its century of service. On Independence Day in 2014, Calvin and Jill Hall celebrated their wedding amid Lakemont's fireworks show. (Courtesy of Eric Smyklo Photography.)

Four

FUN AND GAMES

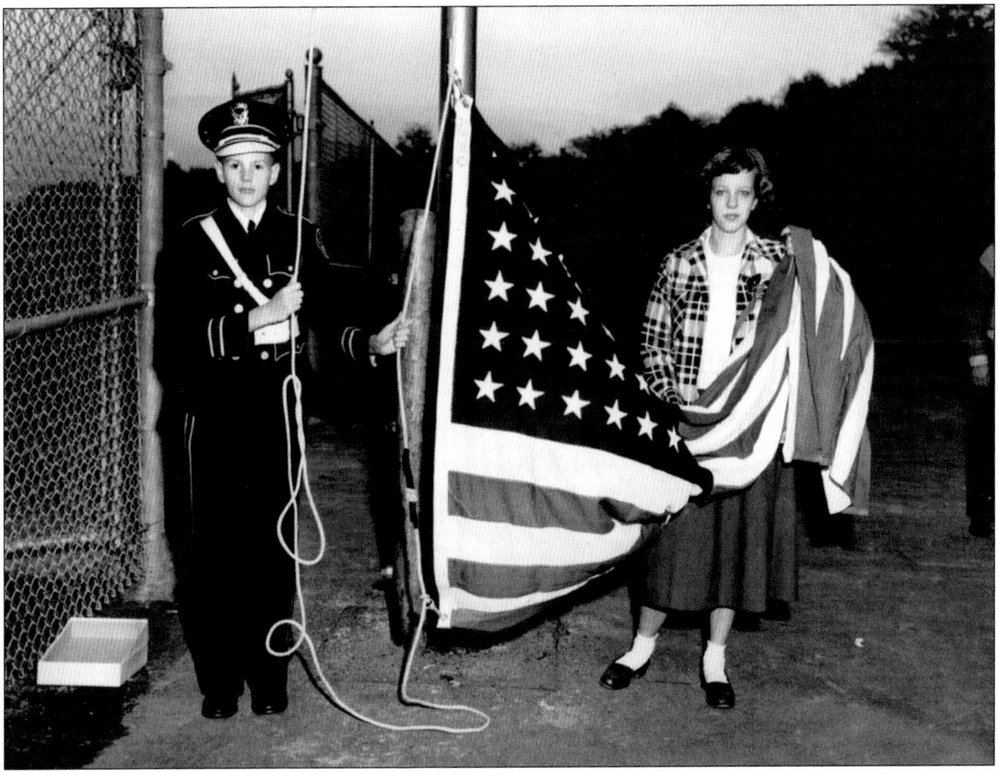

Sports and leisure have long been central to the spirit of Altoona's people. Such zeal was demonstrated on October 6, 1949, at the dedication of the Keith Junior High football field on Twenty-fifth Avenue. Prior to the ceremony, students Charles Espenlaub and Nancy Heller hoisted the flag above the field dedicated to the school's World War II veterans. (Courtesy of AM.)

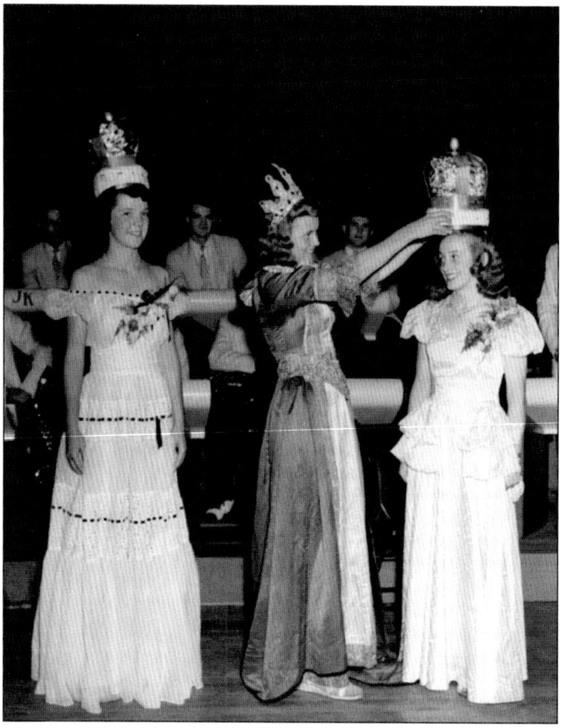

Athletic events were far from the only competitive engagements in Altoona. On August 8, 1947, the Blair County Chamber of Commerce hosted the Potato Blossom Queen pageant. Held at the Jaffa Mosque, the contest crowned Shirley Lee Nee of Bedford and Rose Marie Ellenberger of Warriors Mark as the most outstanding. (Courtesy of BCCC.)

WFBG Radio and Television broadcasted area sports. With the station's initials representing original owner William F. "Bill" Gable, TV broadcasts began on March 1, 1953. Taken in 1953 (the same year the first color televisions were sold), this photograph reveals a daytime show and audience. Engineer Art Rossbach stands with his headset behind the cameraman. (Courtesy of AM.)

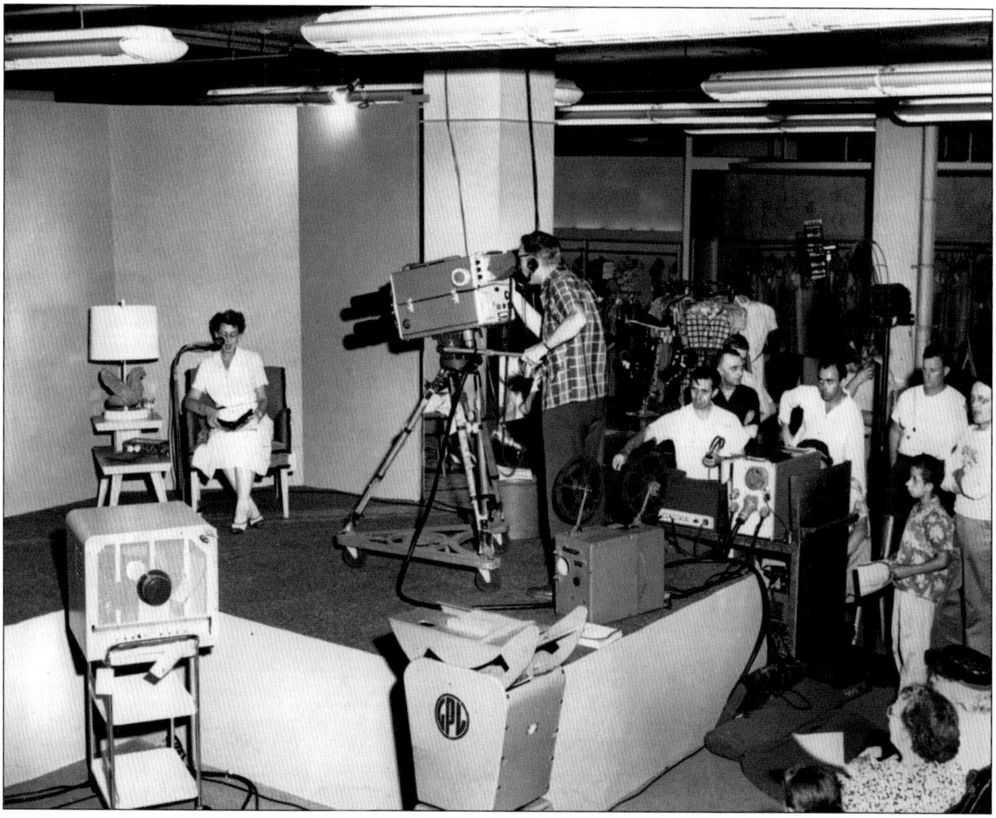

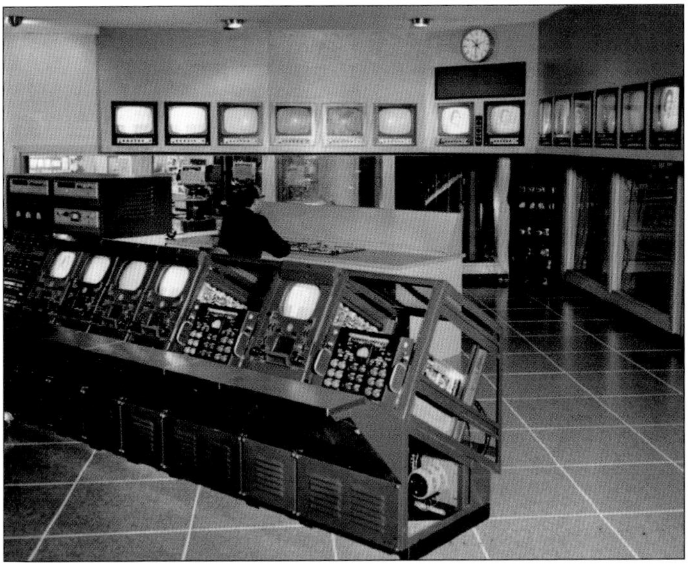

Taken exactly three months before Lee Harvey Oswald's murder was broadcast live on these televisions, this 1963 view shows the interior of WFBG's control room. After Gateway Communications purchased the station in 1972, its call letters were changed to WTAJ to reflect the broader Altoona-Johnstown market. The channel remains a widely watched CBS affiliate. (Courtesy of AM.)

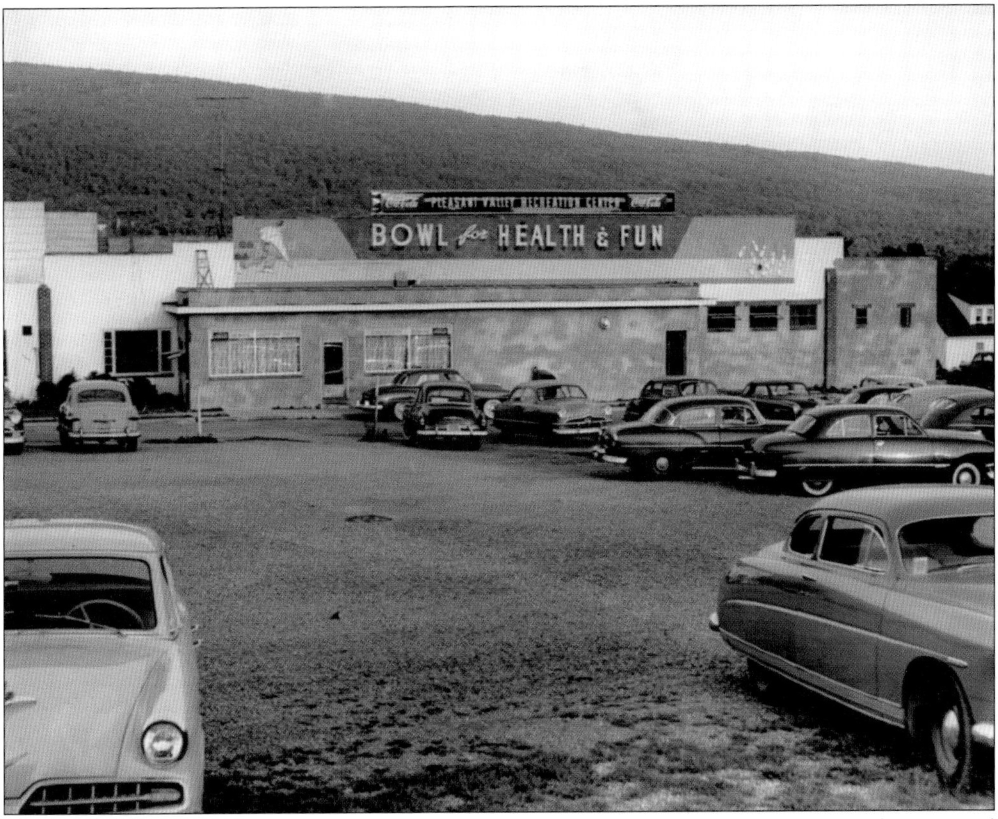

After completing service with the 17th Airborne, Bob DiVentura returned to Altoona and established the Pleasant Valley Recreation Center. Opening the evening prior to Thanksgiving 1948, the lanes have been accommodating patrons ever since. The establishment hosted Pres. Barack Obama for his infamous game of bowling there on March 30, 2008. (Courtesy of BCCC.)

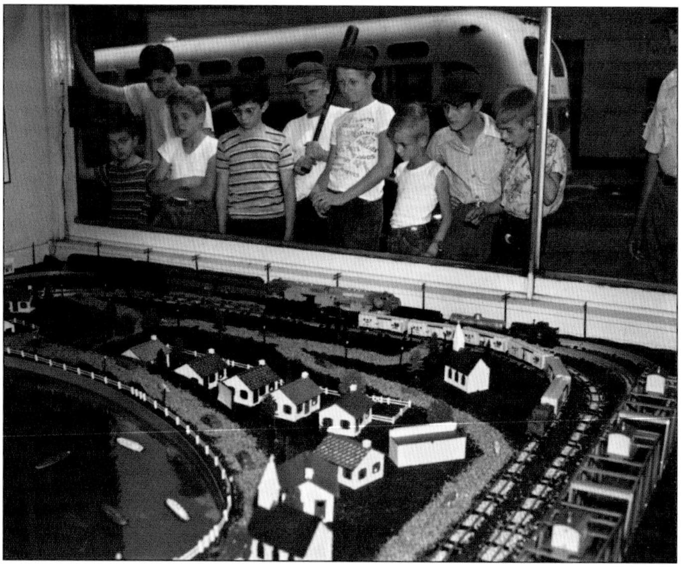

Rothert Company House Furnishers possessed a prime location along Twelfth Street and Twelfth Avenue. This photograph shows a sandlot baseball team taking a stretch during Altoona's centennial celebrations to view Rothert's sales window on August 10, 1949. Considering the livelihood of many locals, model railroading became a popular pastime. (Photograph by Gelon Smith, courtesy of William Burket.)

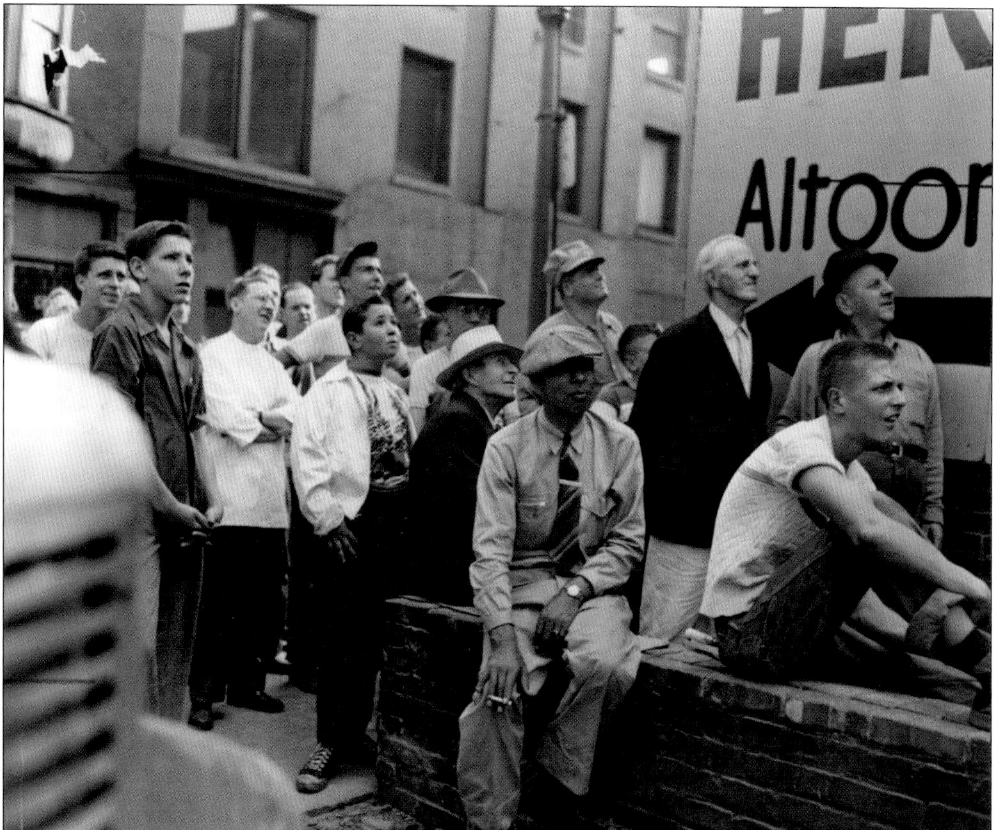

By the 1950s, watching building demolitions became a pastime in and of itself. On August 27, 1951, wide-eyed spectators watched in saddened amazement as a wrecking ball brought down the four-story Penn Theatre on Green Avenue between Tenth and Eleventh Streets. The newspaper advertised the demolition as a free show. (Courtesy of AM.)

Cricket Field along Seventh Street and Chestnut Avenue was constructed in 1898 and hosted the likes of Babe Ruth. This April 10, 1959, photograph was taken the same day as a heated city hall forum discussing the PRR's sale of the site. City council controversially rezoned the area to commercial space. Within a year, the field was replaced by a supermarket. (Courtesy of AM.)

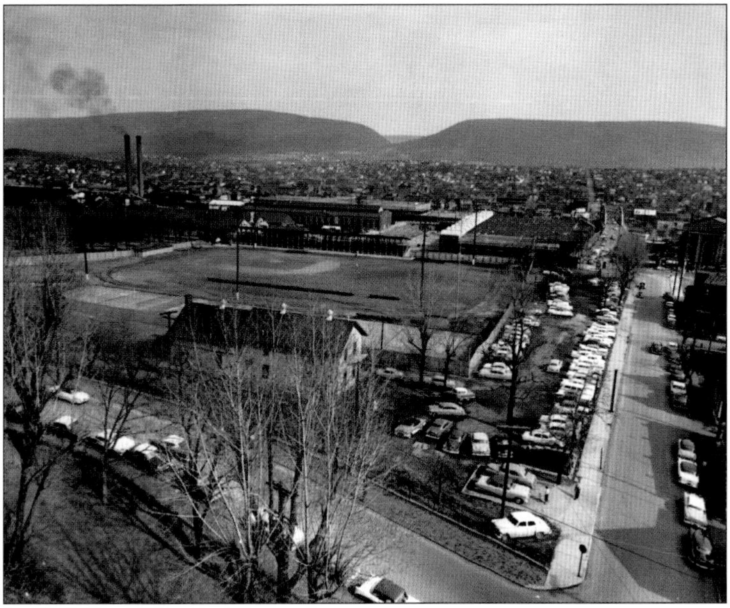

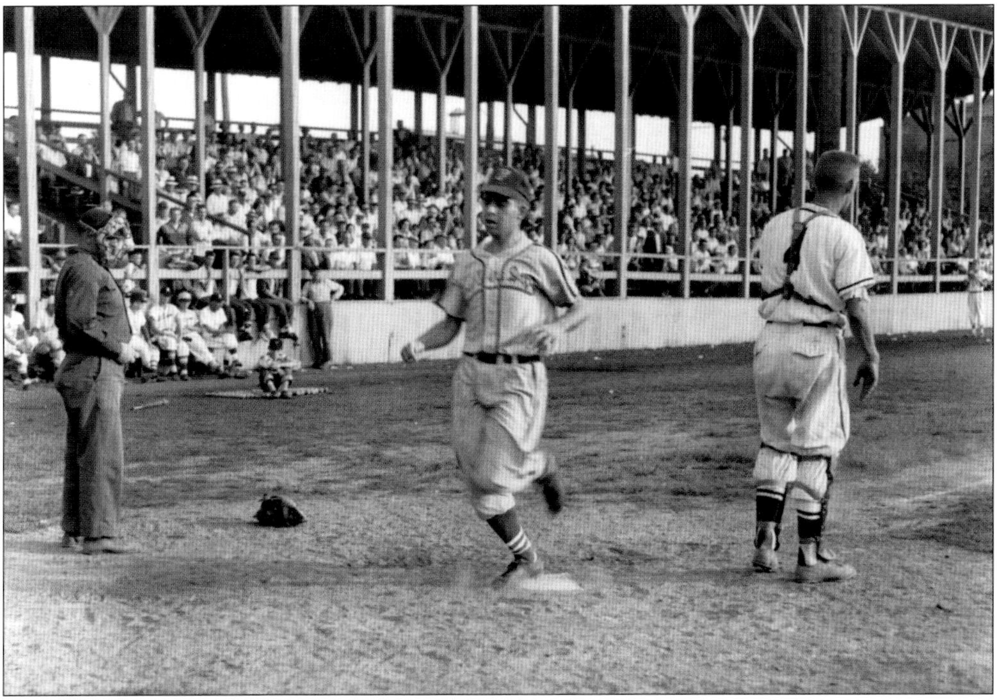

A last hurrah of Cricket Field was the August 1959 National Amateur Baseball Federation Series. Vet's Field stadium was subsequently built on Maple Avenue to host the NABF the following season. Local sportswriter Herb Werner commented, "Let's forget about the departed Cricket Field." For many, that act proved easier said than done. (Courtesy of BCCC.)

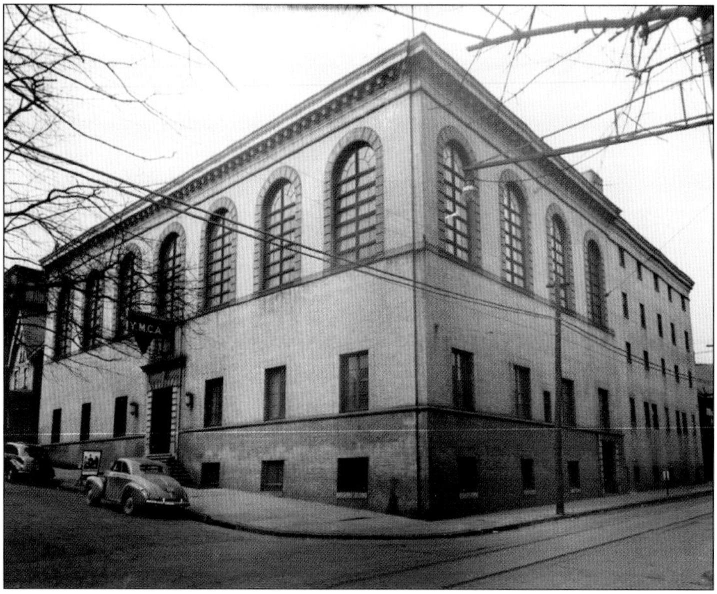

Located at the corner of Ninth Street and Lexington Avenue, Altoona's YMCA was constructed in the 1920s as an arena for local youth to escape the toils of railroad culture. Taken during the third year of the Korean War, this fall 1952 photograph shows a Marine Corps recruitment sign out front. (Courtesy of AM.)

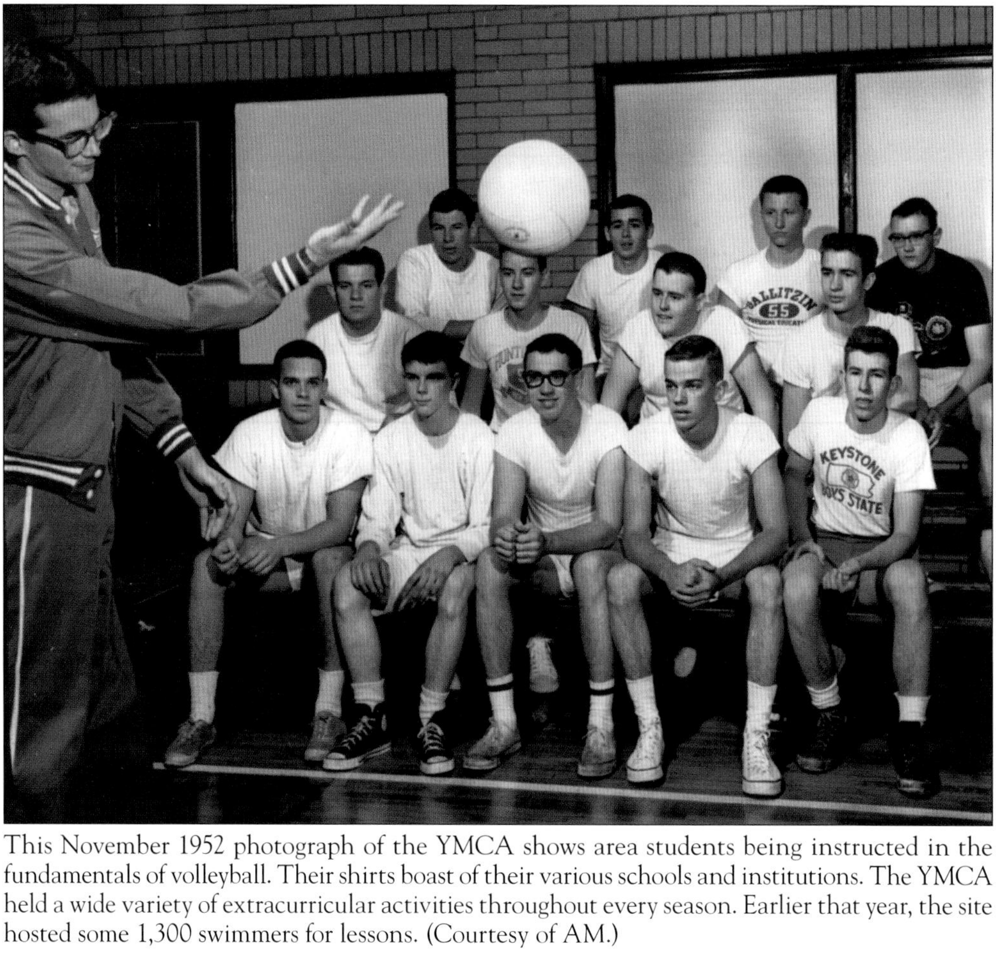

This November 1952 photograph of the YMCA shows area students being instructed in the fundamentals of volleyball. Their shirts boast of their various schools and institutions. The YMCA held a wide variety of extracurricular activities throughout every season. Earlier that year, the site hosted some 1,300 swimmers for lessons. (Courtesy of AM.)

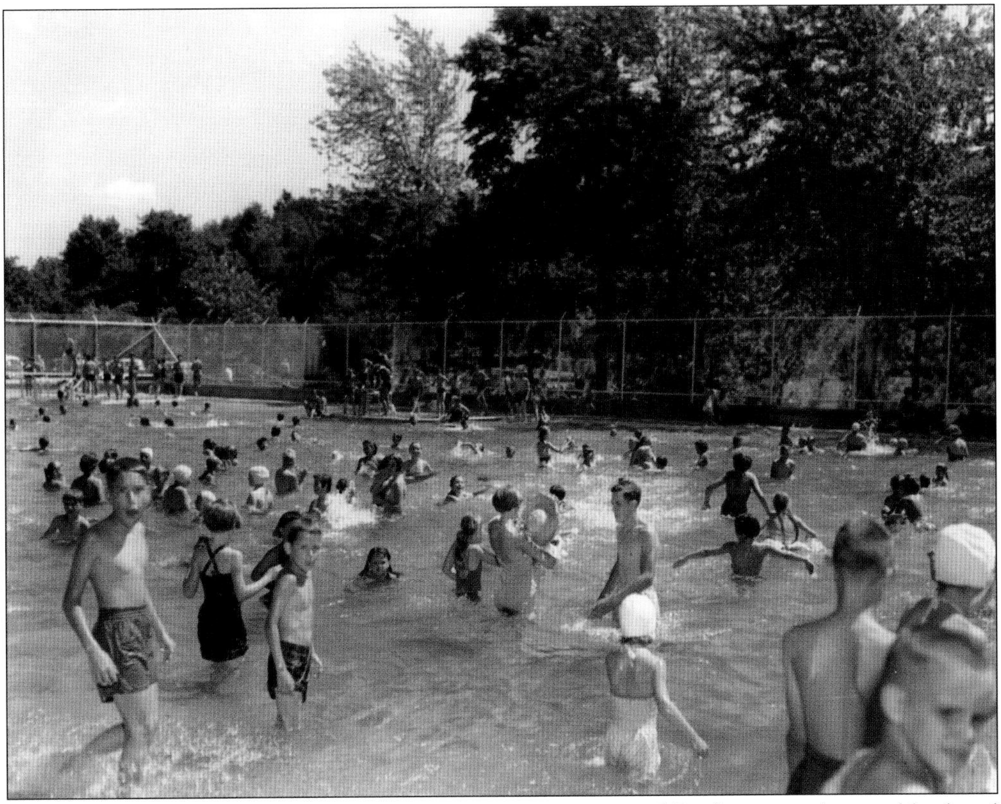

Built in part by student volunteers in 1920, Juniata's Memorial Pool remained a neighborhood staple for nine decades. The children seen here were among 2,500 swimmers who gathered for the August 9, 1958, pool rededication. Connie Notopoulos wrote in her teen column, "Such a mob of kids!" The dilapidated pool was closed in 2009 and demolished in 2013 for a new spray park. (Courtesy of BCCC.)

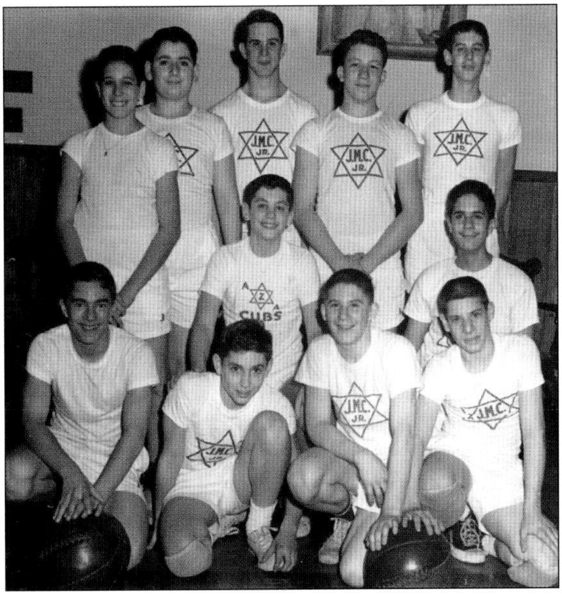

Dedicated on August 21, 1949, the Jewish Memorial Center at Agudath Achim Synagogue was created "for the benefit of the entire community, regardless of race, creed, or color." The center's 1960s basketball team included, from left to right, (first row) Danny Handler, Chuck Cogan, Terry Goldstein, and Jerry Binus; (second row) Eric Krivoy and Jack Snowiss; (third row) Joel Kaber, Dave Dolinger, Arnie Karp, Steve Wolfberg, and Jack Titleman. (Courtesy of the Jewish Memorial Center.)

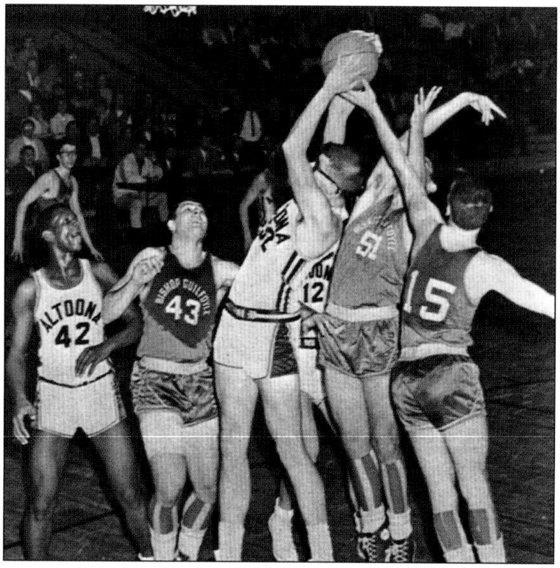

On February 7, 1967, frenzied crowds packed the Jaffa Shrine to watch the city's two high schools, Altoona and Bishop Guilfoyle, play each other in basketball for the first time. Players here include Fred Hatfield (42), Tom Turchetta (43), Pat Nicodemus (shooting), Joe Landolfi (51), and Pat Shute (15). Although Guilfoyle lost 68-62 in overtime, the team won a state Catholic interscholastic title the following month. (Courtesy of BGHS.)

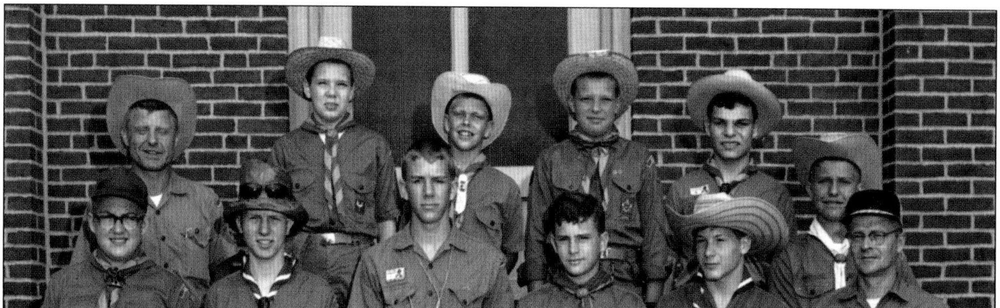

From August 22 to 28, 1965, Troop 23 of St. James Lutheran Church embarked on a 56-mile hike from Pen Mar to Carlisle in what was considered a first-rate adventure. Pictured here from left to right are (first row) Jim Myers, Paul Anderson, Jan Apple, Jim Stevens, Jack Cassarly, and Bob Schmelzlen; (second row) Paul Rhykerd, Steve Barry, Scott Rhykerd, Bill Smith, Sheldon Shapiro, and Glenn Rhykerd. (Courtesy of St. James Evangelical Lutheran Church.)

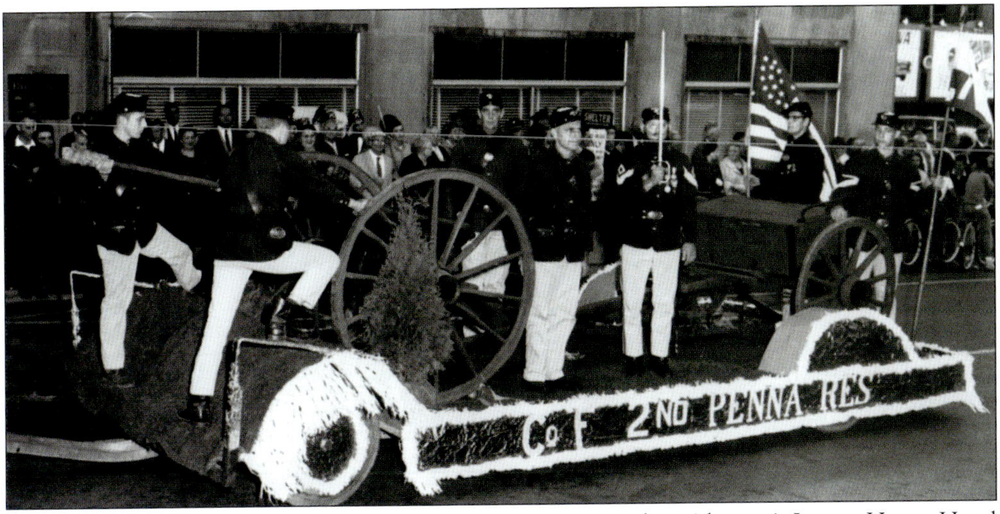

In September 1862, a dozen Northern governors congregated in Altoona's Logan House Hotel to offer their support for Lincoln's Emancipation Proclamation. One century later, Altoonans celebrated that gathering as a political turning point of the Civil War. Taking place in a time rife with racial anxiety, this commemoration was one of the few in the nation to acknowledge emancipation as a legacy of the conflict. Here, Civil War reenactors parade past the Penn Alto Hotel and city hall as spectators look on. (Courtesy of AM.)

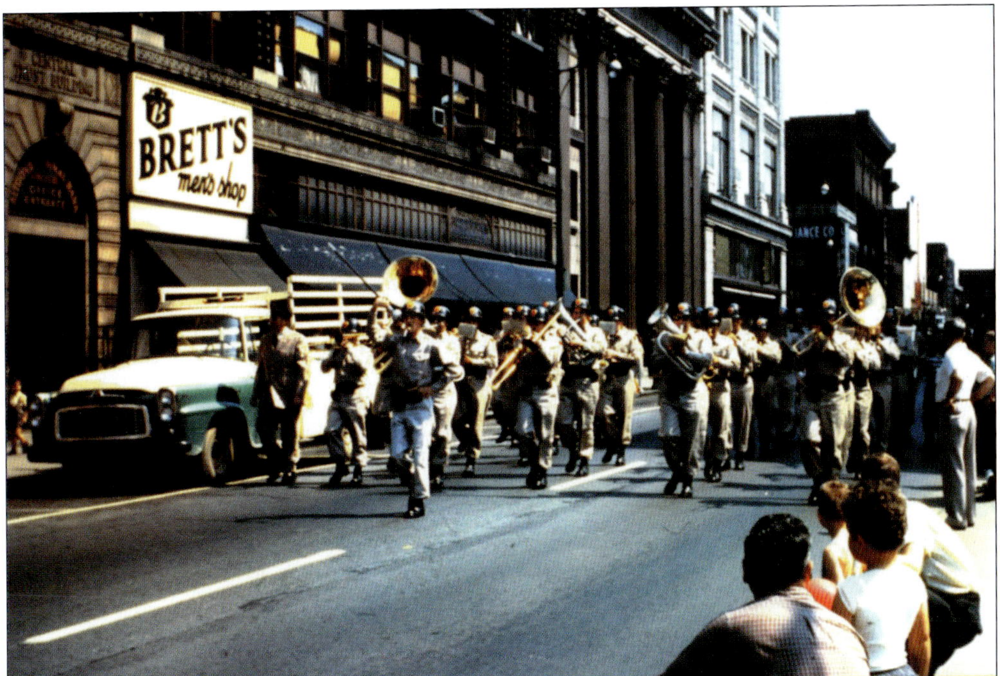

Despite mounting tensions over the escalating Vietnam War, the 28th Infantry Division Band based out of Altoona remained a popular highlight of Memorial Day parades. Chief Warrant Officer James Wolford (far left) is seen here guiding the band down Eleventh Avenue past Brett's Men's Shop in a late-1960s photograph. (Courtesy of David Seidel.)

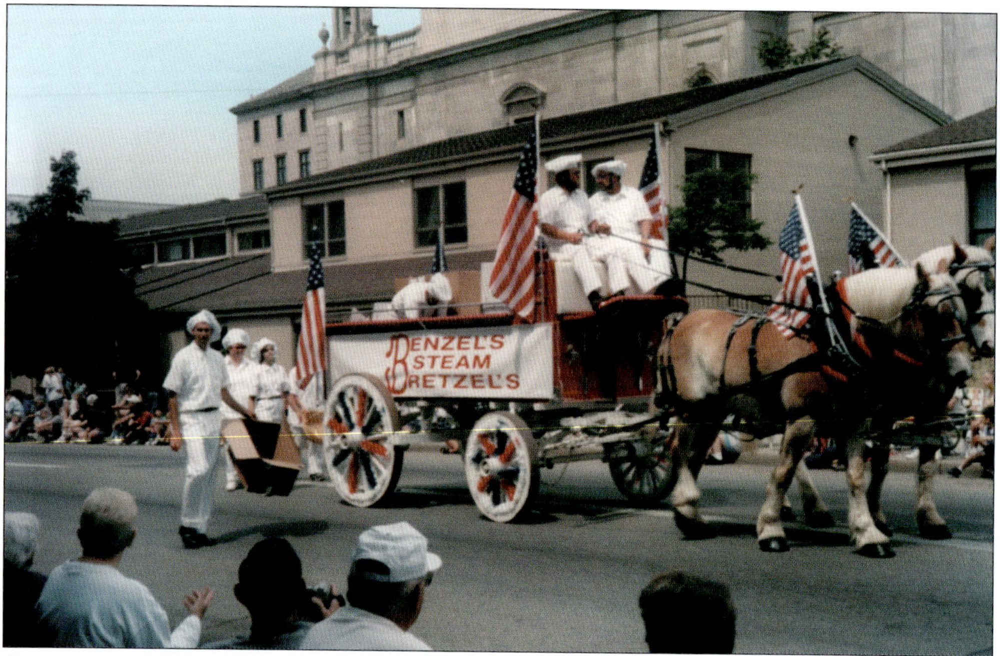

On May 22, 1999, "Half the city paraded through the town while the other half watched" to mark Altoona's sesquicentennial. Thousands rode or walked in the three-hour parade, including employees of Altoona's Benzel's Bretzels, who tossed snacks to spectators. All those involved "felt like family," commented resident Jim Kennedy. (Courtesy of Benzel's Bretzels.)

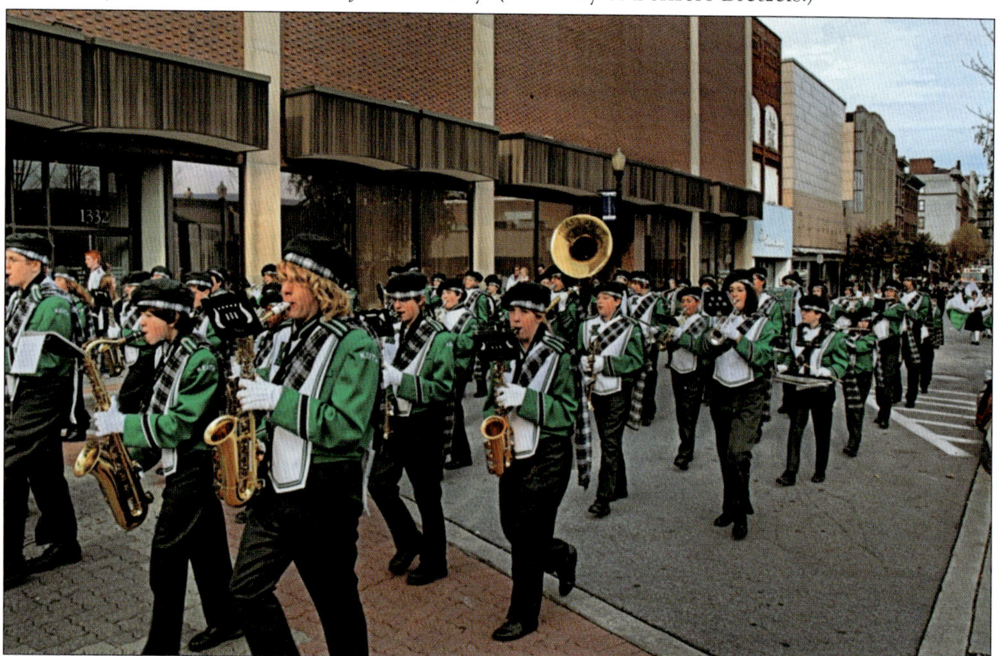

The Keith Junior High School marching band parades down Eleventh Avenue on Veterans' Day in 2007 for the last time. Keith closed less than seven months later when it merged into the city's new junior high. Alumnus Mike Gibbons recalled, "There were great people and great memories that will remain, even after the school is no more." (Courtesy of Bob Airhart.)

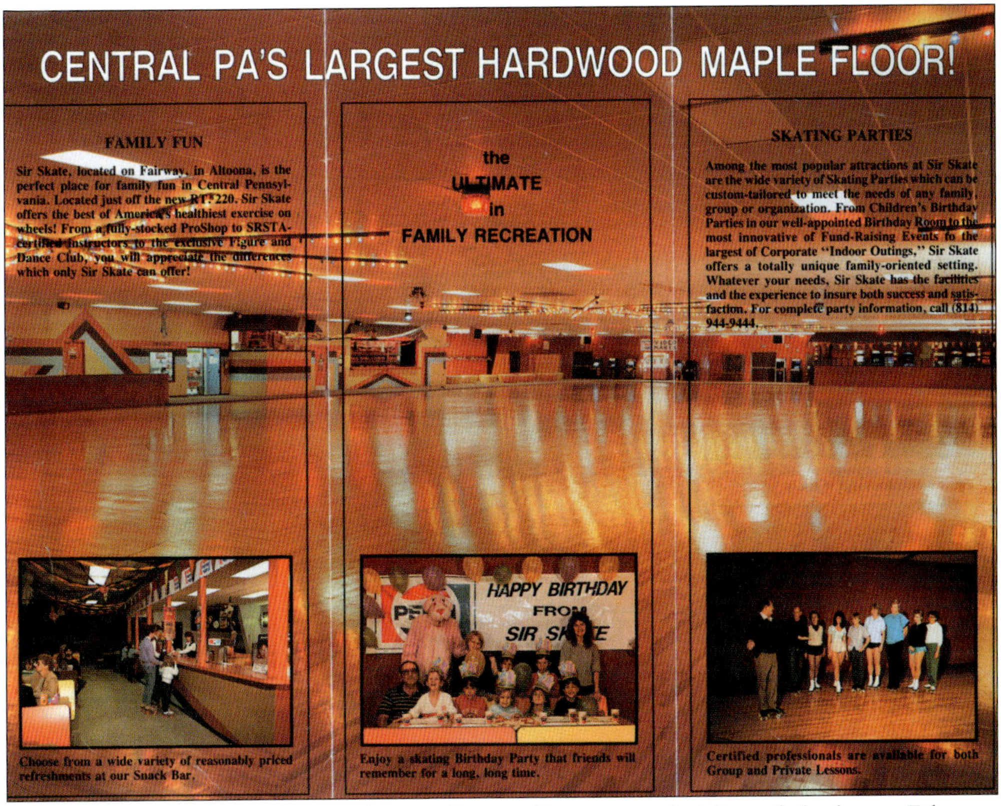

Charging $1.75 for admission, Sir Skate on Fairway Drive opened with much fanfare on February 18, 1981. The heavily used roller rink was a popular venue for birthday parties, as seen in this brochure, until its spring 2000 closing. One parent exclaimed, "What about our kids? Where are they going for entertainment?" (Courtesy of William H. Donnelly Jr.)

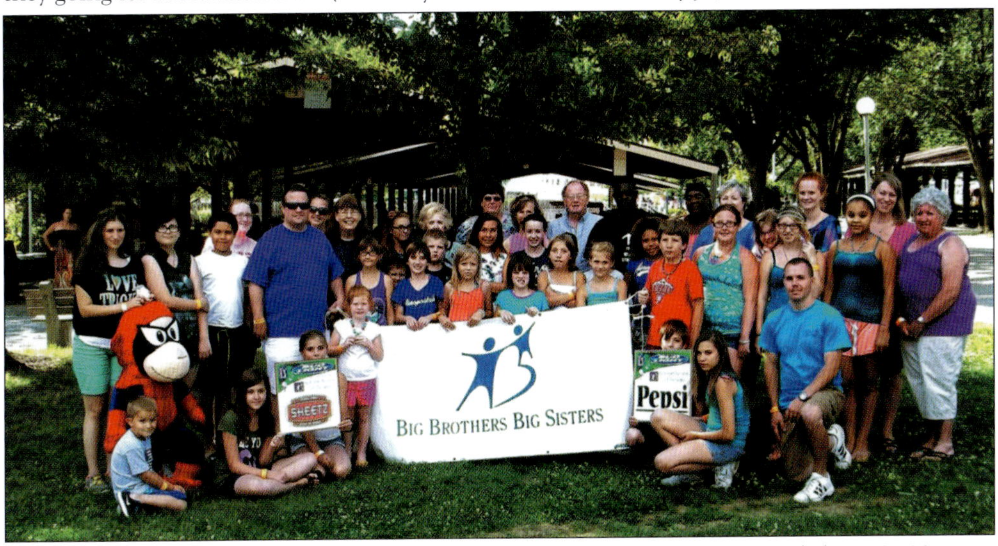

Big Brothers Big Sisters of Blair County was established in 1964 and has since guided over 2,100 young people through challenges and triumphs. On July 17, 2014, the organization celebrated Big Brothers Big Sisters Day at Lakemont Park. (Courtesy of Big Brothers Big Sisters of Blair County.)

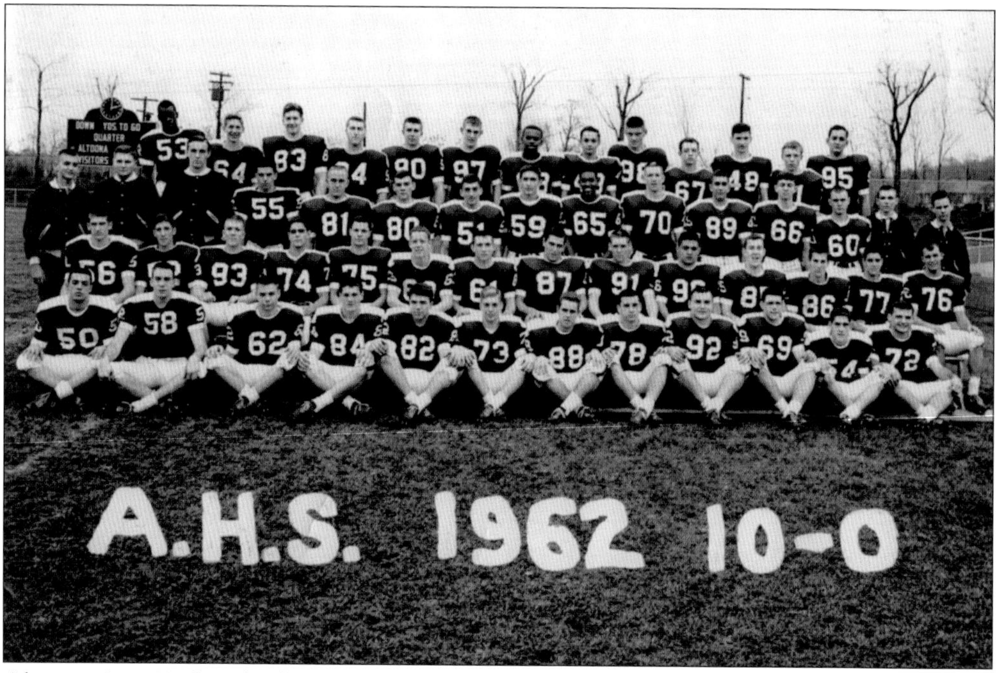

Altoona Area High School football coach Earl Strohm "demanded toughness, grit and a team approach from his players." That sense of conviction came to fruition when his 1962 squad went undefeated with a 10-0 record. Among the team members was future NFL lineman Mike Reid. (Courtesy of AAHS.)

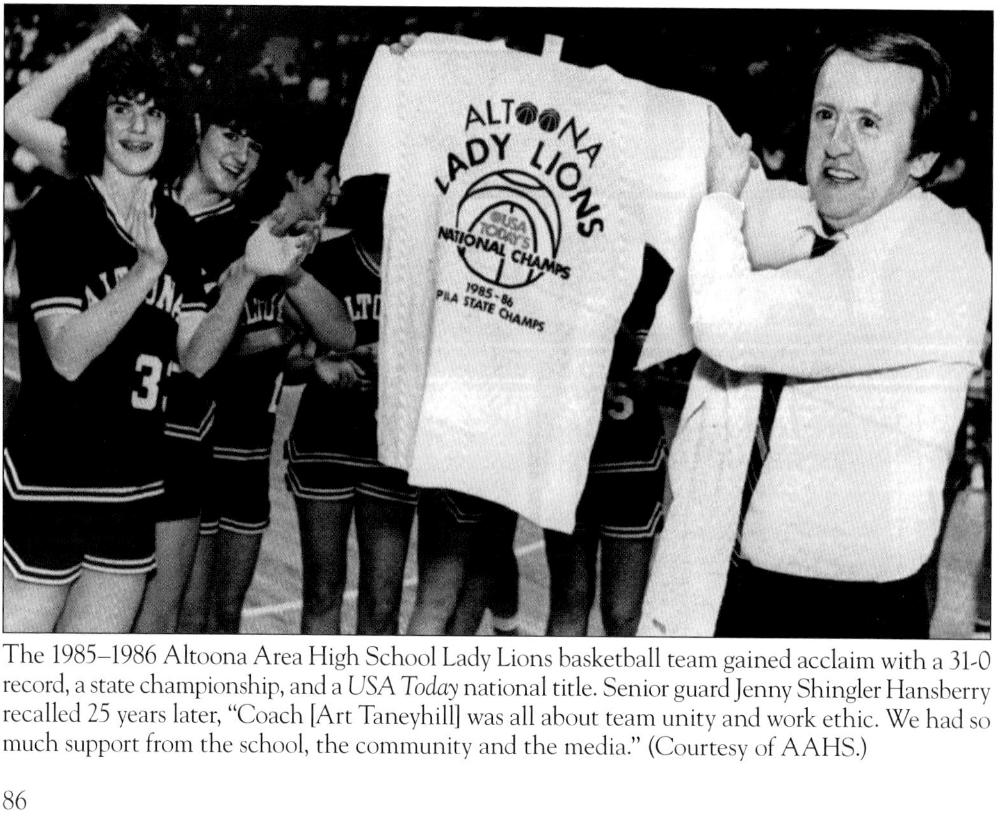

The 1985–1986 Altoona Area High School Lady Lions basketball team gained acclaim with a 31-0 record, a state championship, and a *USA Today* national title. Senior guard Jenny Shingler Hansberry recalled 25 years later, "Coach [Art Taneyhill] was all about team unity and work ethic. We had so much support from the school, the community and the media." (Courtesy of AAHS.)

In 1987, Bishop Guilfoyle High School's football team achieved its first undefeated season in half a century. Defeating Hollidaysburg during the regular season, the team was cheered from the stands by the previous undefeated squad of 1937. Here, coach Tom Irwin oversees a practice on the field now named in his honor. (Courtesy of AM.)

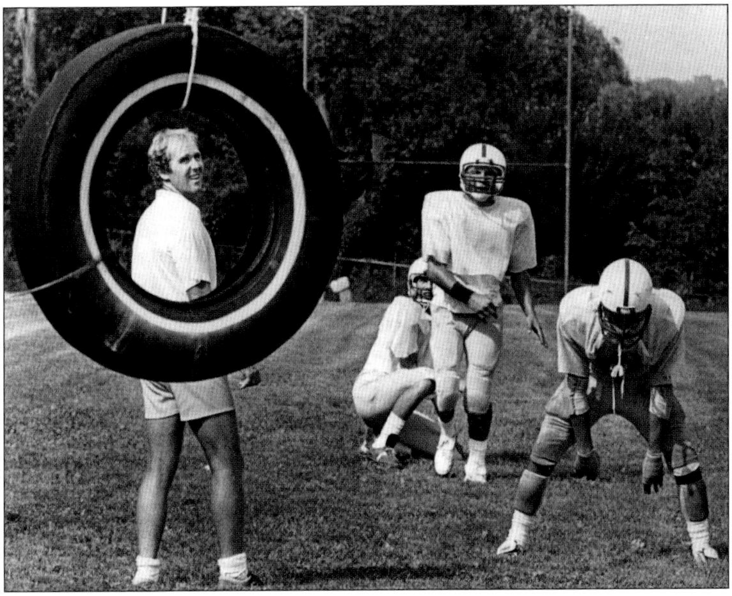

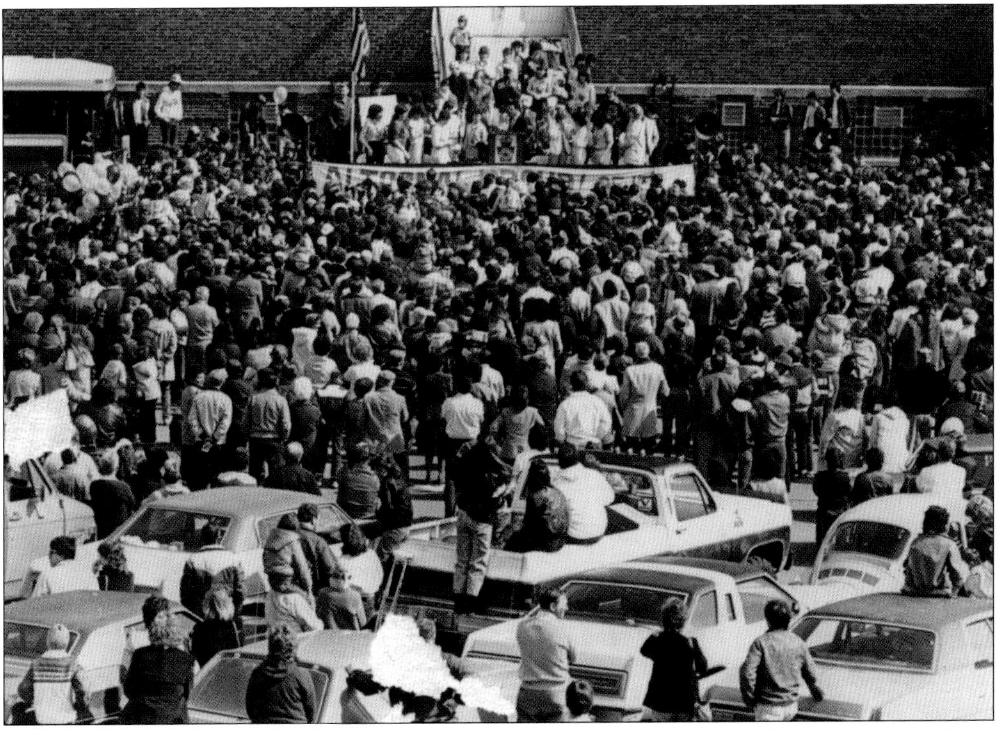

Bishop Guilfoyle High School won the city's first girls' basketball state championship in 1984, defeating Pine Grove in the championship 64-63. The celebratory victory rally at the Jaffa Mosque attracted an estimated 2,000 people. Coach John Frederick and team won another championship in 1991, while successor Mark Moschella has brought home four gold trophies since. (Courtesy of AM.)

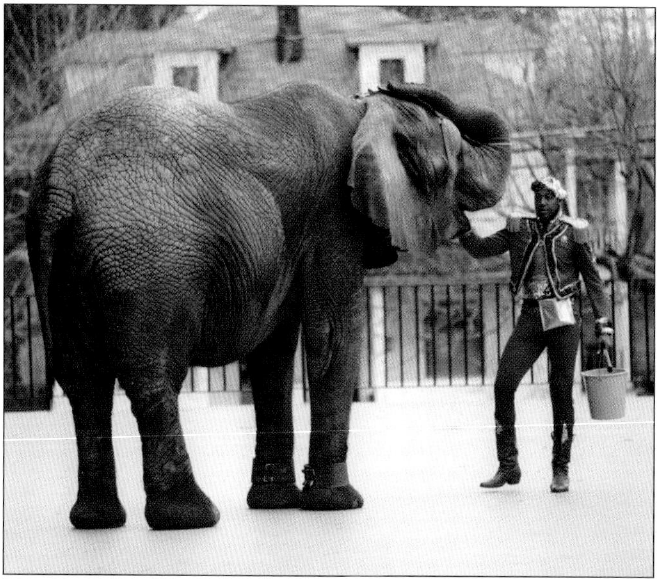

Disaster struck the Jaffa Mosque on April 21, 1993, when a circus elephant named Tyke barreled through the front doors as 4,000 students watched. Police circled the building as trainer Tyrone Taylor placated the animal. While Tyke was pacified that day, the elephant was gunned down by Honolulu police the following year. Tyke's death ultimately raised additional awareness to animal rights. (Courtesy of AM.)

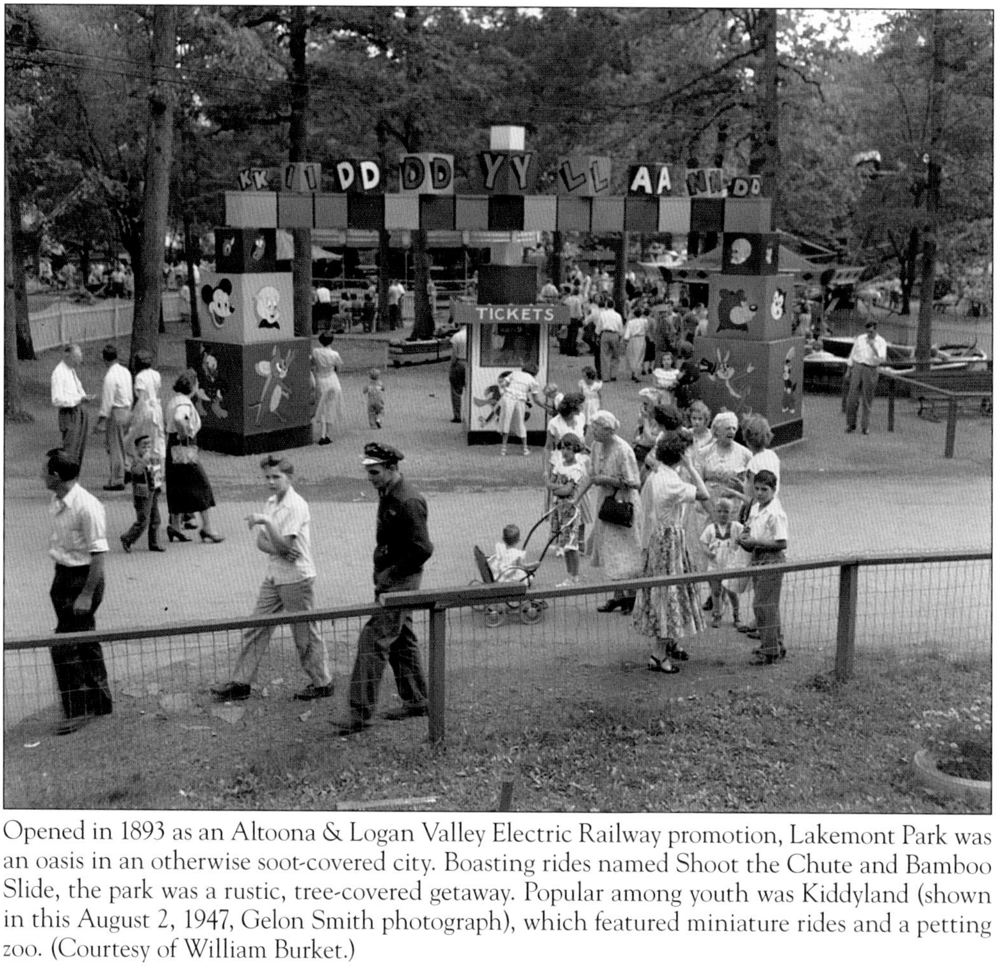

Opened in 1893 as an Altoona & Logan Valley Electric Railway promotion, Lakemont Park was an oasis in an otherwise soot-covered city. Boasting rides named Shoot the Chute and Bamboo Slide, the park was a rustic, tree-covered getaway. Popular among youth was Kiddyland (shown in this August 2, 1947, Gelon Smith photograph), which featured miniature rides and a petting zoo. (Courtesy of William Burket.)

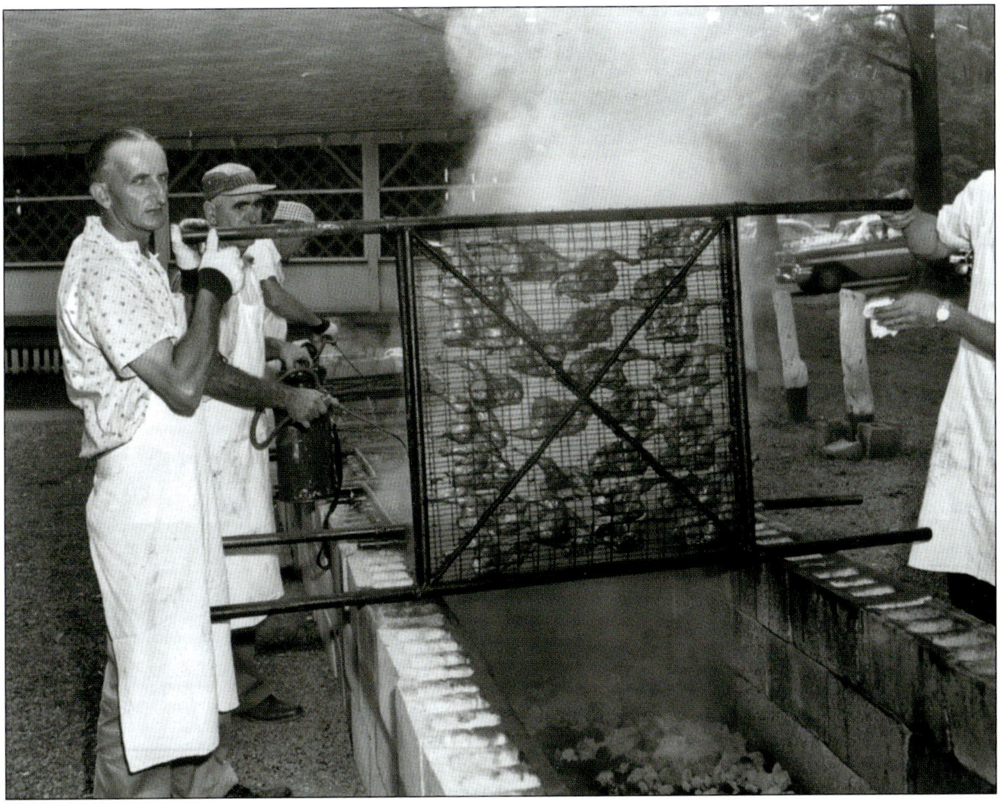

In 1952, the ladies of the Blair County Barbequed Chicken Committee helped initiate a culinary trend that was incorporated into Lakemont Park picnics. The *Altoona Mirror* wrote, "Because of the current interest in the new-fashioned manner of preparing chicken over charcoal pits and its intriguing acceptance by those who have partaken of the tasty morsel, this form of festivity was established as a must." (Courtesy of BCCC.)

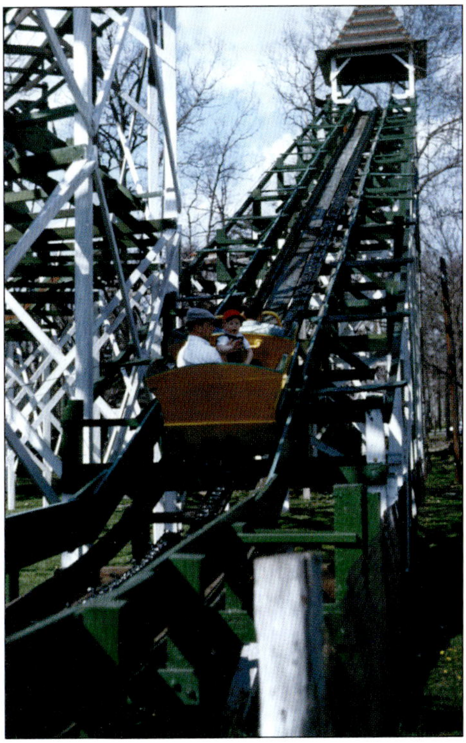

Formerly known as Gravity Railroad, Leap-the-Dips was constructed in 1902 at Lakemont Park. Falling into disrepair, the attraction was closed for nearly 15 years before reopening on Memorial Day 1999. Park visitor Dave Altman exclaimed in 2010, "It is like a time capsule." Leap-the-Dips remains the world's oldest operating wooden roller coaster. Tim (left) and Bobby Seidel are seen riding the coaster in this April 1968 photograph. (Courtesy of David Seidel.)

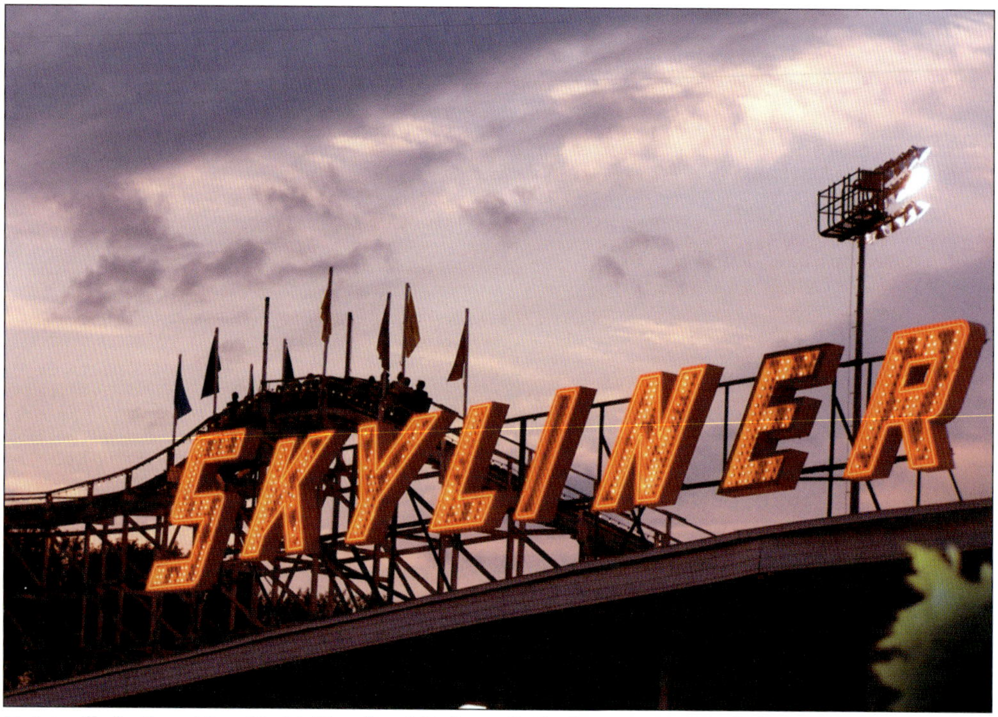

Originally built at New York's Roseland Park in 1960, the impressive Skyliner roller coaster was reconstructed at Lakemont in 1987, following Roseland's closure. Dominating the Altoona Curve baseball club's right field, the ride offers a stunning view at twilight. (Author's collection.)

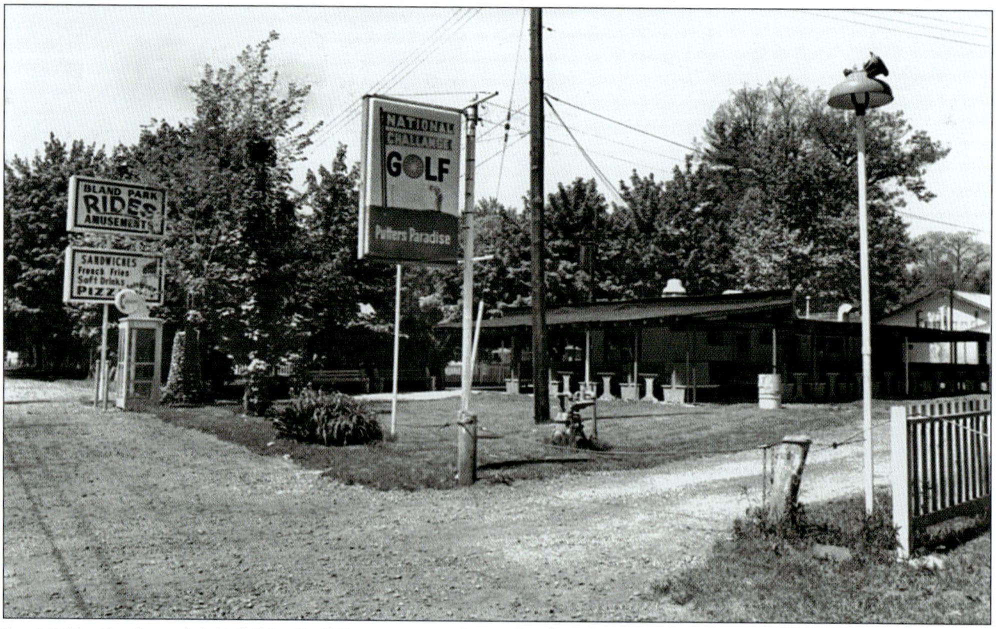

In 1946, Fred and Mafalda DelGrosso purchased Bland's Park in rural Tipton. Located near the former Altoona Speedway, the park grew exponentially as baby boomer families sought entertainment. The resurgence of the park also led to the rise of DelGrosso Foods, a highly successful company specializing in Italian foods. (Courtesy of Blair County Historical Society.)

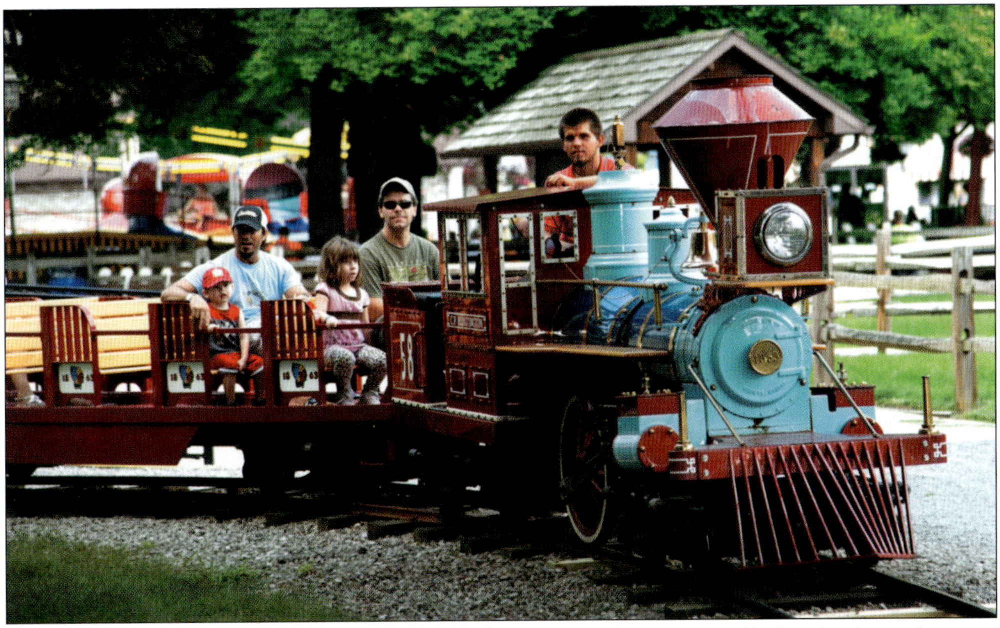

Embracing railroad culture, Bland's Park included a miniature locomotive. 1949 park ads proclaiming, "Enjoy your picnic dinner" in "nature's shade" proved an alluring invitation for citizens of an industrial town. A newer version of the ride on the Tipton Creek Railroad remains popular among families. (Courtesy of DelGrosso's Amusement Park.)

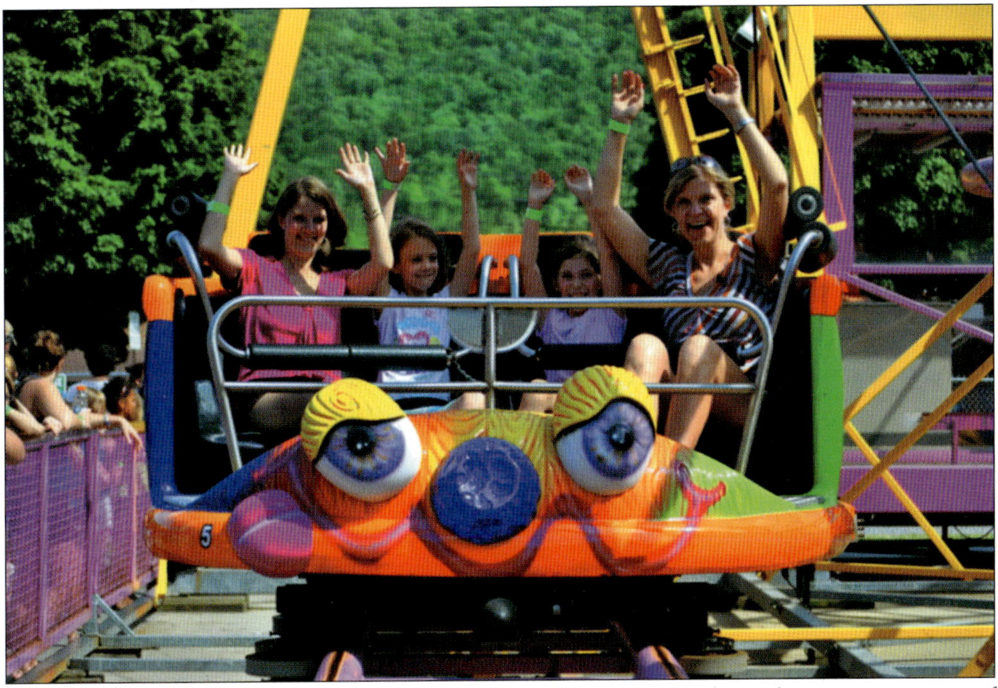

Now known as DelGrosso's Amusement Park, the former Bland's Park operates as one of Pennsylvania's premier destinations for family fun. Pictured here are, from left to right, Jessica Black, Taylor Black, Lyndsey Fleck, and Kim Fleck enjoying the colorful Crazy Mouse roller coaster. The family purchases season passes every year. (Courtesy of Explore Altoona.)

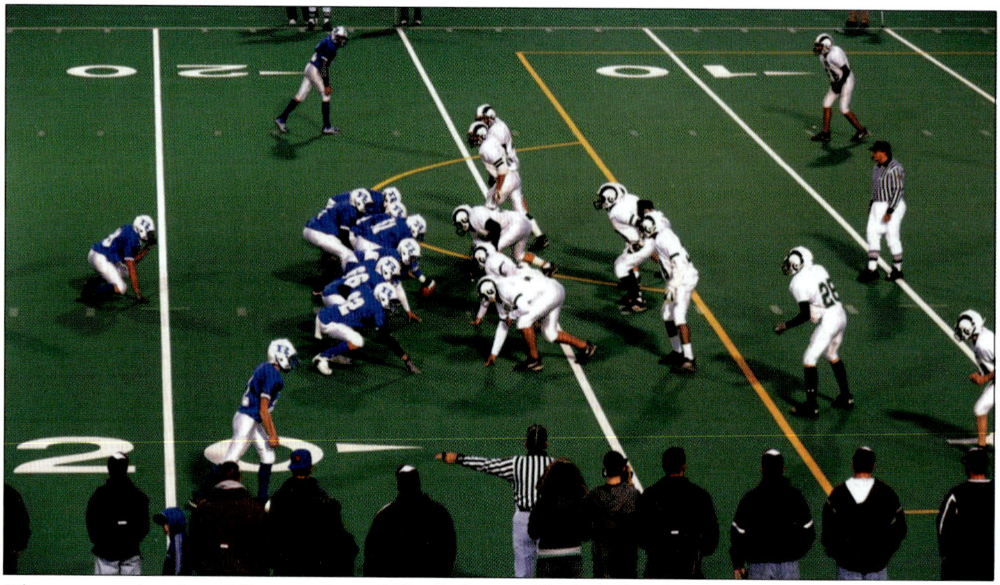

The soon-to-be closed Roosevelt and Keith Junior High Schools met on the gridiron one final time on November 1, 2007, before a crowd of 3,000 at Mansion Park. The 81st time the schools faced off, Keith won 18-14 after four consecutive series losses. Mike Pappas, who had seen every Keith-Roosevelt game since 1989, reflected, "It's hard to see the series end, but change is a constant in life." (Courtesy of David Seidel.)

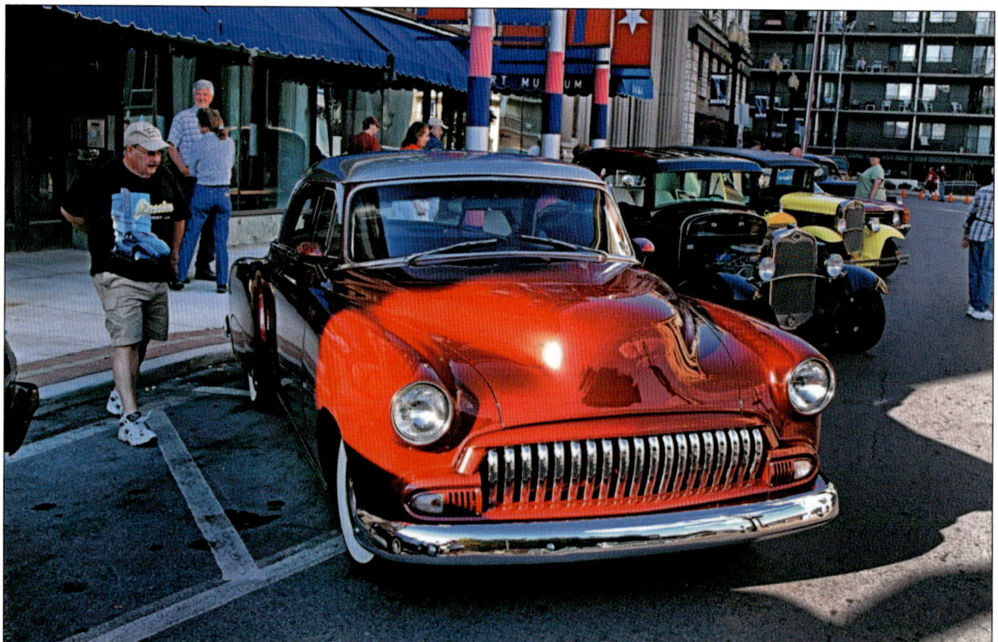

On October 1, 2007, citizens were invited to bring their classic automobiles downtown for a cruise-in. Coordinator Rick Spielvogle noted, "Back in the old days, cruising on Eleventh and Twelfth Avenues was the place to be seen and to see friends." Hosted by the Blair County Antique Auto Club, the event benefitted the Miracle League of Blair County. (Courtesy of Bob Airhart.)

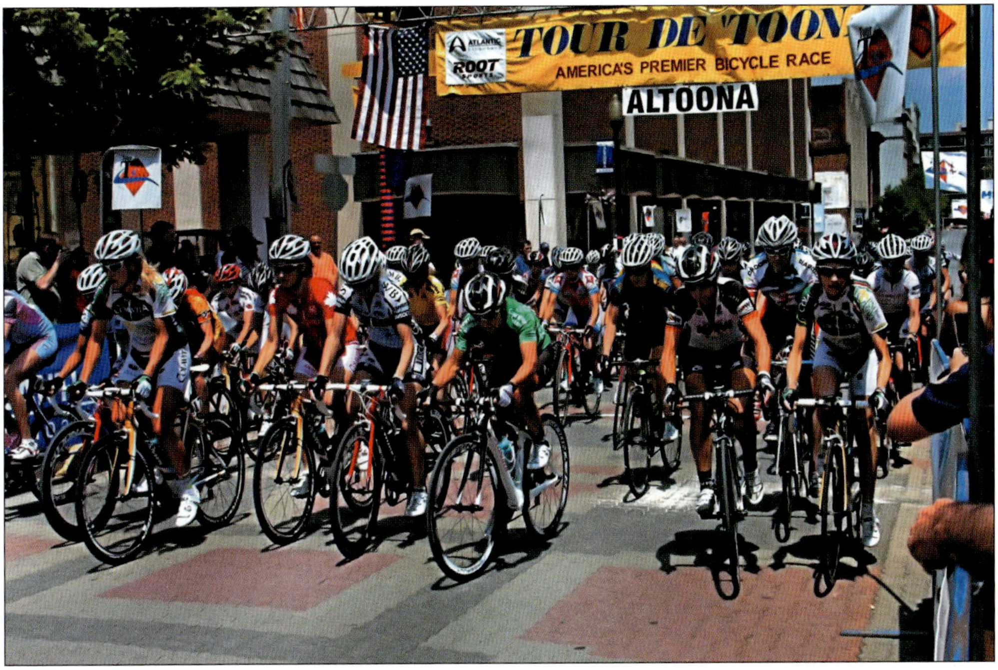

Initiated in 1987, the International Tour de 'Toona became one of the largest pro-am bicycling events in the United States. Stretching through four counties some years, the road races exhibited both male and female cyclists of growing prominence. Beleaguered by financial woes in its later years, the Tour de 'Toona last occurred in July 2011. (Courtesy of Bob Airhart.)

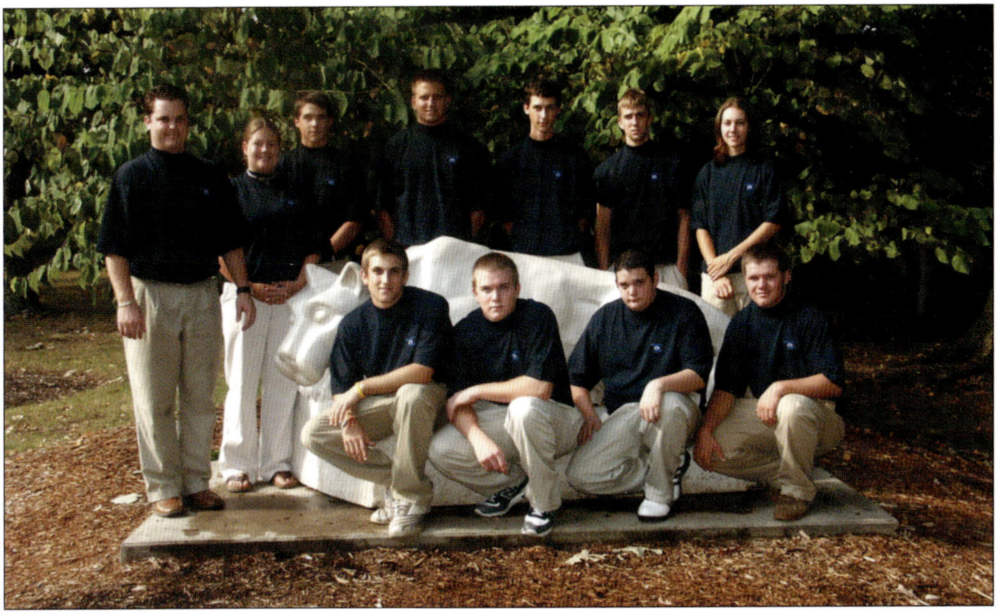

Under the leadership of coach Tom Koehle, Penn State Altoona golf gained four AMCC championships and four NCAA tournament berths. The 2005–2006 team included, from left to right, (first row) Drew Grossman, Mike Richardson, Ryan Koehle, and Aaron Schroeder; (second row) Tom Koehle, Leslie Pavetto, Derek Bailey, Quintin Dziabo, Rick Penatzer, Garrett Pierce, and Jena Smolko. "Golf is a source of pride for our college," Koehle noted. (Courtesy of PSA.)

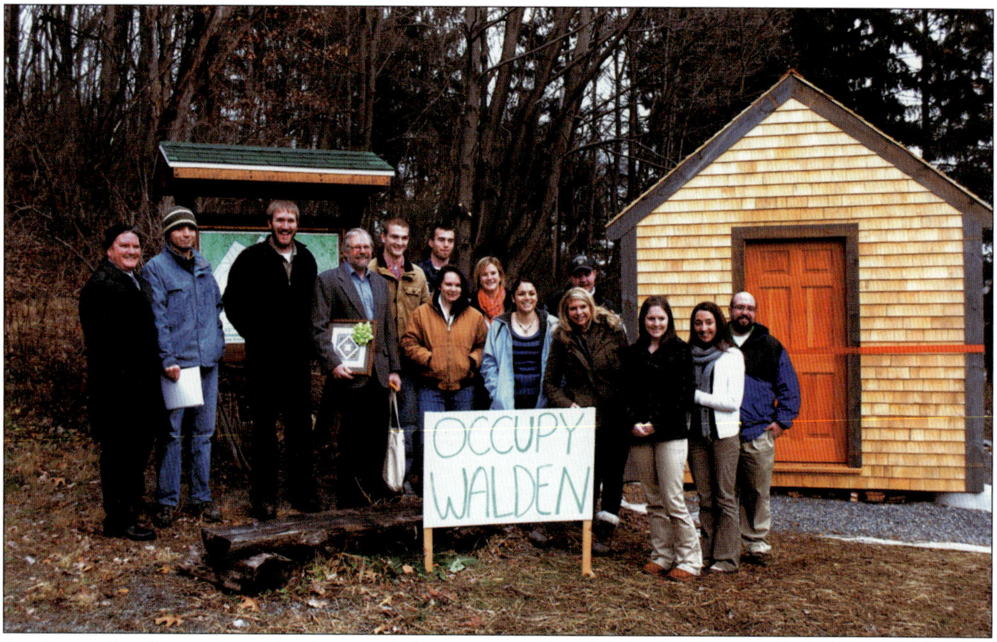

Students, faculty, and staff gather to dedicate a replica of Henry David Thoreau's Walden cabin at Penn State Altoona's Seminar Forest on December 8, 2011. Headed by the English and Environmental Studies programs, students built the cabin near Juniata Gap Road in four days, using predominantly hand tools. Dr. Ian Marshall (holding frame) called the project "an experiment in learning." (Courtesy of PSA.)

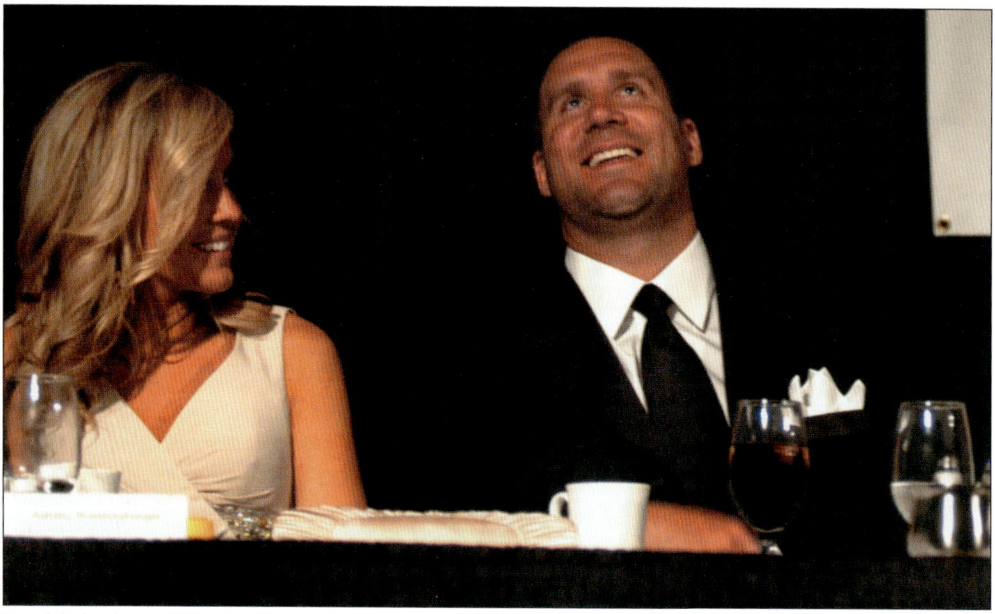

Established in 1987, the Blair County Sports Hall of Fame ceremony was spearheaded by Neil Rudel of the *Altoona Mirror*. The banquet has honored dozens of local athletes who have risen to regional and national notoriety. On April 28, 2012, Pittsburgh Steelers quarterback Ben Roethlisberger welcomed inductees alongside his wife, Ashley, at the Blair County Convention Center. (Photograph by Gary Baranec, courtesy of AM.)

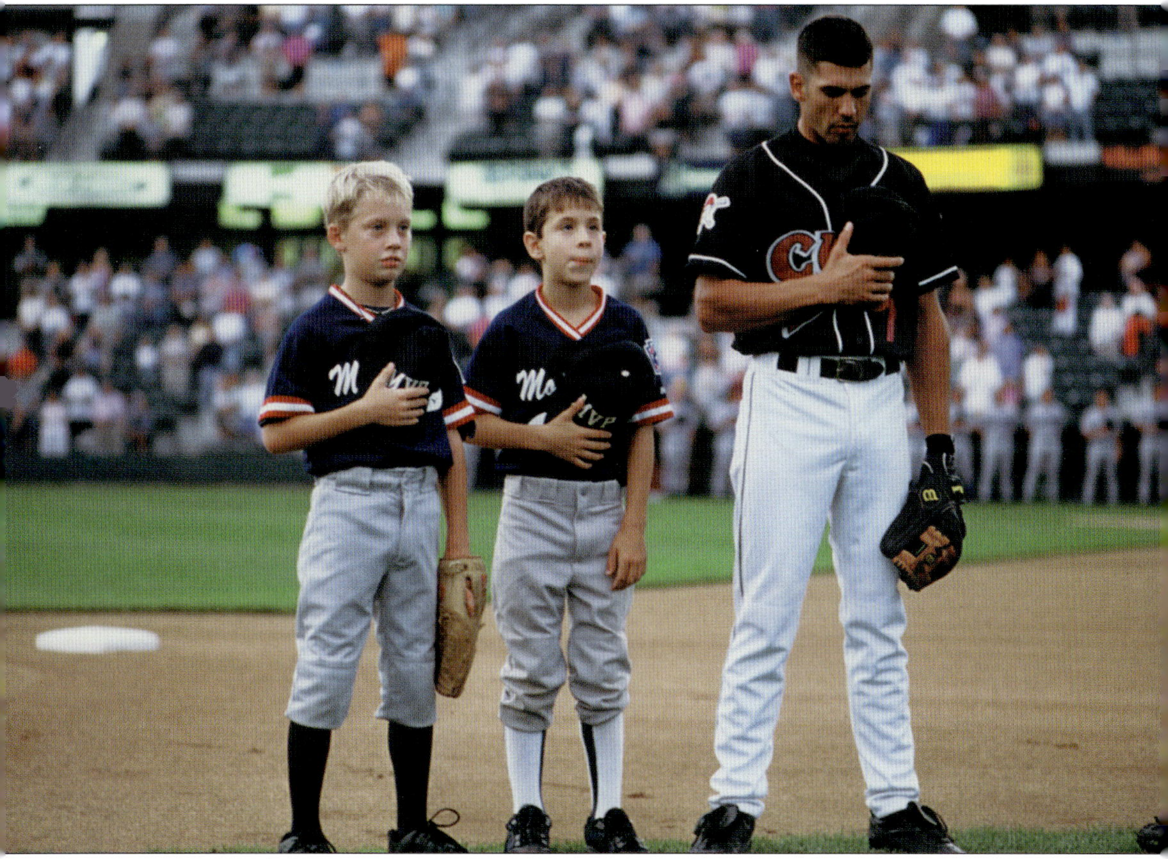

Succeeding the failed Altoona Rail Kings minor-league team in 1999, the Altoona Curve became the Double-A affiliate of the Pittsburgh Pirates. The franchise won the Eastern League championship in 2010. Notable MLB players such as Andrew McCutchen and Pedro Álvarez initiated their professional careers with the team. In this 2000 photograph, second baseman Rob Mackowiak stands alongside little leaguers during the national anthem. The Curve continues to infuse an immense level of regional pride among the people of central Pennsylvania. (Courtesy of Explore Altoona.)